THE FILMMAKERS
BOOK OF THE DEAD

Popcorn Artwork by Dave Lange, Darkmatter Studios

THE FILMMAKER'S BOOK OF THE DEAD

HOW TO MAKE YOUR OWN
HEART-RACING HORROR MOVIE

Danny Draven

ELSEVIER

AMSTERDAM • BOSTON • HEIDELBERG • LONDON
NEW YORK • OXFORD • PARIS • SAN DIEGO
SAN FRANCISCO • SINGAPORE • SYDNEY • TOKYO

Focal Press is an imprint of Elsevier

Focal
Press

Focal Press is an imprint of Elsevier
30 Corporate Drive, Suite 400, Burlington, MA 01803, USA
Linacre House, Jordan Hill, Oxford OX2 8DP, UK

Notices
Knowledge and best practice in this field are constantly changing. As new research and experience
broaden our understanding, changes in research methods, professional practices, or medical
treatment may become necessary.
Practitioners and researchers must always rely on their own experience and knowledge in evaluating
and using any information, methods, compounds, or experiments described herein. In using
such information or methods they should be mindful of their own safety and the safety of others,
including parties for whom they have a professional responsibility.
To the fullest extent of the law, neither the Publisher nor the authors, contributors, or editors,
assume any liability for any injury and/or damage to persons or property as a matter of products
liability, negligence or otherwise, or from any use or operation of any methods, products,
instructions, or ideas contained in the material herein.

Library of Congress Cataloging-in-Publication Data
Draven, Danny.
  The filmmaker's book of the dead/Danny Draven.
     p. cm.
  1. Horror films–Production and direction. I. Title.
  PN1995.9.H6D73 2010
  791.43'6164–dc22

                             2009029535

British Library Cataloguing-in-Publication Data
A catalogue record for this book is available from the British Library.

ISBN: 978-0-240-81206-9

For information on all Focal Press publications
visit our website at *www.elsevierdirect.com*

09 10 11 12 13   5 4 3 2 1

Printed in China

Typeset by: diacriTech, Chennai, India

Cover Artwork & Design by:
Dave Lange
Darkmatter Studios

**FOR MY MUSES
JOSEPHINE & LUCAS**

TABLE OF CONTENTS

PART FIVE · DISTRIBUTION AND MARKETING

WEBSITE CONTENTS FOR DRAVEN'S FILMMAKER'S BOOK OF THE DEAD

Website Extras

Chapter 2 Website Extras:

Cryptz schedule

Darkwalker shooting schedule

Deathbed shooting schedule

Ghost Month Production Schedule

Production Agreement Sample

Chapter 3 Website Extras:

Sample of non-union talent agreement

Chapter 7 Website Extras:

Sample of non-union director's contract

Chapter 15 Website Extras:

Listing of horror distributors

Chapter 16 Website Extras:

As produced sample

Comprehensive CCSL Sample

Comprehensive combined continuity sample

Comprehensive dialogue list sample

Comprehensive spotting list sample

Simple CCSL sample

To access this content, visit the companion website at http://booksite.focalpress.com/ companion/Draven. Use access code **DRA8HL98FR53** to log in.

FOREWORD

By Charles Band

Charles Band (2009).
Photo Credit: Courtesy of Full Moon Features.

Danny Draven is *the* renaissance film dude! From the moment he joined us at Full Moon Pictures almost 10 years ago (at the ridiculously young age of 21!) his love and dedication to the genre along with his uncanny ability to adapt to the never-ending new technologies put him into a unique and very valuable category. Although Danny left Full Moon a few years later to pursue his many independent dreams, we have been associated ever since.

Independent filmmakers are certainly in a new world today where practically anyone can create, produce, and market a film almost single-handedly, and the cost to produce a feature that way is practically zero. Back when I started out in this intoxicating business, you had to have at least $40,000–$50,000 to make a film, you had to shoot it on 35mm, you had to have an expensive answer print to screen it, and ultimately you had to have some form of theatrical distribution to exploit it. Then, you just prayed that your distributor would be at least partially honest and send you a report with some pennies. You were part of an expensive food chain and there were few shortcuts. Today, you can shoot your show on your camcorder in HD, edit and post it on your computer, spit out DVDs, create your own packaging, and start selling your film on the Internet. You may not make a dime, but you can do it all yourself! And if you actually have some talent, then you have a real chance of being discovered, and off you go! That brings me back to Danny Draven. Danny can do it all *and* he is super talented! He can craft a film for very few dollars and make it look like the budget was 10 times what was actually spent. It's not because he is extremely technically proficient (which he is)—it's because the love for his craft shines through and he is truly gifted. This book is a terrific practical guide to filmmaking from someone who doesn't just write about it, but lives it every day.

CHARLES BAND
Full Moon President
May 19, 2009
Hollywood, California

ACKNOWLEDGEMENTS

Every writer is a frustrated actor who recites his lines in the hidden auditorium of his skull.

—ROD SERLING

A VERY SPECIAL THANKS TO
MIKE & MARLENE BROWN

Elinor Actipis
Jane Dashevsky
Amanda Guest
Melinda Rankin
Jeanne Hansen
Jojo Draven & Lucas
Pebbles
Mami & Papi Takim
Albert "Koko" & Siane Soegijopranoto
Stefan Soegiarto
Loui & Ika Sugiyanto
Jason Rouch
Sheena & Shawn Rolsen
Helene Hill
Stuart Gordon
Rick & Angie Irvin
Dave & Sandra Lange
Darkmatter Studios
David DeCoteau
Charles Band, Full Moon Features

Shirley To
Marina Resa
Tom Savini
Lloyd Kaufman, Troma Entertainment
John D. LeMay
Robert Kurtzman
Chuck Williams
Buddy Barnett
Kathe Duba-Barnett
Steven M. Blasini
BenniQue Blasini
Robert Englund
Nancy Booth
Reggie Bannister
Gigi Fast Elk Bannister
Mbencekno, Inc.
Fangoria Magazine
Michael Gingold
Tony Timpone
Debbie Rochon
James Wan
Patricia Dziekan
Michael King
Mac Ahlberg
John Strysik
Herschell Gordon Lewis
Andrea Beesley-Brown
Ryan Brookhart
J. R. Bookwalter, Tempe Entertainment
Del & Sue Howison
Dark Delicasies, Burbank, California (www.darkdel.com)
Jon Sagud, RED Digital Cinema
North American Motion Pictures
Brett Lauter, Pan Global Entertainment
Arriflex
Sound Indeas, Inc., Elliott Zimmerman
Regent Releasing, Jonathon Aubry

Ryan Mantione, Full Moon Features
Draven Lovell
Marc Pilvinsky
Todd Debreceni
Producers Guild of America
Nancy Naglin, *Videoscope* Magazine
Dean Boor, *GoreZone* Magazine
Rue Morgue Magazine
Karoline Brandt
Nathan Barr
Jim Dooley
Matthew Sakevitz
Kwok Ching
Gold Wheel Abbot
Lee Mok-sau
Yeung Gor
Chow Bak-tung

Script Sample Creation for Chapter 22
Line 21 Media Services Ltd.
www.line21cc.com
Da Vinci City Hall provided the original script and it was produced by:
Haddock Entertainment Inc.
www.haddockentertainment.com

Software Contributors
Chris Huntley, Write Brothers, Inc.
Paul Clatworthy, PowerProduction Software
Alejandro Seri, Final Draft, Inc.
Michael Trent, Movie Outline Software
David Parrish, Wide Screen Software, LLC
Logan Ryan, Mariner Software, Inc.
Steve Shepard, Storyist Software
David Johnson, Literature and Latte

Interview Transcriptions
Marlene R. Brown

Danny Draven Back Cover Photo
Michael Helms

Cover Artwork, Design, and Section Illustrations
Dave Lange
Darkmatter Studios
www.darkmatterstudios.com

FOR MORE INFORMATION ON DANNY DRAVEN AND HIS FILMS GO TO:

www.dannydraven.com
www.myspace.com/dannydraven

PART ONE

THE HORROR GENRE

CHAPTER 1
THE MECHANICS OF MONSTERS

> **To make Michael Myers frightening, I had him walk like a man, not a monster.**
>
> **—JOHN CARPENTER**

A beam of light illuminates a dark hallway leading to a door. Something scratches at uneven intervals as Amy wipes the sweat from her brow. Beams of light on the floor become broken as a shape moves on the other side. Amy musters her courage and calls out, "Jamie, is that you?" The scratching stops for a moment as if something were listening and then continues. "Come on…quit messing around. I mean it." She creeps along the wall toward the door, being pulled in by her curiosity. When she gets to the door, the scratching stops. "Jamie?" she says as she leans in closer. Suddenly, a tear-shaped drop of blood lands on her cheek from above. She touches it, smearing the blood across her face in a horizontal line. The sight of blood causes her to freeze in terror. A thunderous thump echoes from above as another drop hits her cheek and drips downward over the horizontal smear, forming an upside-down crucifix. A chattering sound, like teeth biting together in rapid succession, is heard above. She cautiously retreats from the door and tilts her head up. Hanging upside down is a grotesque beast, its fangs like razor-sharp icebergs in a sea of blood. It hovers motionless, looking at her with its soulless black-marble eyes. It smells the sweet aroma of fear oozing from her pores. In a sudden rush of reality she realizes the end has come. In an instant its jaws open and it swoops down upon her, severing her head. Her headless corpse still stands upright as the creature devours her brains in a fountain of gore.

Is that gruesome enough for you? Welcome to the horror genre. If you are going to make a successful, sellable horror film on a low-budget scale, choosing the right monster is the key to your success. Let's face it: independent horror films can't afford A-list Hollywood talent, some occasionally have B-movie actors who have been used excessively or appear for only a few minutes, and others have none. My advice is to treat your monster as your star and put as much money and effort into the makeup and creature effects as possible. This is your main attraction, your box cover and trailer, your Brad Pitt and Angelina Jolie. Make it terrifying.

DEFINING A MONSTER

What is a monster? That question has many answers, but for the sake of this book I'm defining it as any wicked immoral person, supernatural entity, or imaginary creature of myth or fantasy in a work of fiction. Usually it is one dimensional but not flat and boring. In horror films, the monster is your antagonist and drives your narrative. You must infuse it with characteristics and behaviors that help tell the tale, but at the same time make it compelling, sinister, and sometimes empathetic. Like the protagonist, it must also want something, whether it is blood, brains, sex, body parts, DNA, a human form, or just power over another. Establishing what a monster wants or needs for survival will help you define who and what it is. Avoid clichés and making knockoffs of other successful films; you will lose.

The following are the most common types of monsters, along with valuable examples that have inspired me to make horror films.

GHOSTS & THE SUPERNATURAL

One of life's certainties is your demise. Whether you die of old age, are murdered, or die of a disease, you can't live forever—at least in the nonfiction world. After the grim reaper claims your soul, your lifeless body may be cremated, rot in a coffin, be diced up by medical students, or be eaten by a maniac. One day your body—no matter how much surgery and aerobics—will return to the earth as dust. It's unsettling to be reminded of our mortality, but in horror films that is our job. The storyteller's vision of what a ghost looks like, or what may be waiting for us in the spirit world, gives us some hope of an afterlife, whether it is good or bad. In a horror film, it is most likely going to be bad.

I've always felt that less is more with the traditional ghost stories. Alfred Hitchcock once said, "There is no terror in the bang, only in the anticipation of it." This is great advice on all levels of filmmaking, but it's especially helpful when you're working on a limited budget. One of the great success stories of independent horror films is THE BLAIR WITCH PROJECT (1999). This is a movie that showed practically nothing, yet it scared the hell out of you by tricking you into believing it was all real documentary footage. The film was made for a mere $22,000, it was shot in 8 days on digital video, and it has grossed over $240.5 million. It was in *Guinness World Records* for "Top Budget: Box Office Ratio"; that is, for every $1 the filmmakers spent, they made back $10,931. That is success and a house in Malibu.

RECOMMENDED VIEWING

THE CHANGELING (1980), THE OTHERS (2001), GHOST STORY (1981), THE INNOCENTS (1961), JU-ON (2000), THE ENTITY (1981), STIR OF ECHOES (1999), THE DEVIL'S BACKBONE (2001), THE SHINING (1980), DARK WATER (2002), THE HAUNTING (1963), THE AMITYVILLE HORROR (1979), POLTERGEIST (1982).

DEMONS & DEVILS

William Shakespeare once said, "There are more things in heaven and earth, Horatio, than are dreamt of in your philosophy." This type of thinking is what keeps the horror movie industry in business. Stories about demons and devils are as old as creation. The constant battle of good and evil seems unending. They're timeless, mythological archetypes waiting to be retold for each new generation.

In 2002, when I was preparing to produce and direct the film Stuart Gordon Presents DEATHBED (2002), I was turned on to several movies by horror legend Stuart Gordon. One film in particular we analyzed was ROSEMARY'S BABY (1968), and it was then my taste in horror movies changed. The movie inspired many filmmakers, including Stuart, but for me this movie became my new guidebook for horror filmmaking. Roman Polanski, a living master of cinema, takes us inside a cult of witches who usher in the birth of the son of Satan. If anyone in Hollywood has experienced the aftermath of evil, it's Polanski. A year after the film was made, his pregnant wife Sharon

DEMONIC TOYS (1992)
Photo Credit: Courtesy of Full Moon Features.

Tate and her friends were brutally murdered by the Manson family in 1969.

I think most horror fans would agree that William Peter Blatty's adaptation of his novel THE EXORCIST (1973) is the scariest movie made on the subject of demonic possession. It has had the most psychological impact on its audience since its release in 1973, and it also created the most controversy. People fainted and went into hysterics at the theaters, actress Linda Blair had death threats from religious zealots, and Christian evangelist Billy Graham even claimed an actual demon was living in the celluloid of the film reels. "I have no doubt that THE EXORCIST moved people very profoundly," says director William Friedkin. "There is always an attempt to try and label and defuse the impact of something that moves us deeply. Very few people really want to accept the stuff that is going on there as a kind of unknowable phenomenon. It's easier to call it a horror film." Even after all the controversy, the film remains a classic. It spawned several sequels and won two Academy Awards in 1973.

RECOMMENDED VIEWING

THE EXORCIST (1973), DEMONS (1985), NEEDFUL THINGS (1993), THE DEVIL'S ADVOCATE (1997), THE NINTH GATE (1999), SOMETHING WICKED THIS WAY COMES (1983), THE OMEN (1976), ROSEMARY'S BABY (1968), HELLRAISER (1987), TALES FROM THE CRYPT: DEMON KNIGHT (1995), THE SENTINEL (1977), LORD OF ILLUSIONS (1995).

ALIEN LIFE-FORMS

Aliens in horror films provide a great opportunity to use your imagination to the fullest. Imagining what a creature from another world might be like is the most stimulating part of the filmmaking process, and the possibilities are endless. Just remember that an alien in a horror film is not necessarily the same as an alien in a sci-fi film; there is a difference.

A-list Hollywood heavyweight Peter Jackson, who gave us the LORD OF THE RINGS trilogy and the 2005 remake of KING KONG, started his career making low-budget horror films in New Zealand. Over a 4-year period, using his friends as actors, Jackson made the horror/comedy called BAD TASTE (1987) with his own 16mm camera. The movie is about big-headed aliens turning the townsfolk into intergalactic hamburgers for their fast food chain. The film never had a script and was improvised during production; the masks were made in Jackson's mother's kitchen, and he even invented a homemade Steadicam device for $15. Although Jackson funded most of the movie himself, eventually the New Zealand Film Commission gave him some finishing funds to complete the picture. The young Jackson was an innovator and an inspiration to me and many other indie filmmakers.

RECOMMENDED VIEWING

INVASION OF THE BODY SNATCHERS (1978), LIFEFORCE (1985), ALIEN (1979), THE TERROR WITHIN (1989), THE THING (1982), PREDATOR (1987), FROM BEYOND (1986), BAD TASTE (1987), DREAMCATCHER (2003), SPECIES (1995), THE TOM-MYKNOCKERS (1993), BABY BLOOD (1990), THE BLOB (1988).

CLIVE SAYS

" Let's put subtext aside for a moment and consider the creature that cavorts at the centre of any horror movie: the monster. The leader of Hell's Sadean order of Cenobites, ol' Pinhead himself. But where, I am regularly asked, does this nightmare come from? Well, I've already made mention of the sadomasochistic elements, which reflect my own long-standing interest in such taboo areas. Associated with that milieu is the punkish influence, which makes Pinhead the patron Saint of Piercing. But there is also a streak of priestly deportment and high-flown rhetoric in him that suggests this is a monster who knows his Milton as well as he knows his de Sade, and can probably recite the Mass in Latin (albeit backwards). "

—CLIVE BARKER

MADMEN & SERIAL KILLERS

One of the three great Confucian philosophers in China during the Classical period was a man named Hsün-tzu. He once said that "the nature of man is evil; his goodness is only acquired through training." He preached that when a human being is born, his nature consists of instinctual drives that, when left undeveloped, are selfish, anarchic, and antisocial.

It's society and family that mold his behavior until he becomes a disciplined and morally conscious human being. If you want to make a great madman, strip away his training and get to the root of his evil nature. This is the key. The earliest serial killer movie ever made was the German expressionist film THE CABINET OF DR. CALIGARI made in 1920. This is a great example of how, even in the early days of cinema, people craved the emotions of a horror picture.

Clive Barker once said, "Sometimes it's good to be in the hands of a maniac. Just so long as it's in art, not life." Some A-list filmmakers started their careers by putting their audience in the hands of a maniac. In 1963, in Ireland, B-movie legend Roger Corman was making the film THE YOUNG RACERS (1963). At the time, a young Francis Ford Coppola, the multiple Academy Award-winning director who gave us THE GOD-FATHER (1972) and APOCALYPSE NOW (1979), was working as a sound technician on the shoot. With money leftover from the shoot, Corman gave Coppola his first mainstream directing gig, DEMENTIA 13 (1963), a cheap copycat of the Hitchcock hit PSYCHO (1960). Corman allowed Coppola to use the same set, crew, and actors William Campbell, Luana Anders, and Patrick Magee, as long as he could work around Corman's shooting schedule. Coppola made this slasher classic for an estimated $42,000.

In 1972, Wes Craven made a low-budget horror film called LAST HOUSE ON THE LEFT (1972) for an estimated $90,000. The film is about a group of girls that are held captive by a group of psychotic convicts. After the convicts butcher them, the gang seeks refuge in a house owned by the parents of one of the victims. It was based on the Ingmar Bergman film THE VIRGIN SPRING (1960). To this day it is a very realistic and disturbing look at human brutality. In their marketing campaign, the filmmakers used one of the great tag lines: "To avoid fainting, keep repeating, 'it's only a movie…it's only a movie…it's only a movie…'" I found myself chanting this mantra the first time I saw the film.

RECOMMENDED VIEWING

AUDITION (1999), HENRY: PORTRAIT OF A SERIAL KILLER (1986), AMERICAN PSYCHO (2000), HALLOWEEN (1978), THE TEXAS CHAINSAW MASSACRE (1974), SAW (2004), CAPE FEAR (1991), NIGHTBREED (1990), FRIDAY THE 13TH (1980), THE SILENCE OF THE LAMBS (1991), THE LAST HOUSE ON THE LEFT (1972), DEMENTIA 13 (1963), VACANCY (2007).

VAMPIRES

We're all familiar with the charming, exotic, well-dressed creatures that seduce beautiful women on the screen—the romantic antihero. We all know we can kill them with a stake through the heart and sunlight, ward them off with garlic, burn them with holy water, and test our friends by checking in a mirror to see if they have a reflection or not. Despite how many cliché vampire movies have been made, this is no doubt a popular monster and one of my favorites.

In modern times we have an entire underground subculture of followers who model themselves after vampire fiction; they usually distinguish themselves from fictional and folkloric vampires by adding a *y—vampyre*. They glamorize the vampires of popular fiction and emulate their lifestyles through music, nightclubs, role-playing games, web sites, and chat rooms. They are usually drawn to this lifestyle because they were different as children—or just misunderstood—and this alluring lifestyle offers them an escape to an exotic existence where they can shape their identities. Some have been known to participate in blood drinking rituals and other subcultures like Goths, blood fetishism, sadomasochism, and bondage. I don't recommend becoming a vampyre solely for story ideas.

In other occult lores, the vampire is thought of more as a psychic vampire. They believe that they can leave their grave in a spirit form instead of a physical one. These psychic vampires feast on life energy, not physical blood, similar to some Hollywood producers.

Vampirism is an extremely popular subject for low-budget horror films. George Romero's film MARTIN (1977), a low-budget horror film made for an

Art by Dave Lange, Darkmatter Studios.

estimated budget of $80,000, tells a story of a young man who believes he is a vampire. It's interesting to note that this movie isn't about fangs and special effects; rather, it's about razor blades and syringes and an insatiable bloodlust of a misguided youth. This is a superb film to see how a master like George Romero envisioned a new kind of vampire—or perhaps a vampyre.

RECOMMENDED VIEWING

NOSFERATU (1922), THE LOST BOYS (1987), FROM DUSK TILL DAWN (1996), NEAR DARK (1987), DRACULA (1992), FRIGHT NIGHT (1985), BLADE (1998), VAMP (1986), THE HUNGER (1983), SALEM'S LOT (1979), 30 DAYS OF NIGHT (2007), MARTIN (1977), VAMPIRES (1998), VAMPYR (1932), INTERVIEW WITH THE VAMPIRE (1994).

WEREWOLVES & SHAPE-SHIFTERS

Is the idea of a man transforming into a wolf really that far-fetched? After all, when you look at the evolutionary timetables and see a small monkey evolving into modern-day man, it's not that hard to believe. The Greeks have a legend about King Lycaon of Arcadia. The story goes that King Lycaon served Zeus a meal of human flesh. Offended and disgusted, Zeus pushed it away and transformed King Lycaon into a wolf. This is also where the scientific term for werewolf comes from, "lycanthrope." We even see an early account in the Bible. In the book of Daniel (4:15–33), King Nebuchadnezzar showed symptoms of lycanthropy for several years.

In 1999, a scientist attempted to patent a technique for creating animal–human hybrids. The new creatures were said to be bizarre life-forms that no one has seen before. Lucky for mankind, the U.S. Patent and Trademark Office rejected the request, but you can just imagine the possibilities. H. G. Wells created animal–human hybrids in his novel *The Island of Dr. Moreau*, which was published in the 1890s.

Werewolf legends and evidence of animal cults go back for millennia. The beast within cannot be ignored. There may be a wolf in each and every one of us, and these legends can mirror the animal that exists in us. What happens to people when they give in to these primal urges? A horror film is born.

RECOMMENDED VIEWING

WOLF (1994), THE HOWLING (1981), DOG SOLDIERS (2002), AN AMERICAN WEREWOLF IN LONDON (1981), SILVER BULLET (1985), WOLFEN (1981), BAD MOON (1996), GINGER SNAPS (2000), CURSED (2005), THE WOLF MAN (1941), AN AMERICAN WEREWOLF IN PARIS (1997), FULL ECLIPSE (1993), SLEEPWALKERS (1992), ISLAND OF LOST SOULS (1932), THE COMPANY OF WOLVES (1984).

ZOMBIES & THE UNDEAD

Zombies give us a look at ourselves after we die. They are beings that should not be. They are reanimated corpses out for blood and brains, or they're just trapped in a rotting body roaming the countryside because hell was full.

In the Victorian era, postmortem photographs—that is, photos of dead people—were the second most common type of photograph, especially in the United States. Usually this was the only photograph ever taken of the person. Also during the era, most households had a parlor, or "death room," in which deceased family members were laid out for final respects and then photographed, and the picture was sent to friends, family, and loved ones. History shows us that humans want to remember the dead, but horror filmmakers show us that sometimes we must bring them back.

Several Hollywood directors started their careers by making classic zombie films, such as George Romero with NIGHT OF THE LIVING DEAD (1968), made for an estimated $114,000; and LORD OF THE RINGS writer/director Peter Jackson with his zombie splatter fest DEAD-ALIVE (1992). Sam Raimi's classic THE EVIL DEAD (1981), made for only $50,000 and shot on 16mm film by a group of friends over several years, is to this day a great example of what one can do with an ultra-low budget, a creative mind, and determination. It's interesting to note that Raimi's inspiration was a student project called EQUINOX (1970) that was made for only $6,500.

The TRANCERS series.
Photo Credit: Image courtesy of Full Moon Features

RECOMMENDED VIEWING

NIGHT OF THE LIVING DEAD (1968), CITY OF THE LIVING DEAD (1980), DEAD-ALIVE (1992), RE-ANIMATOR (1985), EVIL DEAD II (1987), SHAUN OF THE DEAD (2004), RETURN OF THE LIVING DEAD (1985), 28 DAYS LATER...(2002), THE SERPENT AND THE RAINBOW (1988), RESIDENT EVIL (2002), PHANTASM (1979).

DISEASE, PLAGUE & PARASITES

We have all been sick at some stage of our lives, and the thought of an unseen or microscopic villain inside us makes most people squirm. I encourage you to remember the experience of having a fever, chills, food poisoning, vomiting, or one of the many other ails of the body. For a person to be at the mercy of the body and its ability to fight off a cold, sore throat, cancer, or other sickness, it quickly reminds us of our mortality. In our modern-day world, especially with the looming threat of bioterrorism, this subject in horror films is a realistic and valid one.

There are several writer/directors that started their careers by making low-budget horror films dealing with parasites and disease. David Cronenberg's first feature film was SHIVERS (1975), which was made for an estimated budget of $179,000 (CAD) and was Canada's most profitable film made to date in 1975. First time writer/director Eli Roth made CABIN FEVER (2002), a film about a group of teens who rent a cabin in the woods and fall victim to a flesh-eating virus. The film was made for $1.5 million and grossed approximately $30.5 million at the box office internationally. The film launched young Eli Roth's career and was Lionsgate Home Entertainment's highest grossing horror film in 2003.

RECOMMENDED VIEWING

CABIN FEVER (2002), RABID (1977), KANSEN (2004), THE OMEGA MAN (1971), SHIVERS (1975), I AM LEGEND (2007), PARASITE (1982), BRAIN DAMAGE (1988).

HUMAN HYBRIDS

One way to create a great monster is to take a human being and fuse him or her with an opposite, or something horrific. For example, in David Cronenberg's THE FLY (1986), eccentric scientist Seth Brundle

(Jeff Goldblum) is experimenting with a set of "Telepods" that allows instantaneous teleportation of an object from one pod to another. He has been successful transporting inanimate objects, but when he tries a live baboon the result is a grotesque monstrosity. After working out some bugs, no pun intended, he successfully transports a second baboon with no apparent harm. Inspired by his success and frustrated by his love life, he decides to try it on himself. As the pod doors close, a common house-fly slips into the chamber, unseen by Brundle. Moments later he emerges from the pod, seemingly normal. For the rest of the film we see him change into something fantastic: Brundle Fly. Part human, part fly.

Looking out your window into Mother Nature you will be surprised at the animals and creepy crawlers that can inspire you to create your own hybrid monster. If you carefully study the creatures' habits, eating rituals, hunting tactics, and mating behaviors, you will invent some original hybrids for your story. For example: vampires (human–bat), werewolves (human–beast), and cyborgs (human–machine).

As human beings, we think of ourselves as masters of our universe: we've landed on the Moon, split the atom, and tamed the beasts of nature. Seeing ourselves as anything less than perfect or at the bottom of the food chain may be disturbing to most. Horror films should tear apart the normal and make it abnormal. When we see something unnatural, it makes us squirm. When we create a monster that is half human, we empathize more, but at the same time we are repulsed by that other half. Adding the part-human factor to a monster helps the audience feel as if this, too, could happen to them, and it makes them empathetic. It makes the creature both fantastic and tragic, but also real.

The following are some examples of human hybrids as seen in horror films:

HUMAN & MACHINE

TERMINATOR (1984), BLADE RUNNER (1982), GHOST IN THE MACHINE (1993), BRAINSCAN (1994), CHRISTINE (1983), PULSE (Japanese version, 2001), TETSUO: THE IRON MAN (1989).

HUMAN & PLANT

SWAMP THING (1982), LITTLE SHOP OF HORRORS (1986), INVASION OF THE BODY SNATCHERS (1978), ATTACK OF THE KILLER TOMATOES! (1978), ACACIA (2003).

WES SAYS

"*I just felt that Freddy was the paradigm of the threatening adult. Freddy stood for the threatening side of male adulthood. He was the ultimate bad father. It's a sickness where youth is hated. Childhood and innocence are hated. From the very beginning that's how I saw him.*"

—WES CRAVEN on A NIGHTMARE ON ELM STREET

ADAPTATIONS OF CLASSICAL LITERATURE

For those of you who are fans of classical horror literature, I encourage you to consider an adaptation. Most of the works of horror masters Edgar Allan Poe and H. P. Lovecraft are in the public domain, which means the copyright has expired and you can use the material for free. There are numerous short stories and novels that have fantastic creatures that have not yet been adapted to the screen or perhaps just need a retelling. This is a great place to start because your star is the classical author himself.

RECOMMENDED VIEWING

NECRONOMICON: BOOK OF THE DEAD (1993), THE RESSURRECTED (1992), RE-ANIMATOR (1985), DAGON (2001), THE UNNAMABLE (1988), DREAMS OF THE WITCH-HOUSE (2006), THE CURSE (1997), THE BLACK CAT (2007), CASTLE OF BLOOD (1964), THE PIT AND THE PENDULUM (1961), DIE, MONSTER, DIE! (1965).

KILLING STYLE & WEAPON RECOGNITION

You must establish early on how your monster is a threat. If your protagonist and your audience aren't absolutely terrified of the monster, you have no movie. If your monster is a physical being, how does he kill? For a slasher film, you must choose a recognizable weapon. In HALLOWEEN (1978) it's a kitchen knife; in the NIGHTMARE ON ELM STREET films, Freddy uses his razor-sharp glove on his right hand. In a supernatural film it may be through possession or manipulating inanimate objects to kill. Establishing these elements early in the story will help you in writing and also directing.

ADMIRATION OF THE MONSTER

When creating a monster, you should make it so wicked and fantastic that your characters and the audience admire it and its special abilities. Your monster must have strength of epic proportions, have the ability to break the laws of reality, jump to other dimensions of existence, reanimate the dead, break through walls, or whatever your mind can create. All great monsters have something that is attractive; usually it is power, strength, or supernatural abilities. This is a common theme in horror films. How many have you seen where the scientist admires the acid-like blood of an alien species, or the reproduction rate of a female mutated rat, or the way it eats its victims?

KNOW THY MONSTER

There is no magic formula to making a great movie monster. However, it's refreshing when I see new monster ideas or people reinventing old ones. You should be encouraged to create your own monster, madman, or malevolent forces of antagonism unlike anything the world has ever seen. There are no shortcuts to being original. Look inside yourself and you will be surprised at the monsters that lurk in your subconscious waiting to be born.

INTERVIEW BOX

ROBERT ENGLUND ACTOR, DIRECTOR

AKA Freddy Krueger from the NIGHTMARE ON ELM STREET Films

Robert Englund (2005).
Source: Wikipedia.

www.RobertEnglund.com

ROBERT ENGLUND returned to the West Coast where he had grown up after 5 years of success in regional theater. His very first audition landed him a starring role in the 1973 film BUSTER AND BILLIE directed by Daniel Petrie.

Far from living the classic hand-to-mouth existence of a struggling actor, Englund worked steadily through the 1970s playing best friends, bad guy #1, and southern rednecks and starring opposite Henry Fonda, Susan Sarandon, Jeff Bridges, Sally Field, and Arnold Schwarzenegger, among others.

In the 1970s, regarded as the second golden age of American movies, Englund was privileged to work for such classic film directors as Robert Aldrich, Robert Mulligan, J. Lee Thompson, Bob Rafelson, and John Milius.

During this time, Englund was living in Malibu, fishing off his porch at high tide, and surfing, when not slogging through traffic on the seemingly endless rounds of interviews and callbacks that fill the days of every working actor. He guest starred in scores of TV shows and worked alongside some of the biggest stars of that decade, including Barbra Streisand, Richard Gere, Burt Reynolds, and Charles Bronson.

Finally, audiences could put a name to his familiar face when Englund was cast as Willie the friendly alien in the hit miniseries and subsequent weekly TV show V. Within weeks, Englund went from questions like, "Didn't I go to high school with you?" to "Aren't you that lizard guy on TV?" Twenty-five years later Willie still generates fan mail from science fiction devotees both in the United States and around the world.

The series was a huge success. As a result Englund figured he would be eternally typecast as a sweet and lovable alien. To counterbalance this public image, he looked for a role that would allow him to demonstrate another side of his talents. During one hiatus from filming the series, he auditioned for a hot young director making an interesting low-budget horror movie for the independent studio New Line Cinema. Englund's interview with Wes Craven landed him the role of the burn-scarred dream demon, Freddy Krueger, in A NIGHTMARE ON ELM STREET and launched him into horror history.

Englund's portrayal of Freddy Krueger blasted him into the pop culture vernacular as heir apparent to the horror icons of the past, destined to stand alongside Bela Lugosi's Dracula and Boris Karloff's monster in FRANKENSTEIN.

After more than 70 feature length films, four TV series, and countless episodic guest star roles, Englund is now directing as well as acting, and he is exploring the world of reality television and Internet programming.

DRAVEN: *Your character Freddy Krueger from the* NIGHTMARE ON ELM STREET *films is one of the most influential screen monsters in the history of horror films. What are the mechanics underneath that made Freddy such an unforgettable screen monster, and why?*

ENGLUND: It is a combination of the character's sense of humor and Freddy's physicality in which I bring to the role as a trained actor. He's not only reminiscent of the familiar boogie man of myth and fairy tale but he also represents a very real sexual threat. These factors combined with the nightmare/bad dream trope make him a novel and contemporary villain.

DRAVEN: *In the horror genre, what are the biggest mistakes you see filmmakers make when creating a monster?*

ENGLUND: Instead of erring in the direction of originality, filmmakers tend to borrow from preexisting creations that everyone is familiar with. That could be monsters, creatures, or villains that they have already seen in other movies or read about in books or comics. Established monsters can be reinterpreted, freshened up, e.g. the vampires in 30 DAYS OF NIGHT (2007) and the damaged heroine/killer from MAY (2002).

DRAVEN: *What is the best way for a new director to communicate with an actor on set?*

ENGLUND: Directors need to respect the fact that all actors work differently. Directors should be able to adapt to each actor's needs. Some actors require discipline, some require pampering, and others should be left alone. All actors should be encouraged to bring their ideas to the project. It is also important that the director communicate so that all departments are on the same page.

DRAVEN: *What do actors really want from a director?*

ENGLUND: I don't know about others, but I want the director's vision communicated to me. I also want the director to be open to my ideas.

DRAVEN: *In your vast experience in the genre, what do you think are the key elements to a great cinematic death scene?*

ENGLUND: Surprise. I think my favorite death scene is Harry Dean Stanton's in THE MISSOURI BREAKS (1976) directed by Arthur Penn.

DRAVEN: *In the horror genre, what are your favorite screen monsters, and why?*

ENGLUND: The BRIDE OF FRANKENSTEIN (1935), the creature from the Id in

continued on the next page

continued from the previous page

FORBIDDEN PLANET (1956), the giant squid from 20,000 LEAGUES UNDER THE SEA (1954), the Cyclops from THE 7TH VOYAGE OF SINBAD (1958), Norman Bates from the original PSYCHO (1960), William Finley as Emil Breton in SISTERS (1973), John Cassavetes in ROSEMARY'S BABY (1968), the alien in ALIEN (1979) and its sequels, Klaus Kinski in NOSFERATU (1979), the stick man/insect in MIMIC (1997), and Angela Bettis in MAY (2002). They all surprised me with their original performances or designs, captured my imagination when I was young, or thrilled me as an adult.

DRAVEN: *What are some of the things that annoy you about low-budget films in today's digital revolution?*

ENGLUND: I am more annoyed by overproduced, money-wasting event films that rely on CGI and fail to deliver proper thrills.

DRAVEN: *In today's world of distribution, there is a glut in the marketplace with too many independent horror films being made. Some producers seem to recycle the same star actors, over and over again, ad nauseam. What are your thoughts on this?*

ENGLUND: There is too much product of all types these days. There are too many teen comedies, too many mediocre thrillers, too many chick movies, etc. When producers are fortunate enough to luck into a popular character, of course they are going to exploit it. Franchises are inevitable. The popularity of an actor dictates how many movies he will be in. The profits from a successful bad movie/franchise can fund several low-budget, independent movies. Movies beget movies.

DRAVEN: *Where do you think the future of the horror film is headed?*

ENGLUND: I'd like to see some classic period horror revisited as a source, maybe some Edgar Allan Poe or Brothers Grimm.

DRAVEN: *What does Freddy Krueger think of my book?*

ENGLUND: He couldn't put it down but ruined his copy turning pages with his glove on.

Notes On Writing Weird Fiction

By H.P. Lovecraft

NOTES ON WRITING WEIRD FICTION
BY H. P. LOVECRAFT

My reason for writing stories is to give myself the satisfaction of visualising more clearly and detailedly and stably the vague, elusive, fragmentary impressions of wonder, beauty, and adventurous expectancy which are conveyed to me by certain sights (scenic, architectural, atmospheric, etc.), ideas, occurrences, and images encountered in art and literature. I choose weird stories because they suit my inclination best—one of my strongest and most persistent wishes being to achieve, momentarily, the illusion of some strange suspension or violation of the galling limitations of time, space, and natural law which forever imprison us and frustrate our curiosity about the infinite cosmic spaces beyond the radius of our sight and analysis. These stories frequently emphasise the element of horror because fear is our deepest and strongest emotion, and the one which best lends itself to the creation of Nature-defying illusions. Horror and the unknown or the strange are always closely connected, so that it is hard to create a convincing picture of shattered natural law or cosmic alienage or "outsideness" without laying stress on the emotion of fear. The reason why *time* plays a great part in so many of my tales is that this element looms up in my mind as the most profoundly dramatic and grimly terrible thing in the universe.

H. P. Lovecraft (1890-1937).

Conflict with time seems to me the most potent and fruitful theme in all human expression.

While my chosen form of story-writing is obviously a special and perhaps a narrow one, it is none the less a persistent and permanent type of expression, as old as literature itself. There will always be a certain small percentage of persons who feel a burning curiosity about unknown outer space, and a burning desire to escape from the prison-house of the known and the real into those enchanted lands of incredible adventure and infinite possibilities which dreams open up to us, and which things like deep woods, fantastic urban towers, and flaming sun-sets momentarily suggest. These persons include great authors as well as insignifi-cant amateurs like myself—Dunsany, Poe, Arthur Machen, M. R. James, Algernon Blackwood, and Walter de la Mare being typical masters in this field.

As to how I write a story—there is no one way. Each one of my tales has a differ-ent history. Once or twice I have literally written out a dream; but usually I start with a mood or idea or image which I wish to express, and revolve it in my mind until I can think of a good way of embodying it in some chain of dramatic occurrences capa-ble of being recorded in concrete terms. I tend to run through a mental list of the basic conditions or situations best adapted to such a mood or idea or image, and then begin to speculate on logical and naturally motivated explanations of the given mood or idea or image in terms of the basic con-dition or situation chosen.

The actual process of writing is of course as varied as the choice of theme and initial conception; but if the history of all my tales were analysed, it is just pos-sible that the following set of rules might be deduced from the *average* procedure:

1. Prepare a synopsis or scenario of events in the order of their abso-lute *occurrence*—*not* the order of their narration. Describe with enough fulness to cover all vital points and motivate all incidents planned. Details, comments, and estimates of consequences are sometimes desirable in this tempo-rary framework.

2. Prepare a second synopsis or scenario of events—this one in order of *narration* (not actual occurrence), with ample fulness and detail, and with notes as to changing perspective, stresses, and climax. Change the original synopsis to fit if such a change will increase the dramatic force or general effectiveness of the story. Interpolate or delete incidents at will—never being bound by the original conception even if the ultimate result be a tale wholly dif-ferent from that first planned. Let additions and alterations be made whenever suggested by anything in the formulating process.

3. Write out the story—rapidly, flu-ently, and not too critically—following the *second* or narrative-order synopsis. Change incidents and plot whenever the developing process seems to suggest such change, never being bound by any previous design. If the development sud-denly reveals new opportunities for dramatic effect or vivid story telling, add whatever is thought advantageous—going back and reconciling the early parts to the

continued on the next page

continued from the previous page

new plan. Insert and delete whole sections if necessary or desirable, trying different beginnings and endings until the best arrangement is found. But be sure that all references throughout the story are thoroughly reconciled with the final design. Remove all possible superfluities—words, sentences, paragraphs, or whole episodes or elements—observing the usual precautions about the reconciling of all references.

4. Revise the entire text, paying attention to vocabulary, syntax, rhythm of prose, proportioning of parts, niceties of tone, grace and convincingness of transitions (scene to scene, slow and detailed action to rapid and sketchy time-covering action and vice versa…etc., etc., etc.), effectiveness of beginning, ending, climaxes, etc., dramatic suspense and interest, plausibility and atmosphere, and various other elements.

5. Prepare a neatly typed copy—not hesitating to add final revisory touches where they seem in order.

The first of these stages is often purely a mental one—a set of conditions and happenings being worked out in my head, and never set down until I am ready to prepare a detailed synopsis of events in order of narration. Then, too, I sometimes begin even the actual writing before I know how I shall develop the idea—this beginning forming a problem to be motivated and exploited.

There are, I think, four distinct types of weird story; one expressing a *mood or feeling*, another expressing a *pictorial conception*, a third expressing a *general situation, condition, legend or intellectual conception*, and a fourth explaining a *definite tableau or specific dramatic situation or climax*. In another way, weird tales may be grouped into two rough categories—those in which the marvel or horror concerns some *condition* or *phenomenon*, and those in which it concerns some *action of persons* in connexion with a bizarre condition or phenomenon.

Each weird story—to speak more particularly of the horror type—seems to involve five definite elements: (a) some basic, underlying horror or abnormality—condition, entity, etc.—, (b) the general effects or bearings of the horror, (c) the mode of manifestation—object embodying the horror and phenomena observed—, (d) the types of fear-reaction pertaining to the horror, and (e) the specific effects of the horror in relation to the given set of conditions.

In writing a weird story I always try very carefully to achieve the right mood and atmosphere, and place the emphasis where it belongs. One cannot, except in immature pulp charlatan-fiction, present an account of impossible, improbable, or inconceivable phenomena as a common-place narrative of objective acts and conventional emotions. Inconceivable events and conditions have a special handicap to over come, and this can be accomplished only through the maintenance of a careful realism in every phase of the story *except* that touching on the one given marvel. This marvel must be treated very impressively and deliberately—with a careful emotional "build-up"—else it will seem flat and unconvincing. Being the principal thing in the story, its mere existence should overshadow the characters and events. But the characters and events must be consistent and natural except where they touch the single marvel. In relation to the central wonder, the characters should shew the same overwhelming emotion which similar characters would shew toward such a wonder in real life. Never have a wonder taken for granted. Even when the characters are supposed to be accustomed to the wonder I try to weave an air of awe and impressiveness corresponding to what the reader should feel. A casual style ruins any serious fantasy.

Atmosphere, not action, is the great desideratum of weird fiction. Indeed, all that a wonder story can ever be is *a vivid picture of a certain type of human mood*. The moment it tries to be anything else it becomes cheap, puerile, and unconvincing. Prime emphasis should be given to *subtle* suggestion—imperceptible hints and touches of selective associative detail which express shadings of moods and build up a vague illusion of the strange reality of the unreal. Avoid bald catalogues of incredible happenings which can have no substance or meaning apart from a sustaining cloud of colour and symbolism. These are the rules or standards which I have followed—consciously or unconsciously—ever since I first attempted the serious writing of fantasy. That my results are successful may well be disputed—but I feel at least sure that, had I ignored the considerations mentioned in the last few paragraphs, they would have been much worse than they are.

RECOMMENDED SOFTWARE PROGRAMS

Here are some recommended software programs to get you started writing your script:

Final Draft
www.finaldraft.com

Movie Outline
www.movieoutline.com

Contour
http://www.marinersoftware.com/

Movie Magic Screenwriter
www.screenplay.com

Storyist
www.storyist.com

Scrivener
www.literatureandlatte.com

PART TWO

PREPRODUCTION

CHAPTER 2
GETTING STARTED

There is nothing more satisfying than having a script you believe in, a clear vision of your film, and the determination to get the movie made no matter what the consequences. When you get to this point, you can read the rest of this book…

Before you do anything else, it's important that your script is fine-tuned and *ready for production*. I was up against crazy deadlines and delivery schedules when I was a producer for hire, and sometimes the scripts would be rushed. The biggest mistake was that some films were going into production with a script that wasn't ready. This causes all kinds of disasters on set, such as continuity problems, gaps in the story, character inconsistencies, and just general goofs—and it shows in the final product. These are all issues that should be worked out in the script development stage, but all too often on low-budget films it happens on set.

When your script is green-lit, it's time to get your movie into production and out into the world, hopefully within one year or less.

FINANCING

I'm often asked how I get financing for a film. It's not easy, especially for new filmmakers who may not have any credits. For your first feature or short, I think it's best to self-finance your project. I know not all of us are rolling in money, but for the price of a car these days you can make

an impressive first feature. The chances of you raising millions of dollars for your first independent epic are slim. Just be honest with yourself and your accomplishments, and always look at your projects from the investor's point of view. If you were an investor, would you hand over hundreds of thousands of dollars to a new filmmaker with little or no experience? Maybe…maybe not. It's much easier to get investors after you have a proven track record or at least a show reel. But how do you get there?

There are some fine books out there about financing, business plans, and how to get other people's money. I recommend you read all of them. However, I'll be frank with you: I've never done any of that. I started out with no friends or family in the business and no connections at all. I knew no one in Hollywood when I first moved to town. All the money for my films has come through networking with the right people. Just because you make a great business plan for your film doesn't guarantee anyone will read it. The budget is never how much you want to raise; rather, it's how much the investor is willing to spend. When you know that number, you can conform your indie movie to fit the budget.

PRODUCTION AGREEMENT SAMPLE (DOWNLOAD)

This is an example of a typical agreement for the financing, production, and distribution of a motion picture.

web file: Production_Agreement_SAMPLE.pdf

(Note: throughout the book, you will sometimes see files listed like this – this indicates that they can

be downloaded from the companion website, at http://booksite.focalpress.com/companion/Draven. Instructions for accessing the site are given in the Table of Contents, after the web material listing).

FILM VERSUS DIGITAL

When I'm preparing a film, the decision to shoot digital or on film is always the first question I ask myself. I consider a lot of factors when deciding on a shooting format for the production, such as budget, tech and crew requirements, overall look, and final delivery requirements. There is a lot of debate going on among filmmakers who argue that one format is better or cheaper than the other. I think both formats are great professional options, but it's important not to turn your nose up at one or the other and always be open to all possibilities. Film has been around for over 100 years; it is still going strong and is a standard for making motion pictures. Digital production is as common as ever and also a great format of choice. The two formats are, of course, very different. After all, film is a photochemical process and digital is zeros and ones. I don't believe one is better than the other. It's simply a matter of personal taste. If I want a movie to look like digital, I'll shoot digital; if I want it to look like film, I'll shoot film. Each format has its place depending on your artistic needs. It's up to you to choose.

There are some amazing digital cinema cameras out there, such as the RED ONE camera, which seems to be revolutionizing digital cinema production. It's quite impressive and a popular high-end digital option for independents. They also have the SCARLET, EPIC, and a 3D model; it's truly amazing stuff.

The RED ONE digital camera.
Photo Credit: RED Digital Cinema (www.red.com).

The RED 3D digital Camera
Photo Credit: RED Digital Cinema (www.red.com)

The ARRIFLEX S16 camera (Super 16mm).
Photo Credit: ARRIFLEX (www.arri.com).

The ARRIFLEX 435 Xtreme camera (35mm).
Photo Credit: Arriflex (www.arri.com).

YOUR PRODUCTION COMPANY

Set Up a Company – It's vital to make a motion picture under the umbrella of a corporation. This could be a C corporation, S corporation, or, more commonly for motion picture production, a limited-liability company (LLC). This is for you and your investors' protection.

Get a Production Account – You must make sure to set up a separate bank account for your production funds. This includes getting a business checkbook, credit cards, ATM cards, and a personalized banker. A word of warning: never mix personal and production funds. When I was starting out, I tried to save money by running an entire production through my own personal bank account. I mixed my personal expenses with my production funds and lost track very quickly. I used my personal credit cards for most things and was confident I would just reimburse myself later. Needless to say, the film went over budget, and I had accumulated thousands of dollars in debt that I had to pay off over the next several years.

Get a Production Office – A production office is your communication hub. You must establish a central location where people can call and get someone on the phone at all times. This can be at a home office or a temporary rental space; I prefer the latter. The following checklist describes the communication and operations infrastructure that I set up first.

PRODUCTION OFFICE CHECKLIST

Phone & Voice Mail – One dedicated office phone number with voice mail is best. To avoid confusion, do not give out too many numbers.

Email & Internet – Establish one central email address for all communication with the cast and crew, and have a dedicated high-speed connection to the Internet.

Fax Machine – Your fax machine should be on a dedicated line. Even in an age of PDF files and digital signatures, this is used a lot during production for contracts, deal memos, and other production correspondence that requires actual signatures.

Production Web Site – If you set up a dedicated, password-protected web site, you can save time and money by posting all relevant production information on the site. This can include schedules, actor sides, script revisions, meal menus, up-to-date call times, and maps to locations. This works great; it centralizes all communication to one source and keeps the phones from ringing too much with questions from the cast and crew. If you do this, make sure your cast and crew members are Internet savvy, and instruct them to check the site daily.

Copy Machine – You can buy an inexpensive copy machine that will do the trick, or lease one if your production is larger. Don't be without it!

Office Supplies – Make sure you have plenty of ink, paper (regular, three-hole punch, and colored paper for revisions), staples, and paper clips to last the duration of the shoot.

ACORD™ CERTIFICATE OF LIABILITY INSURANCE

DATE (MM/DD/YYYY)
11/28/2006

PRODUCER	THIS CERTIFICATE IS ISSUED AS A MATTER OF INFORMATION ONLY AND CONFERS NO RIGHTS UPON THE CERTIFICATE HOLDER. THIS CERTIFICATE DOES NOT AMEND, EXTEND OR ALTER THE COVERAGE AFFORDED BY THE POLICIES BELOW.

PRODUCER: THE INSURANCE AGENT

Phone No.   Fax No.

INSURERS AFFORDING COVERAGE	NAIC #
INSURER A: EFM - Empire Fire and Marine Insurance Company	
INSURER B:	
INSURER C:	
INSURER D:	
INSURER E:	

INSURED: YOUR PRODUCTION COMPANY

Phone No.   Fax No.

COVERAGES

THE POLICIES OF INSURANCE LISTED BELOW HAVE BEEN ISSUED TO THE INSURED NAMED ABOVE FOR THE POLICY PERIOD INDICATED. NOTWITHSTANDING ANY REQUIREMENT, TERM OR CONDITION OF ANY CONTRACT OR OTHER DOCUMENT WITH RESPECT TO WHICH THIS CERTIFICATE MAY BE ISSUED OR MAY PERTAIN, THE INSURANCE AFFORDED BY THE POLICIES DESCRIBED HEREIN IS SUBJECT TO ALL THE TERMS, EXCLUSIONS AND CONDITIONS OF SUCH POLICIES. AGGREGATE LIMITS SHOWN MAY HAVE BEEN REDUCED BY PAID CLAIMS.

INSR LTR	ADD'L INSRD	TYPE OF INSURANCE	POLICY NUMBER	POLICY EFFECTIVE DATE (MM/DD/YY)	POLICY EXPIRATION DATE (MM/DD/YY)	LIMITS	
EFM		**GENERAL LIABILITY** [X] COMMERCIAL GENERAL LIABILITY CLAIMS MADE [X] OCCUR GEN'L AGGREGATE LIMIT APPLIES PER: POLICY PROJECT LOC	4568AS	12/01/2006	12/20/2006	EACH OCCURRENCE	$ 1,000,000
						DAMAGE TO RENTED PREMISES (Ea occurence)	$ 100,000
						MED EXP (Any one person)	$ 5,000
						PERSONAL & ADV INJURY	$ 1,000,000
						GENERAL AGGREGATE	$ 1,000,000
						PRODUCTS - COMP/OP AGG	$ 1,000,000
		AUTOMOBILE LIABILITY ANY AUTO ALL OWNED AUTOS SCHEDULED AUTOS HIRED AUTOS NON-OWNED AUTOS				COMBINED SINGLE LIMIT (Ea accident)	$
						BODILY INJURY (Per person)	$
						BODILY INJURY (Per accident)	$
						PROPERTY DAMAGE (Per accident) Max per Auto / Max Aggregate	$ Excluded / Excluded
		GARAGE LIABILITY ANY AUTO				AUTO ONLY - EA ACCIDENT	$
						OTHER THAN AUTO ONLY: EA ACC / AGG	$ / $
		EXCESS/UMBRELLA LIABILITY OCCUR CLAIMS MADE DEDUCTIBLE RETENTION $				EACH OCCURRENCE	$
						AGGREGATE	$
							$
							$
							$
		WORKERS COMPENSATION AND EMPLOYERS' LIABILITY ANY PROPRIETOR/PARTNER/EXECUTIVE OFFICER/MEMBER EXCLUDED? If yes, describe under SPECIAL PROVISIONS below				WC STATU-TORY LIMITS / OTH-ER	
						E.L. EACH ACCIDENT	$
						E.L. DISEASE - EA EMPLOYEE	$
						E.L. DISEASE - POLICY LIMIT	$
EFM		**OTHER** Miscellaneous Rented Equipment		12/01/2006	12/20/2006	Coverage $ 350,000	Deductible 2,500

DESCRIPTION OF OPERATIONS / LOCATIONS / VEHICLES / EXCLUSIONS ADDED BY ENDORSEMENT / SPECIAL PROVISIONS

*Split Dates apply to all coverages in the specified section.

Certificate Holder is named as an Additional Insured and Loss Payee as their interests may appear.

Coverage Location: United States & Canada

Production: UNTITLED GHOST STORY

All coverages expire at 12:01 a.m. Standard Time.

CERTIFICATE HOLDER	CANCELLATION
THE PERSON or COMPANY WHO YOU ARE INSURING Phone No. Fax No.	SHOULD ANY OF THE ABOVE DESCRIBED POLICIES BE CANCELLED BEFORE THE EXPIRATION DATE THEREOF, THE ISSUING INSURER WILL ENDEAVOR TO MAIL **1** DAYS WRITTEN NOTICE TO THE CERTIFICATE HOLDER NAMED TO THE LEFT, BUT FAILURE TO DO SO SHALL IMPOSE NO OBLIGATION OR LIABILITY OF ANY KIND UPON THE INSURER, ITS AGENTS OR REPRESENTATIVES. AUTHORIZED REPRESENTATIVE

ACORD 25 (2001/08)   90844-155580-120903   © ACORD CORPORATION 1988

Insurance certificate example (Page 1).

ADDITIONAL COVERAGE DETAILS

DATE (MM/DD/YY)

INSURED **YOUR PRODUCTION COMPANY**

The following is attached to and made part of certificate 155580-12

Policy Details	Coverage	Limit	Deductible
Inland Marine			
Company:	Empire Fire and Marine Insurance Company		
Policy Number:			
*Period:	12/01/2006 - 12/20/2006: 19 Day(s)		
	Miscellaneous Rented Equipment	350,000	2,500
	Props, Sets & Wardrobes	Excluded	
	Negative Film or Videotape	Excluded	
	Faulty Stock, Camera & Processing	Excluded	
	Extra Expense	Excluded	
	Third Party Property Damage	Excluded	
	Hired/Non-Owned Physical Damage-Aggregate	Excluded	
	Hired/Non-Owned Physical Damage-Per Vehicle	Excluded	
	Terrorism	Included	

*All coverages expire at 12:01 a.m. Standard Time.

Coverage is not afforded for stunts & pyrotechnics.

For a complete listing of coverages, terms, conditions and exclusions, please view your policy.

155580-

Insurance certificate example (Page 2).

Get Insurance – Production insurance is mandatory to protect yourself, your cast and crew, and everything your production team touches. A certificate of insurance is usually required by location owners, equipment rental houses, and other service providers. I've had people break bones, lights fall on heads, equipment destroyed, hands burned, and grips fall off of ladders! Usually, the lower the budget and the more inexperienced crew people are, the higher the possibility for injury or damage.

When you are talking to an insurance agent, it's wise to lay out all the facts and emphasize that your production is low risk. You should make it clear you are making a low-budget film with a small crew, no pyrotechnics, no firearms, no large trucks, etc. It's good to add the workers' compensation option to your policy, and it's also an incentive for crew members to work on your show knowing they are covered if anything were to happen.

THE SCRIPT PREPARATION

Lock & Number – Before you can break down your script, you must lock it to prevent any further changes. Locking a script is simply assigning scene numbers to all scenes and locking in the page numbers. After you lock the script, you can start breaking it down.

The Script Breakdown – For your script to be scheduled and budgeted, it must be broken down. I use the screenwriting program Final Draft to write the script and its companion program, Tagger, to import the script and break it down. When it is broken down in Tagger, the file is exported as a .sex file (don't get a dirty mind here, it really is a .sex file), and that can be imported into a scheduling program like Movie Magic's EP Scheduling or Gorilla.

GHOST MONTH breakdown in Final Draft Tagger.

Distribute Shooting Scripts – After your shooting script is locked, it's time to make copies and distribute it to everyone involved. This ensures that everyone is working off of the same material and scene numbers. You can save money by emailing everyone the shooting script as a PDF file or other digital file format.

Script Revisions – If you wish to make revisions after the script is locked, you must do so without altering the preexisting scene numbers. This avoids the need to print an entirely new draft each time a revision is made, and it ensures that all departments will not get confused. For example, if a new scene is written and needs to be inserted between scenes 21 and 22, the new scene will be numbered 21A. Page numbers are handled in a similar way. When looking at a revised script, the revisions are marked with asterisks in the right-hand margins of the revision pages. A script with a lot of revision pages is sometimes called a colored script or rainbow script because of its multicolored pages.

SCRIPT REVISION COLORS

In the United States, the standard color order is as follows: white (FFFFFF), blue (0000FF), pink (FFCBDB), yellow (FFFF00), green (00FF00), goldenrod (DAA520), buff (F0DC82), salmon (FA8072), cherry (FFB7C5), and tan (D2B48C). After that it starts over again with white. Other countries often include other paper colors.

BUDGETING TIPS & TRICKS

When budgeting a motion picture, it's always best to use a software application that specializes in film production. Don't use Excel or Word to do a budget. There are several software budgeting applications on the market. I use Movie Magic's EP Budgeting software to create my budgets. If you are a student, they offer affordable academic versions.

Reserve Money – Film production is not an exact science, and you should allow for that uncertainty in your budget. Usually, it's 10 to 20 percent of your entire budget.

Flat Fees – When negotiating rates for cast and crew, I have found that it's always better to talk in terms of flat rates. A flat fee sounds a lot better than an hourly rate, and it is much easier to budget.

Pay Fair – Always pay a fair rate to everyone. In my experience, cast and crew members talk to one another more than they talk to you. If you paid one person higher or lower than another for the same job, there may be some hard feelings or even a mutiny.

Money in the Bank – Never, never, never go into production without your *entire* budget in your bank account. I have been in hot water on several productions because I was waiting on cash flow from my executive producers, and they were having financial troubles. A word of warning: if an executive producer ever wants to cash flow your production a little at a time, *don't do it!* It's *your* reputation on the line if you don't pay your cast and crew, not the executive producer's.

Film Stock – The best way to get a good deal on film stock is to call a dealer, tell them you are an independent producer, and negotiate. Always get a bid from another place, then see who is willing to earn your business by giving you the best deal. It's a bidding war for your business. The more you buy, the bigger the break.

If you are considering shooting on ends, it comes in several types: *super shorts* (200–240 ft), *short ends* (250–290 ft), *long short ends* (300–390 ft), *recan 400* (400 ft), *medium ends* (450–690 ft), *long ends* (700–1,000 ft), *general recans* (usually full loads that were put into the camera but never exposed except for maybe a few feet; this could be a 400 or 1,000 ft recan) and *buy-backs* (brand new film that was left over from a production). I think shooting on ends is risky business, and I suggest you don't do it. I considered shooting 35mm short ends on GHOST MONTH, but instead we shot all brand new film stock and I saved money. Shooting new film can actually save you money if you consider the following:

1. **Less loading time using 1,000-ft loads (approximately 11 minutes on 35mm):** There is no need for a dedicated loader. Your second assistant cameraperson (AC) can double duties as a loader. Make sure you hire a second AC/loader.

2. **More productive time:** Fewer rollouts during the day means more productive time to get your pages shot.

3. **Quality assurance:** Although secondhand stock is supposed to be tested, labeled, and stored properly, you can never be too sure about it. It's refreshing to know your stock is new, was properly stored, and is ready to shoot.

A top sheet budget example in Movie Magic's EP Budgeting software.

Cash on Set – You must make sure you always have cash on set. You will need it for everything from running to the store for more coffee creamer, to gas money, to bribing the locals to be quiet while you shoot sound.

SCHEDULING TIPS & TRICKS

To create your schedules, it's best to use a software program that specializes in movie scheduling. Check out Movie Magic's EP Scheduling software. Movie Magic also offers affordable academic versions for students.

The First Day – It's best to always schedule the first day of shooting as a light, easy day. This is when the crew members adjust to one another and the overall pacing is determined for the entire shoot. Never schedule special effects, monster scenes, or any complicated setups on the first day; it's usually best to stick to dialog-only scenes.

Split Days Work Best – In my experience, the best way to schedule a movie is by *split days*—on a 12-hour day you split the day and the night evenly by scheduling from noon to midnight. If possible, avoid those 5 a.m. call times!

The Cast & Crew Funnel Effect – Every day the cast and crew is on set, you're paying for it. When scheduling and budgeting, you want to shoot out as many actors and crew members as possible. I call this a funnel effect because I start at the top and schedule as many people together as possible, then work my way down the schedule like a funnel until the cast and crew slowly disappears from the schedule. For example, you may not need to shoot sound on all days, or you may not need that extra camera assistant or grip for the entire shoot. If you want to save money, scheduling is the key to maximizing your productivity and budget.

Turnaround Time – You must make sure the crew has at least a 12-hour turnaround time. This includes if you go over the hours scheduled, you must adjust the following day to allow the extra time. If you don't, they will raise hell, and no work will get done the next day. Do not overwork your crew. It's counterproductive. They need to sleep and stay sharp and focused, and so do you!

Weather Backup Plans – It's important to check weather updates each and every day of the shoot. You should have a backup plan for every day built into your schedule.

A bare-bones crew is all we needed on this night.

Do not wait until it rains or snows to figure it out; you will have a lot of people standing around waiting on someone to instruct them what to do next.

The following is the final shooting schedule from my film GHOST MONTH. Everything from cast members to props can be tracked on a schedule board with numbers and IDs. I always include the wardrobe ID numbers on the strips so actors are never confused about what clothes they should be in during the scheduled scene.

COLOR CODING KEY

WHITE STRIP: A DAY INTERIOR scene.
YELLOW STRIP: A DAY EXTERIOR scene.
GREEN STRIP: A NIGHT EXTERIOR scene.
BLUE STRIP: A NIGHT INTERIOR scene.

CAST IDS KEY

ALYSSA: CAST ID 1
MISS WU: CAST ID 2
AUNT CHEN: CAST ID 3
BLAKE: CAST ID 4
JACOB: CAST ID 5
NICOLE: CAST ID 6
TESSA: CAST ID 7
CRAWLING GHOST: CAST ID 8
LITTLE BROTHER: CAST ID 9
HAIR GHOST: CAST ID 10
MEI-LING: CAST ID 11
CAB DRIVER: CAST ID 12

"GHOST MONTH" SHOOTING SCHEDULE

Shooting December 4th, 2006 to December 14th, 2006

10 Day Shoot

DAY 1

Monday, December 4, 2006

6:00AM - 6:00PM

Sheet #: 19 2/8 pgs	Scene: 18	EXT	MOUNTAIN RANCH HOUSE Establishing Shot of House.	Day	CAST ID: WARDROBE ID:
Sheet #: 3 4/8 pgs	Scene: 2	EXT	MOUNTAIN RANCH HOUSE / DRIVEWAY Taxi drops Alyssa off at house.	Day	CAST ID: 1, 12 WARDROBE ID: 1A
Sheet #: 55 1/8 pgs	Scene: 54	EXT	SERIES SHOT: ALYSSA WHISTLING WHIL Alyssa whistling while cleaning.	Day	CAST ID: 1 WARDROBE ID: 1D, 1P
Sheet #: 14 2 2/8 pgs	Scene: 13	EXT	OUTDOOR PATIO Alyssa and Miss Wu talk about Feng Shui.	Day	CAST ID: 1, 2 WARDROBE ID: 1B, 1P, 2B
Sheet #: 48 4/8 pgs	Scene: 47	EXT	BACK DOOR / TRASH AREA A voice calls Alyssa's name. She follows trail...	Day	CAST ID: 1 WARDROBE ID: 1E
Sheet #: 56 1/8 pgs	Scene: 55	EXT	SERIES SHOT: ALYSSA TURNING BACK A Alyssa turns back after she hears her name.	Day	CAST ID: 1 WARDROBE ID: 1E
Sheet #: 26 6/8 pgs	Scene: 25	EXT	OUTDOOR PATIO Alyssa cleaning and whistling.	Day	CAST ID: 1, 2 WARDROBE ID: 1D, 1P, 2D
Sheet #: 49 3/8 pgs	Scene: 48	EXT	OUTDOOR PATIO Alyssa finds small door to walkway.	Day	CAST ID: 1 WARDROBE ID: 1E
Sheet #: 5 2 2/8 pgs	Scene: 4	INT	FRONT ROOM / LIVING ROOM Alyssa is welcomed to house.	Day	CAST ID: 1, 2 WARDROBE ID: 1A, 2A
Sheet #: 6 3/8 pgs	Scene: 5	INT	STAIRWAY TO BASEMENT Miss Wu and Alyssa go down the stairs.	Day	CAST ID: 1, 2 WARDROBE ID: 1A, 2A
Sheet #: 20 1/8 pgs	Scene: 19	INT	SERIES SHOT: ALYSSA WASHES THE WII Alyssa washes windows.	Day	CAST ID: 1 WARDROBE ID: 1C

Sheet #: 21	Scene: 20	INT	SERIES SHOT: ALYSSA IS DUSTING THE (Day Alyssa is dusting the counters.	CAST ID: 1
1/8 pgs				WARDROBE ID: 1C, 1P
Sheet #: 22	Scene: 21	INT	SERIES SHOT: ALYSSA SCRUBS THE FLC Day Alyssa scrubs the floor.	CAST ID: 1
1/8 pgs				WARDROBE ID: 1C, 1P
Sheet #: 112	Scene: 111	EXT	SIDE OF THE HOUSE Night Alyssa tries to leave. Miss Wu knocks her out.	CAST ID: 1, 2
1 pgs				WARDROBE ID: 1H, 2K

End Day # 1 Monday, December 4, 2006 -- Total Pages: 8 7/8

DAY 2

Tuesday, December 5, 2006

7:00AM - 7:00PM

Sheet #: 32	Scene: 31	INT	KITCHEN / PHONE AREA (Intercut) Day Alyssa calls Nicole to talk.	CAST ID: 1
2 6/8 pgs				WARDROBE ID: 1L
Sheet #: 34	Scene: 33	INT	KITCHEN Day Miss Wu comes home and sees her in a Chinese dress.	CAST ID: 1, 2
6/8 pgs				WARDROBE ID: 1L, 2D
Sheet #: 59	Scene: 58	INT	KITCHEN Day Alyssa is washing the dishes.	CAST ID: 1
2/8 pgs				WARDROBE ID: 1F, 1P
Sheet #: 60	Scene: 59	INT	FRONT ROOM Day Blake pays a unexpected visit.	CAST ID: 1, 4
2 2/8 pgs				WARDROBE ID: 1F, 4B
Sheet #: 62	Scene: 61	INT	FRONT ROOM Day Miss Wu kicks Blake out and yells at Alyssa.	CAST ID: 1, 2, 4
1 1/8 pgs				WARDROBE ID: 1F, 2F, 2G, 4B
Sheet #: 61	Scene: 60	EXT	OUTDOOR PATIO Day Blake and Alyssa talk. Miss Wu comes home..	CAST ID: 1, 2, 4
1 4/8 pgs				WARDROBE ID: 1F, 2F, 2G, 4B
Sheet #: 66	Scene: 65	EXT	SERIES SHOT: BLAKE AND MEI-LING KISI Day Blake and Mei-Ling Kissing.	CAST ID: 4, 11
1/8 pgs				WARDROBE ID: 4C, 11B
Sheet #: 67	Scene: 66	INT	SERIES SHOT: MEI-LING ARGUING AND Y Night Mei-Ling arguing and yelling at Miss Wu.	CAST ID: 2, 11
1/8 pgs				WARDROBE ID: 2C, 11C
Sheet #: 68	Scene: 67	INT	SERIES SHOT: MEI-LING BLOODY AND BF Night Mei-Ling bloody and bruised.	CAST ID: 11
1/8 pgs				WARDROBE ID: 11A
Sheet #: 7	Scene: 6	INT	BRICK BASEMENT (SET) Day Miss Wu shows Alyssa the brick basement.	CAST ID: 1, 2
1 pgs				WARDROBE ID: 1A, 2A
Sheet #: 51	Scene: 50	INT	BRICK HOLE (SET) Night Alyssa wakes up in hole. Sees a young man crying...	CAST ID: 1, 8
7/8 pgs				WARDROBE ID: 1E

End Day # 2 Tuesday, December 5, 2006 -- Total Pages: 10 7/8

DAY 3

Wednesday, December 6, 2006

7:00AM - 7:00PM

Sheet #: 23 1 1/8 pgs	Scene: 22	EXT	**COURTYARD** Alyssa steps on ashes & offends ghosts.	Day	CAST ID: 1, 2, 8 WARDROBE ID: 1C, 1P, 2C
Sheet #: 25 3/8 pgs	Scene: 24	EXT	**COURTYARD / DOORWAY AREA** Alyssa comes back to reality.	Day	CAST ID: 1, 2 WARDROBE ID: 1C, 1P, 2C
Sheet #: 57 1/8 pgs	Scene: 56	EXT	**SERIES SHOT: ALYSSA STEPPING ON TH** Alyssa stepping on the ash and sweeping it up.	Day	CAST ID: 1 WARDROBE ID: 1C, 1P
Sheet #: 29 3/8 pgs	Scene: 28	INT	**ALYSSA'S BEDROOM** Alyssa finds Chinese Dress	Day	CAST ID: 1 WARDROBE ID: 1D, 1L
Sheet #: 35 4/8 pgs	Scene: 34	INT	**ALYSSA'S BEDROOM** Alyssa finds picture of Mei-Ling.	Day	CAST ID: 1 WARDROBE ID: 1L
Sheet #: 8 1 2/8 pgs	Scene: 7	INT	**ALYSSA'S BEDROOM** Miss Wu shows Alyssa her bedroom.	Day	CAST ID: 1, 2 WARDROBE ID: 1A, 2A
Sheet #: 58 6/8 pgs	Scene: 57	INT	**ALYSSA'S BEDROOM** Miss Wu puts picture of Zhong Kui on door.	Day	CAST ID: 1, 2 WARDROBE ID: 1J, 1K, 2F, 2G
Sheet #: 36 5/8 pgs	Scene: 35	INT	**HALLYWAY / THE LOCKED ROOM** Alyssa tries to get in room and sees ghost.	Day	CAST ID: 1, 8 WARDROBE ID: 1L
Sheet #: 65 3 3/8 pgs	Scene: 64	INT	**LIVING ROOM / BAR AREA** Miss Wu has a talk with Alyssa about Blake and Mei-Ling.	Night	CAST ID: 1, 2 WARDROBE ID: 1F, 2G
Sheet #: 11 4/8 pgs	Scene: 10	INT	**ALYSSA'S BEDROOM** Alyssa wakes up and looks out window.	Night	CAST ID: 1 WARDROBE ID: 1J
Sheet #: 13 2/8 pgs	Scene: 12	INT	**ALYSSA'S BEDROOM** Alyssa goes back to bed.	Night	CAST ID: 1 WARDROBE ID: 1J
Sheet #: 18 2/8 pgs	Scene: 17	INT	**ALYSSA'S BEDROOM** Alyssa prays. Something is under her bed.	Night	CAST ID: 1, 8 WARDROBE ID: 1J

End Day # 3 Wednesday, December 6, 2006 -- Total Pages: 9 4/8

DAY 4

Thursday, December 7, 2006

10:00AM - 10:00PM

Sheet #: 82 1/8 pgs	Scene: 81	EXT	**WOODS / BACK OF BARN** Alyssa walks down the trail.	Day	CAST ID: 1 WARDROBE ID: 1G
Sheet #: 83 1 6/8 pgs	Scene: 82	EXT	**HORSE STABLES** Alyssa confronts Blake about picture.	Day	CAST ID: 1, 4 WARDROBE ID: 1G, 4D

| Sheet #: 27 | Scene: | EXT | BARN AREA | Day | CAST ID: 1, 4 |
| 3 pgs | 26 | | Alyssa meets Blake. | | WARDROBE ID: 1D, 4A |

| Sheet #: 115 | Scene: | INT | BRICK HOLE (SET) | Night | CAST ID: 1, 2 |
| 3 2/8 pgs | 114 | | Alyssa wakes up in hole. Miss Wu tells story. | | WARDROBE ID: 1H, 2K |

| Sheet #: 117 | Scene: | INT | BRICK HOLE (SET) | Night | CAST ID: 1 |
| 3/8 pgs | 116 | | Alyssa finds key, and gets out of hole. | | WARDROBE ID: 1H |

| Sheet #: 85 | Scene: | EXT | WOODS / BARN AREA | Night | CAST ID: 1, 4 |
| 1 6/8 pgs | 84 | | Alyssa snoops around. She sees Blake digging. | | WARDROBE ID: 1G, 4D |

| Sheet #: 89 | Scene: | EXT | SERIES SHOT: POV OF WOODS/BARN AR | Night | CAST ID: 4 |
| 1/8 pgs | 88 | | Alyssa's POV. Blake stares at her in distance. | | WARDROBE ID: 4D |

| Sheet #: 88 | Scene: | EXT | SERIES SHOT: POV OF WOODS/BARN AR | Night | CAST ID: 4 |
| 1/8 pgs | 87 | | Alyssa's POV from Binoculars of Blake Working. He leaves | | WARDROBE ID: 4D |

| Sheet #: 114 | Scene: | EXT | WOODS | Night | CAST ID: 4 |
| 1/8 pgs | 113 | | Blake spies on Miss Wu. | | WARDROBE ID: 4E |

End Day # 4 Thursday, December 7, 2006 -- Total Pages: 10 5/8

DAY 5

Friday, December 8, 2006

12:00PM NOON - 12:00AM MIDNIGHT

| Sheet #: 91 | Scene: | EXT | OUTDOOR PATIO | Day | CAST ID: 1, 10 |
| 5/8 pgs | 90 | | Alyssa sees reflection of ghost in mirror. | | WARDROBE ID: 1H |

| Sheet #: 50 | Scene: | INT | TINY HOUSE (SET) | Day | CAST ID: 1, 8 |
| 6/8 pgs | 49 | | Alyssa discovers bizarre room and has encounter. | | WARDROBE ID: 1E |

| Sheet #: 101 | Scene: | INT | CLOSET (SET) | Night | CAST ID: 1, 10 |
| 5/8 pgs | 100 | | Alyssa is trapped in closet with Hair Ghost. | | WARDROBE ID: 1H |

| Sheet #: 28 | Scene: | INT | ALYSSA'S BEDROOM / CLOSET (SET) | Day | CAST ID: 1 |
| 3/8 pgs | 27 | | Alyssa finds wood trunk in closet. | | WARDROBE ID: 1D |

| Sheet #: 63 | Scene: | INT | BRICK BASEMENT (SET) | Day | CAST ID: 1, 8 |
| 6/8 pgs | 62 | | Alyssa Drops key and finds hole. | | WARDROBE ID: 1F |

| Sheet #: 24 | Scene: | INT | BRICK BASEMENT (SET) | Night | CAST ID: 1, 8 |
| 5/8 pgs | 23 | | Alyssa has her first encounter. | | WARDROBE ID: 1C, 1P |

| Sheet #: 52 | Scene: | INT | BRICK BASEMENT (SET) | Night | CAST ID: 1 |
| 7/8 pgs | 51 | | Alyssa wakes up in brick basement. Ghost voices surroun | | WARDROBE ID: 1E |

| Sheet #: 92 | Scene: | INT | BRICK BASEMENT (SET) | Night | CAST ID: 1, 8, 10 |
| 5/8 pgs | 91 | | Alyssa wakes up in brick basement. Ghosts appear. | | WARDROBE ID: 1H |

| Sheet #: 41 | Scene: | INT | INSIDE BRICK WALL (SET) | Night | CAST ID: 1, 10 |
| 3/8 pgs | 40 | | Alyssa is trapped in wall with Hair Ghost. | | WARDROBE ID: 1J |

Sheet #: 118 1/8 pgs	Scene: 117	INT	**STAIRWAY TO BASEMENT** Alyssa comes up the stairs.	Night	CAST ID: 1 WARDROBE ID: 1H
Sheet #: 121 1/8 pgs	Scene: 120	INT	**STAIRWAY TO BASEMENT** Alyssa bolts up the stairs.	Night	CAST ID: 1 WARDROBE ID: 1H
Sheet #: 107 2/8 pgs	Scene: 106	INT	**ALYSSA'S BEDROOM / CLOSET DOOR (O** Alyssa is spit out of the door.	Night	CAST ID: 1 WARDROBE ID: 1H
Sheet #: 100 3/8 pgs	Scene: 99	INT	**ALYSSA'S BEDROOM / CLOSET DOOR (O** Alyssa gets pulled into closet by Black Hair.	Night	CAST ID: 1 WARDROBE ID: 1H
Sheet #: 43 2 3/8 pgs	Scene: 42	INT	**MISS WU'S BEDROOM** Alyssa and Miss Wu talk about Jacob.	Night	CAST ID: 1, 2 WARDROBE ID: 1J, 2D
Sheet #: 39 3/8 pgs	Scene: 38	INT	**ALYSSA'S BEDROOM / HALLWAY** Alyssa comes into hallway.	Night	CAST ID: 1, 8 WARDROBE ID: 1J
Sheet #: 53 3/8 pgs	Scene: 52	INT	**ALYSSA'S BEDROOM** Alyssa wakes up. The Hair Ghost is above her on the bed.	Night	CAST ID: 1, 10 WARDROBE ID: 1J
Sheet #: 64 2/8 pgs	Scene: 63	INT	**DINING ROOM / KITCHEN** Alyssa is cleaning dinner table.	Night	CAST ID: 1, 2 WARDROBE ID: 1F, 1P
Sheet #: 119 6/8 pgs	Scene: 118	INT	**FRONT ROOM** Alyssa and Miss Wu fight. Alyssa knocks her out.	Night	CAST ID: 1, 2 WARDROBE ID: 1H, 2K
Sheet #: 116 2/8 pgs	Scene: 115	INT	**FRONT ROOM** Miss Wu looks around the house.	Night	CAST ID: 2, 10 WARDROBE ID: 2K

End Day # 5 Friday, December 8, 2006 -- Total Pages: 10 7/8

DAY OFF - SATURDAY, DECEMBER 9, 2006 - DAY OFF

GET SOME REST - RELAX - DON'T PLAY THE SLOTS!

DAY 6

Sunday, December 10, 2006

7:00AM - 7:00PM

Sheet #: 84 2 6/8 pgs	Scene: 83	INT	ARKHAM AGENCY OFFICE Jacob meets Tessa for a little information.	Day	CAST ID: 5, 7 WARDROBE ID: 5F, 7B
Sheet #: 31 7/8 pgs	Scene: 30	INT	ARKHAM AGENCY OFFICE / KITCHEN (Inte Tessa talks to Alyssa	Day	CAST ID: 7 WARDROBE ID: 7A
Sheet #: 2 6/8 pgs	Scene: 1	EXT	DESERT AND MOUNTAIN AREA Alyssa takes cab to House.	Day	CAST ID: 1, 12 WARDROBE ID: 1A
Sheet #: 46 1/8 pgs	Scene: 45	EXT	SERIES SHOT: JACOB AND ALYSSA LAYI Jacob and Alyssa on grass talking.	Day	CAST ID: 1, 5 WARDROBE ID: 1Q, 5D
Sheet #: 45 1/8 pgs	Scene: 44	EXT	SERIES SHOT: JACOB, CLEAN CUT AND H Jacob kissing Alyssa.	Day	CAST ID: 1, 5 WARDROBE ID: 1N, 5C
Sheet #: 30 1 pgs	Scene: 29	INT	KITCHEN / PHONE AREA (Intercut) Alyssa answers phone & talks to Tessa	Day	CAST ID: 1 WARDROBE ID: 1L
Sheet #: 81 4/8 pgs	Scene: 80	INT	ALYSSA'S BEDROOM Alyssa finds Mei-Ling's Diary.	Day	CAST ID: 1 WARDROBE ID: 1G
Sheet #: 69 1/8 pgs	Scene: 68	INT	SERIES SHOT: MS WU FINDS THE NOTE C Miss Wu finding Mei-Ling's note on the bed.	Day	CAST ID: 2 WARDROBE ID: 2J
Sheet #: 16 7/8 pgs	Scene: 15	INT	JACOB'S TRASHY ROOM Jacob calls Alyssa looking for her.	Day	CAST ID: 5 WARDROBE ID: 5A

End Day # 6 Sunday, December 10, 2006 -- Total Pages: 7 1/8

DAY 7

Monday, December 11, 2006

12:00PM NOON - 12:00AM MIDNIGHT

Sheet #: 33 2 6/8 pgs	Scene: 32	INT	NICOLE'S PLACE / KITCHEN (Intercut) Nicole talks to Alyssa.	Day	CAST ID: 1, 6 WARDROBE ID: 6A
Sheet #: 74 2/8 pgs	Scene: 73	INT	NICOLE'S PLACE / HOME OFFICE Nicole answers the phone.	Night	CAST ID: 1, 6 WARDROBE ID: 6B
Sheet #: 76 2 4/8 pgs	Scene: 75	INT	NICOLE'S PLACE (Intercut with outdoor pa Nicole talks to Alyssa.	Night	CAST ID: 1, 6 WARDROBE ID: 6B
Sheet #: 77 3/8 pgs	Scene: 76	INT	NICOLE'S PLACE / HOME OFFICE Nicole hears noise and investigates.	Night	CAST ID: 6 WARDROBE ID: 6B
Sheet #: 80 2/8 pgs	Scene: 79	INT	NICOLE'S PLACE / HOME OFFICE Jacob tears up room and finds address.	Night	CAST ID: 5 WARDROBE ID: 5E
Sheet #: 78 2/8 pgs	Scene: 77	INT	NICOLE'S PLACE / HALLWAY Nicole walks down dark hallway.	Night	CAST ID: 6 WARDROBE ID: 6B
Sheet #: 79 1 7/8 pgs	Scene: 78	INT	NICOLE'S PLACE / KITCHEN Jacob kills Nicole.	Night	CAST ID: 5, 6 WARDROBE ID: 5E, 6B

Sheet #: 73	Scene:	EXT	**OUTDOOR PATIO** Night	CAST ID: 1, 8
1/8 pgs	72		Alyssa calls Nicole.	WARDROBE ID: 1J, 1K
Sheet #: 75	Scene:	EXT	**OUTDOOR PATIO (Intercut)** Night	CAST ID: 1, 8
2 4/8 pgs	74		Alyssa talks to Nicole.	WARDROBE ID: 1J, 1K
Sheet #: 44	Scene:	EXT	**JACOB'S CAR** Night	CAST ID: 5
2/8 pgs	43		Jacob sleeping in car.	WARDROBE ID: 5B
Sheet #: 47	Scene:	EXT	**INT. JACOB'S CAR** Night	CAST ID: 5
1 2/8 pgs	46		Jacob wakes up and calls Alyssa and freaks out on phone	WARDROBE ID: 5B

End Day # 7 Monday, December 11, 2006 -- Total Pages: 12 3/8

DAY 8

Tuesday, December 12, 2006

12:00PM NOON - 12:00AM MIDNIGHT

Sheet #: 4	Scene:	EXT	**COURTYARD** Day	CAST ID: 1, 2, 3
1 5/8 pgs	3		Alyssa meets Aunt Chen and Miss Wu at Door.	WARDROBE ID: 1A, 2A, 3A
Sheet #: 93	Scene:	EXT	**OUTDOOR PATIO** Day	CAST ID: 1, 2, 3
3/8 pgs	92		Miss Wu and Aunt Chen help Alyssa inside.	WARDROBE ID: 1H, 2K, 3A
Sheet #: 120	Scene:	INT	**BRICK BASEMENT (SET)** Night	CAST ID: 1, 2, 3, 8, 10
2 3/8 pgs	119		Alyssa bricks Miss Wu inside. Miss Wu dies.	WARDROBE ID: 1H, 2K, 3A
Sheet #: 122	Scene:	INT	**FRONT ROOM / DOORWAY AREA** Night	CAST ID: 1, 4, 5, 8, 10
2 2/8 pgs	121		Jacob Tries to kill Alyssa. Blake fights him. Jacob dies.	WARDROBE ID: 1H, 4E, 5G
Sheet #: 54	Scene:	INT	**LIVING ROOM** Night	CAST ID: 1, 2, 3, 8
2 pgs	53		Miss Wu tells Alyssa she offended the ghosts.	WARDROBE ID: 1J, 1K, 2E, 3A

End Day # 8 Tuesday, December 12, 2006 -- Total Pages: 8 5/8

DAY 9

Wednesday, December 13, 2006

4:00PM - 4:00AM

Sheet #: 113	Scene:	EXT	**COURTYARD** Night	CAST ID: 2
1/8 pgs	112		Miss Wu does more offerings.	WARDROBE ID: 2K
Sheet #: 17	Scene:	EXT	**COURTYARD** Night	CAST ID: 1, 2, 3
3 pgs	16		Alyssa joins ritual and Miss Wu tells the story.	WARDROBE ID: 1B, 2B, 3A
Sheet #: 12	Scene:	EXT	**COURTYARD** Night	CAST ID: 2, 3
2/8 pgs	11		Alyssa's POV of strange ritual.	WARDROBE ID: 2A, 3A

Sheet #: 96	Scene: 95	EXT	COURTYARD — Night Miss Wu and Aunt Chen burn more offerings.	CAST ID: 2, 3 WARDROBE ID: 2K, 3A
1/8 pgs				
Sheet #: 86	Scene: 85	EXT	COURTYARD — Night Miss Wu and Aunt Chen doing nightly ritual.	CAST ID: 2, 3 WARDROBE ID: 2H, 3A
1/8 pgs				
Sheet #: 70	Scene: 69	EXT	COURTYARD — Night The Crawling Ghost eats the offerings.	CAST ID: 8 WARDROBE ID:
2/8 pgs				
Sheet #: 102	Scene: 101	INT	ALYSSA'S BEDROOM IN PAST — Night Alyssa sees the truth about Mei-Ling and Miss Wu's broth	CAST ID: 1, 2, 3, 9, 11 WARDROBE ID: 1M, 2H, 3A, 9A, 11D
1 pgs				
Sheet #: 103	Scene: 102	INT	SERIES SHOT: MISS WU AND AUNT CHEN — Night Miss Wu and Aunt Chen wrap up Mei-Ling.	CAST ID: 2, 3, 11 WARDROBE ID: 2H, 3A, 11D
1/8 pgs				
Sheet #: 104	Scene: 103	INT	SERIES SHOT: MISS WU AND AUNT CHEN — Night Miss Wu and Aunt Chen brick Mei-Ling into wall.	CAST ID: 2, 3, 11 WARDROBE ID: 2H, 3A, 11D
1/8 pgs				
Sheet #: 105	Scene: 104	INT	SERIES SHOT: THEY STUFF THE MAN INT — Night Miss Wu and Aunt Chen stuff man in urn.	CAST ID: 2, 3, 9 WARDROBE ID: 2H, 3A, 9A
1/8 pgs				
Sheet #: 106	Scene: 105	INT	SERIES SHOT: THEY CLOSE THE METAL — Night They close the metal grate and lock it.	CAST ID: 2, 3 WARDROBE ID: 2H, 3A
1/8 pgs				
Sheet #: 87	Scene: 86	EXT	OUTDOOR PATIO / STAIR AREA — Night Alyssa spies on Blake with binoculars.	CAST ID: 1 WARDROBE ID: 1G
2/8 pgs				
Sheet #: 90	Scene: 89	EXT	OUTDOOR PATIO / STAIR AREA — Night Alyssa jumps at the sight of him and runs inside.	CAST ID: 1 WARDROBE ID: 1G
1/8 pgs				
Sheet #: 123	Scene: 122	EXT	ALYSSA'S NEW HOME / PORCH — Night Alyssa does the offerings. End of movie stinger.	CAST ID: 1, 2, 5 WARDROBE ID: 1R, 2K, 5G
6/8 pgs				
Sheet #: 40	Scene: 39	INT	KITCHEN — Night Alyssa encounters the Hair Ghost.	CAST ID: 1, 10 WARDROBE ID: 1J
3/8 pgs				
Sheet #: 42	Scene: 41	INT	KITCHEN — Night Alyssa wakes up from her encounter.	CAST ID: 1, 2, 3 WARDROBE ID: 1J, 2D, 3A
5/8 pgs				
Sheet #: 95	Scene: 94	INT	KITCHEN — Night Miss Wu tells her about the last night of Ghost Month.	CAST ID: 1, 2, 3 WARDROBE ID: 1H, 2K, 3A
1 5/8 pgs				
Sheet #: 72	Scene: 71	INT	KITCHEN / PHONE AREA — Night Alyssa grabs the phone.	CAST ID: 1 WARDROBE ID: 1J, 1K
2/8 pgs				

End Day # 9 Wednesday, December 13, 2006 -- Total Pages: 9 3/8

DAY 10

Thursday, December 14, 2006

4:00PM - 4:00AM

| Sheet #: 9 | Scene: 8 | INT | HALLYWAY / THE LOCKED ROOM — Night
Alyssa sees lights under door & hears voices. | CAST ID: 1, 2
WARDROBE ID: 1A |
| 3/8 pgs | | | | |

Sheet #: 97 / 3/8 pgs	Scene: 96	INT	HALLWAY / THE LOCKED ROOM Alyssa hears noises. Room opens.	Night	CAST ID: 1 WARDROBE ID: 1H
Sheet #: 10 / 1 7/8 pgs	Scene: 9	INT	DINING ROOM Alyssa has dinner in new house.	Night	CAST ID: 1, 2, 3 WARDROBE ID: 1A, 2A, 3A
Sheet #: 37 / 1 6/8 pgs	Scene: 36	INT	LIVING ROOM Alyssa asks about Mei-Ling.	Night	CAST ID: 1, 2, 3 WARDROBE ID: 1D, 2D, 3A
Sheet #: 98 / 7/8 pgs	Scene: 97	INT	THE LOCKED ROOM Alyssa finds altar and has a revelation.	Night	CAST ID: 1 WARDROBE ID: 1H
Sheet #: 109 / 7/8 pgs	Scene: 108	INT	THE LOCKED ROOM Aunt Chen dies.	Night	CAST ID: 3 WARDROBE ID: 3A
Sheet #: 108 / 2/8 pgs	Scene: 107	INT	HALLWAY / THE LOCKED ROOM Aunt Chen hears a noise and goes to the room.	Night	CAST ID: 3 WARDROBE ID: 3A
Sheet #: 111 / 2/8 pgs	Scene: 110	INT	HALLWAY / THE LOCKED ROOM Miss Wu finds Aunt Chen. Dead.	Night	CAST ID: 2, 3 WARDROBE ID: 2K, 3A
Sheet #: 110 / 7/8 pgs	Scene: 109	INT	ALYSSA'S BEDROOM Alyssa hides from Miss Wu. She goes out the window.	Night	CAST ID: 1, 2 WARDROBE ID: 1H, 2K
Sheet #: 71 / 2/8 pgs	Scene: 70	INT	ALYSSA'S BEDROOM Alyssa can't sleep.	Night	CAST ID: 1 WARDROBE ID: 1J, 1K
Sheet #: 99 / 3/8 pgs	Scene: 98	INT	ALYSSA'S BEDROOM Alyssa compares notes, and discovers they are Miss Wu's	Night	CAST ID: 1 WARDROBE ID: 1H
Sheet #: 94 / 2/8 pgs	Scene: 93	INT	ALYSSA'S BEDROOM Alyssa wakes up and leaves room.	Night	CAST ID: 1 WARDROBE ID: 1H
Sheet #: 38 / 2/8 pgs	Scene: 37	INT	ALYSSA'S BEDROOM Alyssa wakes up and leaves room.	Night	CAST ID: 1 WARDROBE ID: 1J

End Day # 10 Thursday, December 14, 2006 -- Total Pages: 8 5/8

SMILE! THAT'S A WRAP ON PRINCIPAL PHOTOGRAPHY

SCHEDULE SAMPLES (DOWNLOAD)

CRYPTZ (PDF Download)
web file: CRYPTZ_Schedule_Vertical_Sample.pdf

DARKWALKER (PDF Download)
web file: DARKWALKER_Shooting_Schedule.pdf

Stuart Gordon Presents DEATHBED (PDF Download)
web file: DEATHBED_Shooting_Schedule.pdf

GHOST MONTH (PDF Download)
web file: Ghost_Month_Production_Schedule.pdf

INTERVIEW BOX

DAVID DECOTEAU PRODUCER, DIRECTOR
RAPID HEART PICTURES

David DeCoteau

PLAYING WITH FIRE (2008).
Photo Credit: Courtesy of Regent Releasing/Here! Media.

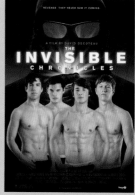

THE INVISIBLE CHRONICLES (2009).
Photo Credit: Courtesy of Regent Releasing/Here! Media.

www.DavidDecoteau.com

DAVID DECOTEAU has produced and directed more than 80 motion pictures over the past 20 years. His passion lies in the creation of popular genre programming made for world consumption. DeCoteau's experience in creating content in countries all over the world makes him a proven choice for exception-ally challenging movie projects. His movies are currently in distribution by Paramount Home Video, 20th Century Fox, Showtime, Blockbuster, HBO, Regent Entertainment, Here!TV, OutTV Canada, Syfy, Full Moon Pictures, and many others. He has worked with and learned from the likes of movie legends James Cameron, Roger Corman,

Wim Wenders, Ken Russell, Charles Band, Gale Anne Hurd, Paul Colichman, and Robert Halmi, Sr.

Some of his many credits include DREAMANIAC (1986), NIGHTMARE SISTERS (1987), CREEPOZOIDS (1987), SORORITY BABES IN THE SLIMEBALL BOWL-O-RAMA (1988), PUPPET MASTER II (1991), PUPPET MASTER III: TOULON's REVENGE (1991), SHRIEKER (1998), WITCHOUSE (1999), THE BROTHERHOOD (2001), THE RAVEN (2007), GRIZZLY RAGE (2007), HOUSE OF USHER (2008), STEM CELL (2009), and PUPPET MASTER 9: AXIS OF EVIL (2009).

DRAVEN: *In your prolific career as a producer and director, you have been known to be a very fast director, sometimes shooting entire feature films in just 4 days. What is the key to being a speedy director on a film set?*

DeCOTEAU: I'm really not that fast—just efficient. I was trained at Roger Corman's New World Pictures. Roger is an extremely efficient movie producer. I learned from him. I also worked as a craft-service person during those early years and watched a director take hours just to figure out where to put the camera. I thought to myself, this is ridiculous! We would work 18-hour days! One day I watched the sun come up twice and I said "Screw this! I'm going to start directing." My father was a gravel plant foreman. He was also a welder and mechanic. I come from a working-class family, and my work ethic is similar to my dad's. Work hard and get your hands dirty if necessary to get the job done. I believe working efficiently actually makes better movies. The cast is happier that they

don't have to wait around, and the crew can go home earlier. I remember watching Ken Russell direct CRIMES OF PASSION (1984). He was so fast, so precise in his direction, and he would only shoot one or two takes and move on. He also edited in the camera so he was able to deliver his director's cut only a few days after we wrapped. Spielberg shot DUEL (1971) in only 10 days, and it's one of his best movies. Sidney Lumet came in 3 weeks ahead of schedule on SERPICO (1973). My belief is that if you have a vision you can move fast and efficiently and get your movie done for a price. I shoot movies on all types of schedules. The 4-day wonder formula is not new. This is how tiny studios like Monogram made movies in the 1940s. My budgets dictate the shooting schedule pure and simple.

DRAVEN: *What is the key to scheduling a low-budget film?*

DeCOTEAU: The AD [assistant director] usually schedules my movies to maximize lighting setups. I like to shoot story in order on any given day. I like to "ease into" a movie. I don't like shooting the tough stuff first. I like to work into the complicated scenes. I can then get a feel for the movie and also see where its weaknesses are and try to fix those. I *never* do a shot list. I *never* storyboard unless the producer needs to see specifically how I want to shoot a VFX scene and he needs to get a bid from an VFX vendor. I play it by ear and shoot the money.

DRAVEN: *What are the advantages and disadvantages of shooting with SAG actors versus nonunion actors?*

continued on the next page

continued from the previous page

SORORITY BABES IN THE SLIME-
BALL BOWL-O-RAMA (1988).
Photo Credit: Courtesy of Full
Moon Features.

WITCHOUSE (1999).
Photo Credit: Courtesy of Full
Moon Features.

DeCOTEAU: Depends. I shoot both union and nonunion movies. Signing with the guild allows you to use name actors, which in some cases helps foreign sales. I have had situations where "names" have been a negative. One distributor asked me if he could not use the name actor on the DVD cover because that particular actor was overexposed in the marketplace. I've been very lucky that I have discovered young actors who have gone on to great success by doing nonunion movies.

DRAVEN: *In today's world, how important is having a star in your film to ensure sales, and why?*

DeCOTEAU: Depends on the star. Depends on the movie. Don't think there is an exact science here. If you look at TWILIGHT (2008) as an example, there were no stars in it, but the film was a big success. Success really does rely on the movie itself most of the time.

DRAVEN: *Do you think shooting two or three cameras saves time during a shoot, or adds more problems?*

DeCOTEAU: When I work in Canada, two-camera is usually mandatory. On GRIZZLY RAGE (2007) I shot four cameras even on dialog. I prefer to use a minimum of two cameras. It's helpful as you get more coverage and you may capture a one-of-a-kind performance and you've got two cameras going. When I shoot 35mm it is usually one camera. Whenever I shoot in Los Angeles, I usually only get one camera because you end up spending all your budget on locations—like a state-owned high school costing $4,000 per day to shoot in.

DRAVEN: *What do you think are the most important elements for a low-budget horror film to have to be sellable in the horror market?*

DeCOTEAU: Originality. Timing. All the planets aligning. Luck. I wish there was a rule book to success in this business. It's a crap shoot. Make the best movie you can make. Harry Novak once said that there is a market for everything; you just have to find it. Help your distributor get the word out. Promote the movie. "You gotta tell 'em to sell 'em."

DR. ALIEN (1989).
Photo Credit: Courtesy of Full
Moon Features.

CREEPOZOIDS (1987).
Photo Credit: Courtesy of Full
Moon Features.

DRAVEN: *With determination and hard work, you are a person who carved his own way into making movies. For aspiring filmmakers, what do you think is the best way to break in to the film business?*

DeCOTEAU: You really have to think outside of the box. I don't think I ever got a directing job from a résumé. It's usually from references and from my terrific agent who has made things happen for me. In most cases, though, I have created my own directing job by developing my own scripts and raising my own finances.

DRAVEN: *How have the new technologies available to filmmakers and new distribution methods changed the way you make and deliver films?*

DeCOTEAU: In a way it has become more difficult. A third of my budget is spent on deliveries. My delivery list is longer that my contract. I used to deliver an answer print and that was it. Now the list is a mile long.

Digital cameras, digital post, and Internet distribution has democratized filmmaking. When I got into the business back in the 80s it was a hermetically sealed business. Now everyone has access. This is a blessing and a curse. Seven thousand feature films were submitted to Sundance last year [2008]. The cream doesn't always rise to the surface. You have to be more than brilliant. You have to be an expert sales person, too. Luck comes in handy as well!

DRAVEN: *THE BROTHERHOOD (2001) marked a stage of your career focused more on gay-themed horror films. Can you tell us what this new subgenre is, how you became involved, and techniques you use in your films that define your work?*

DeCOTEAU: VOODOO ACADEMY was the movie where I realized there might be a larger market for these types of films than I thought. I always knew that gay men and teenage girls love great-looking guys, so I just cast the best-looking and most talented actors I could find. I'm not sure if hiring hot guys makes your movie gay themed, but it sure doesn't hurt. My films are also much less violent and sexual than my 80s/90s films. Foreign sales became crucial, and I didn't want any export/import issue with regard to censorship. Now the films are clean enough to be exported into any country without any cuts. Coarse language was also eliminated so the films

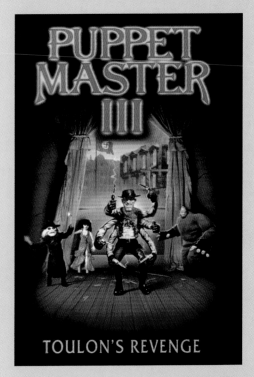

PUPPET MASTER III: TOULON's REVENGE (1991).
Photo Credit: Courtesy of Full Moon Features.

continued on the next page

continued from the previous page

can play on basic cable without cuts. I like to consider my films crossover. One of my films, LEECHES!, not only played on Sci Fi Channel, here! TV, and MTV's Logo channel, but it was also available in both Blockbuster and Wal-Mart. If that's not crossover, I don't know what is.

DRAVEN: *What is the best advice you ever received for how to make movies quickly and cheaply?*

DeCOTEAU: The best advice I ever got from anyone in this business is by watching filmmakers work. I was earning while I was learning. I have young filmmakers approaching me asking me to finance their $3,000 movies all the time. I don't finance other filmmakers anymore with the exception of documentary filmmakers who need a little help in completing their films. But even that is rare.

DRAVEN: *I know you are a lover of shooting on film, especially in the CinemaScope format. In today's digital world, do you think there is still a place for indie filmmakers who want to shoot on film, or is film slowly phasing out to extinction? Is there a sales advantage to shooting on film instead of digital?*

DeCOTEAU: When I started shooting exclusively in 2.35:1 35mm CinemaScope it was out of necessity. Digital had just come into the business and so many filmmakers were making films for 20 bucks and I just couldn't compete at that level—and honestly didn't want to. I decided to aim higher and go for something no one else was doing. Shooting in 35mm was just one more way to make the films special

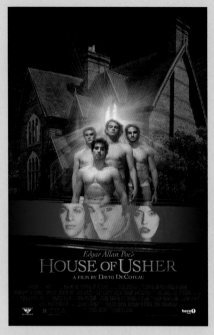

HOUSE OF USHER (2008).
Photo Credit: Courtesy of Regent Releasing/Here! Media.

and give the perception it was bigger and better. It's all about perception in this or any business. Being able to screen a 35mm Scope print in stereo sound at a film market gave buyers the chance to see the movie in the most ideal way. It's so much better than just dropping off a screener and hoping they watch it on a small TV. The screening made it an event and so much more important. Now digital cameras and projection have gotten so good I have made the switch to HD—but high-end HD. I still need to deliver these movies to European broadcasters whose QC specs are extremely high.

CHAPTER 3
CASTING A HORROR FILM

> **You could heave a brick out of the window and hit ten actors who could play my parts. I just happened to be on the right corner at the right time.**
>
> —BORIS KARLOFF

In a lot of indie horror films, the acting is usually the weakest part. The casting choices you make at this stage are the most important decisions you will make for your entire production. It's been said that most of the director's job is choosing the right actors to bring the characters to life. I think that's a great way of looking at it.

THE CASTING PROCESS

The Breakdowns – The breakdowns are a detailed summary of each role you're casting. It's usually a summary of the film's plot, along with character descriptions, age, bio, and any special requirements that may be required. For example, on the following page I've included a partial casting breakdown from Rob Zombie's film HALLOWEEN (2007).

The First Auditions – After you get submissions, you or your casting director will start setting up the first auditions. These initial auditions are usually very quick and intended to find the best candidates for the part. I find it useful to videotape these auditions so I can properly review all performances.

SAMPLE CASTING BREAKDOWN FOR ROB ZOMBIE'S HALLOWEEN*

Start Date: Approximately January 29, 2007

STORY LINE: After being committed for 17 years, Michael Myers, now a grown man and still very dangerous, is mistakenly released from the mental institution (where he was committed as a 10-year old) and he immediately returns to Haddonfield, where he wants to find his baby sister, Laurie. Anyone who crosses his path is in mortal danger.

MICHAEL MYERS (10 YEARS OLD)

Caucasian, 8–12 years old, to play 10. Stringy haired, awkward kid, you get a sense that something is off just by looking at him. He has a very unstable mental state. He enjoys torturing/killing animals and then people. He hates his teenage sister, his stripper mother, and her abusive boyfriend Ronnie. He is, however, protective and very attached to his baby sister, who he calls Boo. This is very disturbing material that we need a very capable young actor for.

LAURIE STRODE

Emancipated or legal 18 to play 17, Caucasian female. Pretty in an unassuming, natural way, this is Michael Meyer's baby sister. She is a normal, real, smart good girl, who is very responsible and caring. The second Michael sees her, he knows. Once he finds her, he will not let go, and Laurie has a strange feeling all day that someone is watching her . . . An actress who is riveting to watch.

ANNIE BRACKETT

Emancipated or legal 18 to play 18, Caucasian, female. PARTIAL NUDITY REQUIRED FOR THIS ROLE. She is LAURIE'S best friend, cute, and curly-haired, full of teen enthusiasm and charm. Borderline bad girl (she rebels, but in a sweet way).

LYNDA

Emancipated or legal 18 to play 18, Caucasian, female. FULL NUDITY WILL BE REQUIRED for this role. She looks like the hot cheerleader type, but has a bad attitude to go with it. She is the girl that convinced you to smoke cigarettes, smoke weed, steal your parents' car and taught you how to French kiss by making out with your older brother. She is all about opportunity.

TOMMY DOYLE

7–12 to play 8 years old, any ethnicity, a cute little boy who talks too much and whose babysitter is LAURIE. He is a mop top of a boy who asks lots of questions, and is filled with fear on Halloween. He believes in the boogey man and the wolf man, and sees Michael Meyers before anyone else does.

JUDITH MYERS

Emancipated or legal 18 to play 16 years old, Caucasian, female. FULL NUDITY REQUIRED FOR THIS ROLE. A celebration of the trailer-trash slut. She dresses inappropriately for her age, and uses her sexuality for mass effect. She flirts with Ronnie even though he is her mom's boyfriend. She and Michael are not close, they fight a lot and she walks in on him while he is masturbating to his photo album of past pet kills. Her response? She calls him a pervert. In no way will this girl ever be a model citizen.

WESLEY RHOADES

14–16 years old to play 14, School-bully #1, ugly, acne-scarred. Teases Michael about his mom's profession.

SHANE WILLIAMS

14–16 years old, WESLEY'S sidekick, overweight, red headed. Also a bully. He tells Michael that he'd like to get physical with his mom, Deborah. He is Wesley's yes man.

*Source: www.Bloody-disgusting.com

It's important that you never hold an audition at your house, apartment, or a public coffee shop. It's simply not safe for the actors and is an unprofessional reflection of you. Always make sure you are casting from a professional office that has a waiting area, restrooms, and water.

The Callbacks – This is when you simply call back all the actors you liked for a second audition, usually with the director and producer present. This is the audition when you want to test them further and ask all the appropriate questions.

Hiring the Actors – At this stage, you have made your final casting decisions and it's time to make offers to the actors. It's important when offering a part to an actor that you are very clear about what you expect of him or her, the pay, and the unpredictable hours and hard work that is required on indie films. Also, make sure any special diets are considered.

NONUNION TALENT AGREEMENT SAMPLE (DOWNLOAD)

** web file: Talent_Agreement_NONUNION_SAMPLE.pdf

(L-R) Erica Edd, Kierstin Cunnington, Marina Resa, Jerod Edington, Shirley To, Rick Irvin, and Danny Draven during a cozy table read for GHOST MONTH in Los Angeles.

The Table Read – The table read is usually the first meeting of all actors in the cast. It's a perfect time for everyone to socialize, get contact information, and discuss the film in more detail. At the table read, we usually just sit around a conference table and do a read though of the entire script. This is a great opportunity for the actors to ask questions and for the director to explain scenes and intentions.

Actors Rick Irvin and Choice Skinner during a rehearsal for a scene in CRYPTZ.

The Rehearsals – The rehearsal stage is usually optional. I like to rehearse with actors because it gives us the opportunity to work together before getting to the set. It's also a great opportunity to work out any last-minute details and character questions. Everyone has a different approach; some directors and actors like to rehearse, and some do not. Do what you think works best for your production.

CASTING THE MONSTER

When casting your monster, or any makeup-effects-heavy part, you should carefully screen the actor. If you cast the wrong person, your shoot could turn into a living nightmare. Also, make sure you do a makeup test with *any* actor who will have special effects makeup applications before you hire the actor. If you don't, and the actor is allergic to something like latex, you could have big problems. I've had several actors on different films have skin reactions to standard makeup. In one case, I had to shoot the actor from only the left side of the face for the rest of the day to avoid showing the skin rash on the cheek.

A corpse getting extensive full-body makeup applied on set.

Shooting a fight scene on the set of DARKWALKER.

Chuck Williams and Danny Draven on set.

On my no-budget film DARKWALKER, I had producer Chuck Williams—who is also an actor—play the monster. That was not by mistake. I knew that the person who needed to fill those shoes had to be a hard-core actor who would take it to the limits. During the shoot, Chuck went through hell and freezing conditions in a paper-thin monster suit and never complained a bit. I often had him lay in a dirty mud puddle, and roll around in it to keep the costume dripping with slime and mud. He even continued producing while in full monster makeup. It's quite funny when you are talking to your producer about details and he is in full monster makeup holding a giant razor-sharp sickle. Most other actors would not have gone through the abuse he did to play that part.

NOTES ON AUDITIONING ACTORS

When I'm choosing my cast, I always come in during the final callbacks and run the actors through a series of tests to determine if they are right for the movie. I want to make sure they are indie film compatible. The most important questions I ask myself at the audition when considering an actor for a part are the following:

How do the actors take direction?
The best way to determine this is to take one scene but direct it differently at least three times. You should note how the actors respond and if they can take your direction.

Can the actors hit their marks?

Some actors may be good at their craft but may not be trained to act for the camera. You should test the actors by giving them several marks to hit during a scene and take note of how well they perform. This is vital when shooting on film. If the actors miss their marks, they will go out of focus and ruin your take and cost you money. The set is no place to teach an inexperienced actor how to hit a mark.

Do the actors ask too many questions and seem to be too needy?

It's important to hire professional actors who do not need to be pampered on set. You are making an indie film, and they must understand that. If your actors are psychologizing their parts too much at the audition, you are probably going to spend more time on the set answering questions instead of shooting.

How do the actors look on camera?

I videotape all the auditions to see how the actors look on camera.

REMEMBER

Make sure all actors you hire are indie compatible.

How do the actors perform with action, fear, or death scenes?

If you have a part with a lot of screaming or a detailed death scene, you really must have the actor perform this in the audition. I've had actors who were talented dramatic performers but terrible screamers, or others who performed death scenes and it looked like a comedy. If these are important moments in your script, you want to make sure they are believable and you can direct them. If you start laughing, so will the audience.

TOP FIVE PLACES ACTORS LOOK FOR JOBS

For this book, I surveyed a lot of actors and asked them to tell me the top five places they look for acting jobs. Here are the results.

Casting Networks: www.lacasting.com

Actors Access Breakdown Services, Ltd.: www.actorsaccess.com

Now Casting Inc.: www.nowcasting.com

Backstage: www.backstage.com

IMDbPro Message Boards: www.imdb.com

These are all great places to post your casting notice for your film. When you accept submissions, try to accept only digital submissions. This is more convenient for everyone, saves money, and helps save the environment.

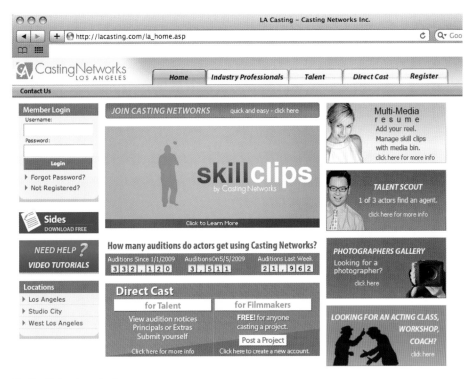

Casting Networks web site.

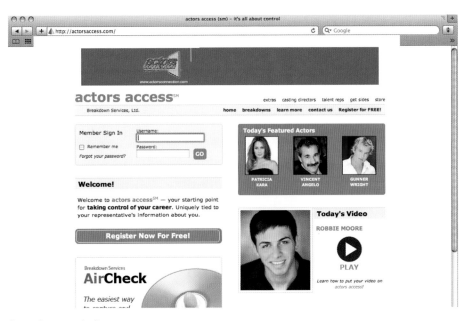

Actors Access web site.

Kulada from Danny Draven's CRYPTZ (2002).

SAG ACTORS

The decision to use professional SAG actors is up to you. There are advantages and disadvantages. You should decide for yourself based on your production needs.

For more information on using SAG actors, check out www.sagindie.com. Information about their low-budget contracts, as well as samples, are provided here. They also offer free classes which is vital for new producers.

NUDITY & VIOLENCE

If your film has nudity or gratuitous violence, you must make the actors aware of this and talk to them about it in detail at the audition. You should never wait until the last minute. The last thing you want is someone who gets cold feet the day the scene is ready to be shot. When actors have a nude scene in a film, they usually get paid a little more for those nude days. I've dealt with shy actors and ones that can't keep their clothes on because they know they get paid more when they come off. It's a crazy world. If it's a hot and steamy simulated sex scene, the actress usually wears what is called a *patch*, and the male actor wears a *sock*; these are to protect their private parts from touching. It's usually best to have a closed set when shooting intimate scenes so the actors are more comfortable. The last thing you want is a crew member gawking

Some actors are happy being covered in blood; they even sing and smile.

Sometimes the floor gets cold, wet, and sticky.

off camera every time someone gets naked. I've had this happen before, and it's creepy to say the least.

When dealing with overly violent scenes, it's best to make sure the actors are comfortable with the material before you hire them. You must understand that some people are more sensitive than others to blood and guts. What you think is gross or funny may make another person light-headed or bring back some traumatic childhood experience. I once hired an actor before they read the script (which was gory), and they had to bail out the day before shooting because they were afraid of bad karma and what their family would think of them after the film was released. Always communicate with your actors before you get on set so there are no surprises.

JOHN D. LeMAY ACTOR

John D. LeMay

JOHN D. LeMAY is a California-based actor whose career in theater began in Normal, Illinois, where he participated in singing and acting in school plays as a young student. After completing a bachelor of science degree at Illinois State University, where he completed a double major in music and musical theater, John moved to Los Angeles in 1985 and made various guest appearances in popular TV series, which included *Remington Steele*, *The Facts of Life*, and Rod Serling's *The Twilight Zone*. In 1987, he landed the leading role in Paramount television's horror syndicated series *Friday the 13th: The Series* as Ryan Dallion, a young antique sleuth who worked with his distant cousin and their retired magician friend to hunt down cursed objects. *Friday the 13th: The Series* was filmed in Toronto, Ontario, Canada. Although

continued on the next page

continued from the previous page

John D. LeMay and Robert Kurtzman on set.

John D. LeMay and co-star Keri Keegan—who played Jessica Kimble—on the set of JASON GOES TO HELL: THE FINAL FRIDAY (1993).

John left to pursue other career goals at the end of the second season, he is best known for his work in the series as Ryan Dallion and is the all-time fan favorite. His web site generates a great deal of interest for both his work from the series (also known under the title *Friday's Curse* in the United Kingdom) and his 1993 starring role in New Line Cinema's FRIDAY THE 13TH film series, part 9, JASON GOES TO HELL: THE FINAL FRIDAY. John has also returned to the stage as a member of the Acting Company at the Alliance Repertory Theatre of Burbank, California and received outstanding critics' reviews for his starring role as a lawyer turned filmmaker in the Alliance production of *Spec*. Recently John has returned to his musical theater roots, appearing in the Ovation Award winning production of *Jekyll and Hyde*.

DRAVEN: *In Friday the 13th: The Series (1987–1989), you played cursed antique sleuth Ryan Dallion. When creating a character like Ryan Dallion, how much of yourself goes into the role, how much is the writers', directors', and producers' input, and how much just happens organically on the set when interacting with the other actors?*

LeMAY: For the role of Ryan Dallion in *Friday the 13th: The Series*, the character cues were initially from the casting director and the information relayed to me from the character breakdowns describing him like the character David Addison, Jr., that Bruce Willis played in the TV series *Moonlighting* (1985–1989). The writing for the character, and the scenes I auditioned with reinforced that idea so, I channeled my best Bruce Willis imitation with his devilish, cocky and flirtatious demeanor. That landed me the role.

After I got the series I spent some time with an early director, Timothy Bond, who cautioned me by saying, "Hey, you don't have to do this Bruce Willis thing because you will just be a second-rate Bruce Willis, so just be the best John D. LeMay you can be instead." It was great advice and I have been forever thankful for it. The best actors are the ones who can bring as

(L–R) John D. LeMay as Ryan Dallion, director David Cronenberg, Louise Robey as Micki Foster, and Chris Wiggins as Jack Marshak.

much of themselves to the part as possible. In an audition it's who can walk into a room and be the most authentic, present, and real. Those actors will own the room. I think the shift was noticeable, and the character emerged after about the fourth episode in the series.

Also, early in production of the series, the producer, Ian Patterson, came up to me and requested I show more fear in response to the scary bits: "John, you are not being scared enough; there are scary things happening here, you can't be stoic watching a monk get smashed in a bed, or getting beheaded by a flying guillotine."

I was again very thankful for the advice. Reacting to special effects that were to be layered in later was new to me, and the series helped me climb a tremendous learning curve.

When you are a regular on a series, the stories keep evolving in ways that always surprise you. As an actor you try to create as much backstory as possible for yourself, but a lot of that is secondary to the writers' impact every week when you get a new script. For storytelling purposes, a lot of backstory information comes to you in bits and pieces. You have to be flexible and willing to go with it. Consequently,

continued on the next page

continued from the previous page

John D. LeMay and Joe Seneca on set of *Friday the 13th: The Series*, the "Voodoo Mambo" episode (1988).

I found the key to grounding myself was the interaction with other actors on the set. Those relationships really helped define who I was week in and week out.

DRAVEN: *The series also stars Louise Robey as the beautiful redhead Micki Foster and Chris Wiggins as the wise Jack Marshak. When all three of you would have scenes together, what is the process you went through among yourselves to make a scene playable?*

LeMAY: Early on we discovered what our job was and how we plugged into the story line. It didn't take too long before we all got into a comfortable rhythm with each other. I remember how important it was for me personally to stay loose. The schedule was an assault on our bodies and minds. It was an exhausting shoot and similar to Guerilla filmmaking. We had to make sure we all stayed healthy week after week. Scenes between the three of us became an exercise in economy. It's all about self-preservation. We learned to work effectively as a unit. I was a bit disappointed to find out that all of our lines were basically interchangeable—it wasn't about character. Our job was to relay exposition and move the story along . . . quickly. Back to more gore.

DRAVEN: *What is it that actors really want from their director?*

LeMAY: Respect! [Laughs] No really . . . we want the director to have good communication skills and make us feel like a collaborator in the process. It's the actor's job to get from point A to point B and have it make sense, and if the actor is having a problem doing that, they may turn to their trusted director to help solve the problem. Specifically with respect to genre films with special effects, the actor needs a director who can relay what the effect is supposed to look like and where it is supposed to be happening. It is then up to the actor to use his or her imagination and hope the effect is a reasonable facsimile of what the director describes and you the actor imagined. Budgets play a role here. I have had my share of disappointments where the effect has been underwhelming and my performance overwhelming. I may not trust that director next time, and they certainly would forever lose my respect. [Laughing]

DRAVEN: *For the aspiring directors out there who may be technical geniuses but lack the*

Kane Hodder as Jason Voorhees and John D. LeMay as Steven Freeman on set of *JASON GOES TO HELL: THE FINAL FRIDAY* (1993) inside the Voorhees house on July 23, 1992.

ability to direct actors, what would be your advice to them?

LeMAY: Cast the right actors and be prepared. The actor gets cast because they bring certain qualities to the process. Hopefully the director has the performer who best suits the role. I imagine that is half the work for the director. A director can't and shouldn't be spending their time on set coaching his actor on how to be the character. They need to be prepared to answer technical questions and assist the actor if they have trouble making sense of a direction, or character motivation.

To understand the process better, an acting class would be a great place to start. There are often acting instructors who will allow you sit in and observe a class. Second, being a technical wizard is a plus and very important for a director, but human beings make films and human beings watch them. Get away from the playback and talk to your performers. Try to avoid yelling directions and never berate your actors in front of the cast and crew.

DRAVEN: *In JASON GOES TO HELL: THE FINAL FRIDAY (1993), you did a lot of hand-to-hand combat scenes with Jason Voorhees (played by Kane Hodder), one of horror cinema's toughest screen villains. Can you describe the creative and technical process behind your favorite fight scene in the film?*

LeMAY: I was pretty confident in my stage combat skills. For two seasons of *Friday the 13th: The Series* I did a lot of stunts, working with stunt coordinator T. J. Scott in Canada. In the series, I fought many emissaries of the devil, and these were not your ordinary fights. You had to have a lot of luck going for you. Once the technical aspects of the fight are set, it is up to the actor to create an environment in which the impossible seems possible.

Kane Hodder was the stunt coordinator on JASON GOES TO HELL, so he choreographed the fight at the Voorhees' house. You have to be on your game with Kane. He is a big guy and you can't read his face under the hockey mask. He has big arms so you don't want to miss one of his arm cues. Oftentimes you get your cues from someone's face; his was all physical cues. A major disadvantage and a bit scary to boot. The adrenaline is always pumping when they yell "Action." Having Kane there

continued on the next page

continued from the previous page

John D. LeMay and Kane Hodder on set during a fight scene.

John D. LeMay and his stunt double preparing before a scene.

(with his black Jason eyes) certainly raised the adrenaline bar. My stunt double got thrown into the jungle gym in the film, so I can't take credit for that. As luck would have it, I was assisted by a conveniently-placed shovel. Not that it helped much. Actually nothing really worked with Jason. The guy just keeps coming. It really was an exhausting fight. I was glad to make it out alive.

DRAVEN: *In terms of acting, how is working in film different from television?*

LeMAY: I really don't see any difference, at least in the projects that I've done in the horror genre. The speed was a bit more hyperactive on the TV series. It always seemed like we were racing to get a shot done. Sometimes you are shooting two different episodes at once, doing pickups from an episode that wrapped last week.

DRAVEN: *If you could chose one horror film or performance in the history of horror cinema that influenced you as an actor, what would it be and why?*

LeMAY: As a kid, I watched the old black and white Universal Studios horror classics like WOLFMAN, DRACULA, and FRANKENSTEIN. Currently, I love watching ABBOTT AND COSTELLO MEET FRANKENSTEIN with my daughter. Classic.

Would have to say I am more a fan of psychological thrillers. One of my favorites is Anthony Hopkins' performance in THE SILENCE OF THE LAMBS (1991). That film had magic; he is a great actor.

Last year I enjoyed watching some old Halloween chestnuts on Turner Classic Movies. There are tons of great films in the genre I have yet to discover. Look . . . when you lived through a horror film, it takes a while before you want to risk triggering the nightmares all over again.

DRAVEN: *On the film set, what is the worst direction you have ever received from a director?*

LeMAY: "Move here and say the line like this."

INTERVIEW BOX
DEBBIE ROCHON ACTRESS

Debbie Rochon weaves her web of celebrity in the genre world of horror.
Photo Credit: Gary Cook

www.DebbieRochon.com

DEBBIE ROCHON has appeared in more than 150 independent horror and cult films. She has written for over a dozen genre magazines over the years and currently is one of the hosts for the Sirius/XM weekly broadcast of Fangoria Radio.

DRAVEN: *What do you think makes a great female protagonist in a horror film?*

ROCHON: One of my favorites to this day has to be the role of Sally as played by Marilyn Burns in the original horror classic THE

TEXAS CHAINSAW MASSACRE (1974). She portrayed all of the qualities that are essential for a strong but realistic female in a horror movie. She was not invincible; she was given obstacles that were physical, mental, and emotional. She was tested and rose to the occasion. I cite her even above the stunning performance Sigourney Weaver gave in the ALIEN film series because what Sally endured was realistic. It could really happen. She wasn't uber-tough, but she had a will to survive that superseded all else. She was scared and abused, but she never gave up. She always continued to have the hope and kept an eye open for the first possible means of escape. The role and performance in this case were extremely believable therefore win my highest accolades. She didn't just scream, she didn't just get up and kick ass; she suffered greatly and found strength within herself to endure until hope turned into reality for her. Even at the end of the film she isn't OK and just happy to be getting away. She is traumatized and shaken and you could well imagine her spending the next couple of years on some serious mind-numbing drugs. For me, that was one of the performances that made the entire film work. All the qualities were born out of real human, female behavior.

DRAVEN: *What do you think makes a great female antagonist in a horror film?*

continued on the next page

continued from the previous page

ROCHON: I think I have to mention one of my favorites, which isn't considered a horror movie. I think the film PLAY MISTY FOR ME (1971) featured one of the scariest antagonists ever because it was very realistic. The more believable the character and story is, the more deeply disturbing a film can be. Jessica Walter knocked the ball out of the park in this film as the obsessed fan of a talk show radio host. The host, played by Clint Eastwood, makes the mistake of having a one-night stand with her, and all bets are off. She becomes impossible to get rid of as she destroys his life one bit at a time. In the horror world I think you have to acknowledge the great Betsy Palmer for her convincing portrayal as the overprotective murderous mommy in the horror classic FRIDAY THE 13th (1980). There is a fine line between playing crazy and just acting plain campy, and these actresses, both with extensive stage and film credits prior to the aforementioned titles, brought a three-dimensional character to the screen.

That is what we all find most disturbing. It's not the unbelievable, but the believable, horrors that could happen next door.

In my opinion, there are a lot of horror movies that integrate both protagonist and antagonist. For example, actress Ellen Page in the film HARD CANDY (2005) is both the hero and the torturer in the film. Ms. Page's character took it upon herself to teach a pedophile a lesson even though she was never actually assaulted by him personally. This probably falls into the antihero category.

DRAVEN: *In your experience, what are the biggest mistakes you see directors—veterans or beginners—make when working with actors on the set?*

ROCHON: There are many, but I think the biggest mistake is shooting from a script that isn't ready. Viewers can forgive a lot of things, but a poorly crafted story is the biggest cinematic sin. People will hang in there through less than perfect camera

Debbie Rochon in
WITCHOUSE 3: Demon Fire.

The money glasses are a
little rose colored as there
is little money involved with
making cult movies.
Photo by Gary Cook.

work, sound design, and even a wooden performance here or there, but if the story is boring or isn't believable, the movie is dead meat. This doesn't mean you can't have outrageous circumstances with bizarre worlds in your movie, but you have to lay down the rules and follow them. How many times have you watched something and wondered, "I thought the women can fly and men can't, but that guy just flew . . . ?" My point being you can set down the craziest rules to your filmatic world and we will follow you. You just have to adhere to your rules and everything will be fine.

I think the next mistake is in the casting department. Once the story is solid you really need to believe the people on your TV otherwise the audience's suspension of disbelief is shattered and you've lost them.

In my experience, I once worked on a film where the filmmaker didn't have insurance, and because of this, my life was altered forever after being injured on a set. I wouldn't want to be a director whose cast was hurt on my set. Besides the legal ramifications, I would find it hard to live with disabling someone permanently. You need insurance on your set or you have no business making a movie. Horror movies are action movies in a lot of ways (e.g., running, jumping, physical stunts) and it's insane to think you don't need it.

DRAVEN: *Have you ever worked with a female horror film director, and if so, how do they differ from their male colleagues?*

ROCHON: There are very few, I have to say, and there have been long stretches between working with them. The first female director I worked with was

From COLOUR FROM THE DARK. Rochon loses her mind in this bloody good adaptation of an H. P. Lovecraft story.

Roberta Findlay when I made two films in the late 80s . . . LURKERS (1988) and BANNED (1989). She was a screamer, but her style was very frank and New York-esque. Her brashness was mostly just accepted, and we all didn't know any better anyway being novices! It ended up being rather funny to watch her direct the cast and crew. She had to be tough because I don't think anyone would listen to her otherwise. I like the energy of working with most women, so I think the comfort level is higher for me. But some

continued on the next page

continued from the previous page

actresses get a lot of their self-esteem from male-specific encouragement. I think both sexes have a lot to offer the role of director. I have just never had the patience for actresses who need to have the full attention of a male director for ego reasons just to be "The Belle of the Ball." I like anyone who works hard, has a vision (even if they're good at making "product" versus "art"), and concerns themselves with the making of the movie, not the movement in their pants.

DRAVEN: *The horror genre has a reputation for exploiting and objectifying women, usually to cater to the predominately young male audience. What are your thoughts on this issue, and do you feel you have been exploited?*

ROCHON: No, I don't feel exploited whatsoever. I think both sexes have equally participated in the exploitation of women. I think there's a place for sexy movies, but as you get older your taste matures. I have no problem watching nudity in film, but what I enjoy now is different than when I was a teenager. I love a good scary horror movie with a solid story, or a well-executed horror–comedy, or even just well done, straight up camp. Exploitation doesn't do anything for me. I have done a lot of exploitation over the years and it didn't corrode my brain, so I think I came out alright. It does ruffle a lot of feathers. You will find people who use it as some sort of proof that you are inferior to them because you've been naked on screen. You can become an easy target to mean-spirited people. I feel like, God willing, if I make it to 90, I will show

all the people in the horror-movie old age home how good I *used* to look.

DRAVEN: *If nudity is required in the script, how does an actress deal with this sensitive issue? What is your experience and how do you deal with this subject?*

ROCHON: I think what saves the most time is to just tell the casting people or director immediately that you don't want to do it if nudity is involved. Never take the part thinking you will deal with it later. Maybe the director won't care and will hire you anyway. Maybe he won't hire you because he's required to deliver X amount of nude scenes per 30 minutes. Never piss everybody off by accepting the role then dropping the bomb that you're not going to strip down the day of the nude scene because you aren't comfortable with it.

I have taken roles that have required nudity, and when it was time for the nude scene, I would either just do it without obsessing over it beforehand, which really just gets you all worried and worked up

From HANGER. During a botched forced abortion, Rochon's character loses her life, but her fetus offspring lives on to exact revenge.

From Colour From The Dark. During the possession, there are reflective moments for Debbie's character Lucia.

anyway, or the opposite happens—I am dreading it. However, I never say a word and just do the scene as well as I can in hopes I will then only have to do minimal takes. I have told directors I wasn't interested in doing a role because of the nudity involved, I have no problem with turning work down. If I like the script, I have usually said yes to nudity because the rest of the movie made it worth it. At the end of the day, I have always looked at the overall picture but also took my bills into consideration as well. I always wanted to be a working actor. Nudity comes with the territory in film.

DRAVEN: *Is the independent horror genre dead?*

ROCHON: The independent horror genre is both dead and undead! I think we need a new, cutting-edge revolution in how we get movies out to viewers. Times have completely changed. No more drive-ins, no more VHS, very little DVD distribution, no TV sales, and very little action on the video on demand download front. I don't know what the next thing will be, but whatever it is, it will save independent horror (and non) movies. This is the frontier that we need to be focused on; what's the new venue? I understand when people say that the indie scene is dead. Most sales have come to a complete standstill, and the self-distribution model hasn't completely taken hold yet. I think something will happen, it always does. If indie film does end up being viewed on iPods or BlackBerries then the filmmakers will adjust to it and shoot more close-ups! We are survivors and will mutate with the times.

DRAVEN: *What are some of the most annoying, penny-pinching things low-budget film producers do when making a film?*

ROCHON: I really don't require much, but if a set doesn't have coffee, water, and a little craft service area, then they really shouldn't be making a movie. These are the basics for your cast and crew to keep them going! I know when Lloyd Kaufman is making a Troma movie he insists on using small cups instead of large ones, but I think that's very smart! How many times do you see half consumed beverages being thrown out? That's why he does it. There's a difference between being a miser and being smart.

I even had one incident where we wrapped the film at about 7 am after shooting all night long—keep in mind this was the last day of the film shoot—and the director said everyone should see the producer after they change to get paid. I changed as fast as a lightening bolt and ran downstairs and poof! The producer was gone. He was never to be seen or heard from again! That was a long time ago but you would be surprised how low some can go. If ever in that situation get the money before you get changed!

CHAPTER 4

THE HORROR FILM CREW

> **I learned to take the first job that you have in the business that you want to get into. It doesn't matter what the job is, you get your foot in the door.**
>
> **—WES CRAVEN**

The key to shooting quickly and efficiently is to hire a *professional* crew and a middle management team (e.g., line producer, assistant directors, unit production manager). The worst thing you can do is to have friends and family fill the positions of professional crew members. A professional crew and middle management team has the experience and knowledge to operate quickly and effectively. They will keep your production running on time and on budget.

DETERMINING CREW SIZE

On my films, I determine crew size based on the needs of the script and the technical needs of the production. When putting together a professional crew for a low-budget film you should always carefully evaluate your needs and ask yourself: Who do we need and who can we do without? I often visit sets of indie filmmakers and see five or more people that didn't need to be hired or jobs that could have been doubled by others. It's important to make sure each person's function on set is justifiable and necessary for the course of the production. In some instances, you may want to consider hiring a person only in preproduction and then not having that person on set on a day-to-day basis. For example, I often do this

The crew setting up for a shot on the set of CRYPTZ.

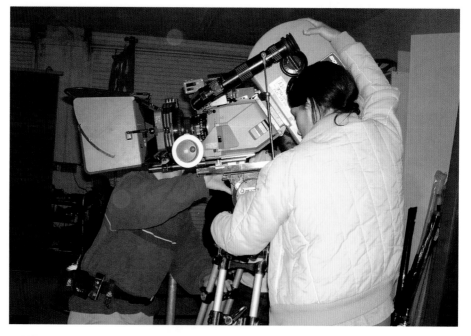

(L–R) The second AC/loader and the first AC reloading a 35mm Movicam Compact camera on the set of GHOST MONTH.

with the wardrobe department. I hire a costume designer in preproduction to do the work for a flat fee and then number all wardrobe changes to easily identify them on the shooting schedule; therefore, there is no need for the costume designer to be present during the shoot. I also usually do not hire a script supervisor mainly because I'm the one editing the film and I know exactly which takes I will use. It is important, however, to have a script supervisor that knows what he or she is doing if you have someone else edit your film.

Another way to keep your crew size small is by doubling crew members' duties. You will pay a higher rate for more duties and responsibilities, but it saves you money in the long run by keeping the crew size small. For example, you can hire a second AC that can double up as a camera loader or an AD that can double as a UPM (unit production manager).

TIPS FOR HIRING CREW

I have found that most crew people will say and agree to almost anything in the interview to get the job. It's vital to put their skills to the test before you hire them, and always get your terms in writing, usually in the form of a deal memo. Here are a few tips:

1. Always go with your gut feeling about a person.

2. Ask a series of technical questions to make sure the applicant can answer accurately as it relates to the job. if possible, have the applicant perform the duties during the interview.

3. Always check professional references.

CASE STUDY: GHOST MONTH

For my film GHOST MONTH, we shot on 35mm with a Moviecam Compact camera, and I had a barebones crew on location in Nevada for 10 days. The 15 member crew consisted of the following: producer/director/line producer, coproducer, assistant director, director of photography, first AC, second AC/loader, gaffer, key grip, grip, key production assistant, key makeup/hair stylist, assistant makeup/hair, production designer, sound mixer, and boom operator.

On the set of GHOST MONTH.

Director of Photography Mike King (center) sets up a low-angle shot on the set of
GHOST MONTH.

NOTES ON USING FREE CREW

I often get asked by aspiring filmmakers to call them if I ever need any help on my next film. I also get the same offer from soccer moms, retired people, family, and the local dentists to help out for free. Filmmaking is exciting, and naturally people are drawn to the behind-the-scenes look at what it takes to make a movie. However, I rarely take anyone up on the offer for one simple reason: *the professional set is not a place to teach lessons.* In fact, during very short shooting schedules, you need to be quick and efficient. The best way to do that is to hire the most experienced people you can afford to get the job done. In some cases there are exceptions. You should be the one to determine if it will benefit the production or not.

You can usually get trained assistants for free. I have helped a lot of students get their first break by working on my set. You can find these people by simply placing ads or calling the local film or trade schools. I often work with an excellent makeup artist named Mark Bautista, who is a good friend of mine. He used to teach at Joe Blasco Makeup School in Hollywood. Students and alumni loved him and always wanted to work with him, so he would always bring a team of free assistants to the set to work on the makeup effects. These guys were always top notch, and Mark would supervise the quality of the work. By having these extra assistants, we were able to save time and money. By working for free,

Mark Bautista (left) with his assistants working on actor Rick Irvin's vampire makeup on the set of CRYPTZ.

Giving a zombie face-lift on set.

FREE CREW

Beware of free, inexperienced crew. They can slow a production down. The less people you have standing around the set, the better. This includes crew, family, and friends.

they got the experience of working on a real set, and we got high-quality work.

POPULAR SITES TO POST CREW CALLS

There are a lot of hungry crew members looking for work out there. I usually start by asking filmmaker friends for recommendations, and if that doesn't turn up any results, I start posting crew calls online. I always get a lot of submissions. It's always best not to be vague about your production. You should always list the crew position requirements, shooting days, format, pay rate, and any other terms or relevant information. Here are some great resources to help you get started:

4 Entertainment Jobs: www.4entertainmentjobs.com

ProductionHUB: www.productionhub.com

Filmstaff: www.filmstaff.com

Entertainment Careers: www.entertainmentcareers.net

Production Jobs: www.findproductionjobs.com

Crew Net: www.crewnet.com

craigslist: www.craigslist.org (in the tv/film/video section)

Indeed: www.indeed.com

CreativeJobsCentral: www.creativejobscentral.com

MovieStaff: www.moviestaff.com

ACTORSandCREW: www.actorsandcrew.com

Mandy: www.mandy.com

ProductionHUB web site.

Crew Net web site.

INTERVIEW BOX

ROBERT KURTZMAN PRODUCER, DIRECTOR, SCREENWRITER, CREATURE AND VISUAL FX CREATOR

Robert Kurtzman

Precinct 13 Entertainment

www.p13entertainment.com

ROBERT KURTZMAN, Hollywood special effects legend and filmmaker, began his career in 1984 when he moved from Ohio to Hollywood and started working as a freelance artist for many of the industry's top special effects creators. His early credits include PREDATOR, EVIL DEAD II, FROM BEYOND, THE HIDDEN, PHANTASM II, INVADERS FROM MARS, NIGHT OF THE CREEPS, and RE-ANIMATOR. In 1988, Robert formed the award-winning KNB EFX Group, Inc. with partners Greg Nicotero and Howard Berger. Over the next 15 years, KNB became one of the most prolific effects studios in Hollywood with hundreds of feature film and television credits, including the SPY KIDS movies, THE CELL, UNBREAKABLE, HOUSE ON HAUNTED HILL, SPAWN, THE FACULTY, Sam Raimi's ARMY OF DARKNESS, DANCES WITH WOLVES, JINGLE ALL THE WAY, THE GREEN MILE, GHOSTS OF MARS, RAT RACE, 13 GHOSTS, VANILLA SKY, THE TIME MACHINE, AUSTIN POWERS: GOLDMEMBER, THE HULK, GHOST SHIP, EVOLUTION, BUBBA HO-TEP, WYATT EARP, John Carpenter's VAMPIRES and IN THE MOUTH OF MADNESS, MISERY, Steven Spielberg's MINORITY REPORT and AMISTAD, Quentin Tarantino's RESERVOIR DOGS, PULP FICTION, KILL BILL Volumes 1 and 2, as well as the television series *Hercules*, *Xena*, *Picket Fences*, *Outer Limits*, *ER*, *Chicago Hope*, and many more.

In 2003, Kurtzman founded Precinct 13 Entertainment/Creature Corps, which is a full-service production facility that handles film, commercials, and music videos as well as special makeup, creature construction, visual effects, editorial and post. P13 and Creature Corps have worked on a wide array of projects with credits that include the effects supervision on HOSTEL, THE DEVIL's REJECTS, 2001 MANIACS, *Mad TV*, and CHILDREN OF THE CORN.

continued on the next page

continued from the previous page

Robert's foray into production began with FROM DUSK TILL DAWN (1996). He wrote the original story, which was adapted by Quentin Tarantino, coproduced the film, and created the eye-popping special effects. His directorial debut was THE DEMOLITIONIST, which was quickly followed by WISHMASTER, a film he directed for Artisan Entertainment and executive producer Wes Craven. WISHMASTER opened as the number one horror film and went on to become the year's most successful independent release.

DRAVEN: *After leaving KNB EFX Group, you formed Precinct 13 Entertainment, a makeup/visual FX studio. Since then you have independently made films such as BURIED ALIVE (2007) and THE RAGE (2007). How is working on huge Hollywood films different from low-budget ones in terms of makeup FX?*

KURTZMAN: On big films you have more time and money and a much bigger crew. You're used to having more research and development (R&D) time to create innovative effects. These days, even on the big films, there really isn't any R&D. You're usually up against an almost impossible deadline when you start the show, but the bigger the show and the more time you have, the more polished the work will look.

On small films you have to really think on your feet and come up with easy, innovative ways to shoot the effects because the schedule and money are so tight. You have to use techniques that are tried and true. Getting your feet wet doing low budget films ultimately prepares you for working on bigger films as the techniques you learn on small pictures always come in handy, even on blockbusters. Sometimes it's the simple things that work best.

DRAVEN: *What are two of the biggest pitfalls you have encountered in making independent films, and what is your advice to help others avoid the pitfalls from happening to them?*

KURTZMAN: Jumping into a film without being prepared and organized.

Never start a film without having secured all the monies and having it in the bank. I've been involved with productions on an FX level that start the film and then halfway through prep or production they have an issue with an investor and someone pulls out on financing. When this happens production usually continues as though nothing is going wrong, and they scramble to fill the financing gap. The work continues, but soon they start not making their payments to the crew on time. They'll have 8 million excuses and will promise you they will make good. However, it doesn't always go down that way, and a lot of times the production folds with crew and talent hung out to dry being owed a lot of money. So as a filmmaker, always have the money in the bank before starting. Putting funding together in pieces is not a good idea.

DRAVEN: *On your independent films, do you shoot on digital or film?*

KURTZMAN: Both. It depends on the film and the financiers. I personally like to shoot digital for various reasons. It streamlines the post process when dealing with digital FX work, and I'm able to move much quicker shooting. I don't have to worry about the

Robert Kurtzman's monster creations.

cost of shooting too much coverage and burning film. Also, I can let the camera roll and keep the actors in the moment without having to cut. I shot my last film for MGM using the Viper (the same camera David Fincher uses on films like ZODIAC), and we were able to get double the amount of coverage, which is a real asset when you get into the edit room.

DRAVEN: *In your experience, what makes a great movie monster and why?*

continued on the next page

continued from the previous page

KURTZMAN: It's all about the story. You can have a great monster, but if it's shot like crap and the story sucks then so does the monster. So it's a combination of things that have to come together to make a great monster movie. Design and execution are key. Also, the less you see the better.

A monster isn't scary unless you can build the suspense around it. It's just a piece of rubber without lighting, music, sound effects, and actors who can convey fear, so all this has to come together to make a great movie monster work.

DRAVEN: *In a new age of digital gore, what are your thoughts for using computers in place of on-set FX? Is one better than the other, or do they compliment each other?*

KURTZMAN: It's a tool and an asset if used properly. One isn't better than the other. There are things that each is great for, and limitations to both. A mix of the two, whenever possible, makes for the best results.

DRAVEN: *For low-budget horror films, what do you think makes the most effective types of monsters? What should filmmakers with big ideas but microbudgets stay away from?*

KURTZMAN: It's best on low-budget films to use more practical effects. Sometimes you have to use digital because you can't afford a crane to fly a puppet around on and you'll never get the puppet to do what you need and your day goes down the tubes while you try to get impossible shots. So shooting plates and adding animated creatures in postproduction is the only way to go. But CGI isn't cheap, as everyone thinks, and if you don't have a post schedule long enough to achieve the effects, then you should rethink your approach to accommodate your budget and schedule.

DRAVEN: *If you could choose three horror films that best demonstrate the use of simple, effective, low-budget FX, what would they be and why?*

KURTZMAN: NIGHT OF THE LIVING DEAD (1968): Very minimal effects but very effective.

THE HOWLING (1981): A low-budget film with a very small FX budget that was able to break new ground in FX techniques. The lighting and staging of the FX were key in creating a successful creature transformation.

FRIDAY THE 13TH (1980): Great gore gags on a shoestring budget. Tom Savini used staging and misdirection to set up great scares and kills using very simple but effective techniques.

DRAVEN: *What do you think are the three most important elements for a low-budget horror film to have?*

KURTZMAN: Good story. Great suspense. Great cast!

There are different kinds of horror films, so you have to consider what the filmmakers are going for. Some are meant to be fun rides and others more cerebral. The most important thing is for the filmmakers to have passion for the material, which ultimately shows in the filmmaking.

DRAVEN: *What is the Robert Kurtzman secret to homemade fake blood?*

KURTZMAN: Karo Syrup, food coloring (red, green, blue) and a dash of clear dish soap to get it to not bead up and flow properly. You just have to eye the coloring to get

Robert Kurtzman's movies.

the right look so it's not too pink or bright red. Every filmmaker likes a different look depending on how they are lighting the film. It's very easy to make the blood too dark and it shows up black on film, so its good to test out the blood on film to make sure it looks good.

CHAPTER 5
PREPRODUCTION TIPS & TRICKS

> **The process of writing and directing drives you to such extremes that it's natural to feel an affinity with insanity that's there. I approach that madness as something dangerous and I'm afraid, but also I want to go to it, to see...to embrace it. I don't know why, but I'm drawn.**
>
> **—DARIO ARGENTO**

When you're making a low-budget film it's crucial to meticulously plan every detail and have a backup plan for every possible disaster scenario you can imagine. The planning stage of a film is vital to bringing your film in on time and budget, a skill that can only help along your career.

I always line produce my own films. After all, no one knows what I'm doing day-to-day better than I do, so it's best if I break down the script, budget, and schedule all the details of my shoot. I am meticulous in the planning stage. After my preproduction planning is completed, I execute it and start delegating it to different departments, and the production is off to a smooth start.

LOCATION TIPS

One of the biggest money savers on an independent film is having a free location. If you were to pay a daily or hourly rate, plus insurance requirements, your budget would skyrocket. During the writing phase, write your story around as many free locations as possible to avoid costly location rentals, especially in Los Angeles.

The Location Scout – When you scout a location, the primary goal is to make sure that it fits the requirements of the script. It's good to have your producer, director, director of photography, and production designer come to the location to scout. If they are not available, you can videotape the location and show it to them later.

LOCATION CHECKLIST

1. **Power** – Make sure the location has house power and that you can use it for your lights. Otherwise, you'll need to bring in a costly generator. Check with your director of photography and/or gaffer regarding sufficient power at the location.

2. **Restrooms** – There must be enough restrooms to cater to your cast and crew size, otherwise you will need to bring in honeywagons or portable toilets, which gets expensive. Always bring your own toilet supplies, unless the location provides them free.

3. **Craft service area** – Make sure there is an area where you can set up craft services and an area where tables and chairs can be set up for the cast and crew to eat meals.

4. **Green room** – There is a lot of waiting on a set, so it's a good idea to designate an area for people to hang out. Usually this is in an area far away from where you'll be shooting so people can talk without disturbing the production.

5. **Makeup/wardrobe room** – Your makeup crew will usually need their own area, preferably with a lot of light and a sink nearby. I usually combine this area with wardrobe.

6. **Parking** – You need to make sure the location provides ample parking for your crew size. If not, see if street parking or paid parking lots are options.

7. **Smoking area** – You should never let anyone smoke inside of a location. Smoking must be done outside and only on breaks. It's unprofessional and potentially hazardous to smoke inside. It's best to post "no smoking" signs, and put a large can with sand in it outside for smokers.

Think ahead, and always have a sink nearby!

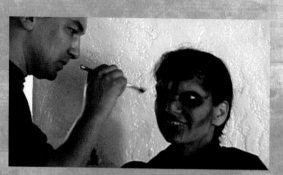

Mark Bautista applying makeup to scream queen Brinke Stevens on the set of HELL ASYLUM.

Rent a House – On GHOST MONTH I wanted a location where I could have complete freedom. We simply called a non-industry-related realtor, and she found us the perfect place: a 6,000 square foot multi-level house in the middle of the desert. We rented it for 2 months and shot the entire film there, and there was even enough room to build sets in the six-car garage.

Marlene Brown and Mike Brown building a set.

Sometimes a large garage can make a great sound stage.

Me living full time on the freezing set of GHOST MONTH in the mountains of Nevada in the winter.

The only difficult hurdle was that the house was empty and 1 hour from civilization, so we had to bring in all the set dressing and furniture. If you decide to go this route, it's best to keep a low profile whenever you're shooting to avoid the authorities showing up and questioning you.

Living on Set – The idea of living on set may seem a bit extreme for most, but it does save money and increase productivity—and no one is ever late! On one of my films, to save money, commute time, and for me to stay focused, I moved into the location for the duration of the shoot. I also had my director of photography, gaffer, wife, and dog living there as well as an occasional stray actor. It was great having the freedom to prep everything for the following day, and it also allowed the director of photography to prelight.

Combining Sets & Locations – When you have locked in a location, it's a good idea to see if there are any other scenes in the script that could be "cheated" at your main location. You should cheat as many as possible. This is a big time and money saver on low-budget films. For example, on GHOST MONTH, I cheated an office and two other apartment interiors for other locations, all in the same house. I also used the exterior and backyard of the house to double for other locations.

Power – Generators are great to have, but they're costly. They require gas refills, expel fumes, are noisy, and draw attention to the location. It's always best to tap into the location's power source or use house power. On GHOST MONTH, we shot the entire film on 35mm. We shot Fuji 250D and Fuji 400T 35mm film stocks, and we didn't have a generator at all. We used house power for the entire shoot.

Porn Sets – I once had the idea that I could save money by shooting on a sound stage, so I found the cheapest one I could: a porn stage. They had plenty of recycled sets, props, and lighting equipment, so we were able to build some custom sets from old ones. The majority of my film DEATH-BED was shot on a porn sound stage (on a flight path!) in a ratty part of North Hollywood.

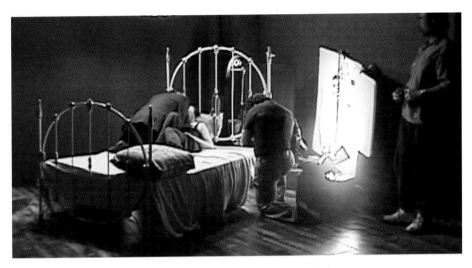

This was shot on a porn stage with recycled walls. We brought our own bed.

EQUIPMENT TIPS

Shoot Holidays & Weekends – Holidays and weekends are a great time to shoot because you usually get good rates during those downtimes. I often shoot films 2 weeks before Christmas for this reason, and I usually get a lot of equipment upgrades for free.

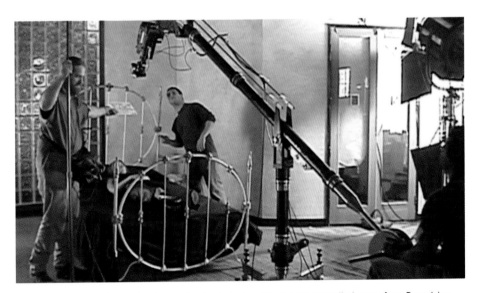

Because we shot on the weekend, we got a great deal on this remote-controlled crane from Panavision.

A homemade skateboard dolly with 12 feet of track.

A homemade rain bar, made with a garden hose and some C stands.

Own, Beg & Borrow – It's always best to own your gear. If you don't own it, do everything you can to beg and borrow it from someone who does. I've saved a lot of money by owning my own equipment and borrowing from generous friends. Sometimes you can make your own.

Prep Days Are Important – Make sure you give your director of photography and/or camera assistants a day of prep with the camera you will be using. It's very important to prep the camera before shooting to avoid doing it on day one.

This is all the equipment we had to shoot GHOST MONTH.

CATERING & CRAFT SERVICES

The Food – It's always best to have your production catered by a professional, low-budget friendly company. I've tried the fast-food chain pizza, tacos, and burgers approach on productions, and it never had a happy ending. Don't do it! Make sure the catering company you hire provides hot meals, both meat and meatless dishes, and more than enough portions for your cast and crew head count. Also, make sure that any special diets are taken into consideration.

Craft Services Table – People tend to be wasteful on sets, so it's a good idea to use small cups and 2-liter bottles for soda and water. Also, only put out small amounts of finger food at a time to avoid waste.

Tables & Chairs – Make sure you have more than enough tables and chairs on set for the cast and crew to use. I've made this mistake before, and people do tend to get cranky when they have to sit on the floor to eat.

WARDROBE TIPS

Ask Actors to Contribute Clothes – Most actors are hip and have a lot of cool clothes, old and new, and enjoy fashioning their characters from their own closet. It's important to ask actors before hiring them to make

Dead girls need to stay healthy too.

Internet access for the undead is also nice.

sure they're open to this idea. For scenes that require blood or where clothing may get damaged, the production should either buy their old clothes or purchase a new wardrobe for that scene. It's always a good idea to buy doubles, especially for scenes that involve blood, fighting, or have the potential to get very dirty.

Thrift Stores – We have saved a lot of money on wardrobe by searching local thrift stores like Goodwill, Salvation Army, and other discount stores. It's not the answer for all your wardrobe needs, but you'll find some bargains.

Collect, Store & Number – When you have locked in the wardrobe required for the characters, you should collect it all and store it in the production office *before* production begins. Do not rely on people to bring it to the set the day of shooting. It's best to wrap each outfit with plastic and number it according to wardrobe ID numbers on the scheduling strips.

CHUCK WILLIAMS PRODUCER, ACTOR

Producer Chuck Williams on set.

www.chuckwilliamsfanclub.com

CHUCK WILLIAMS moved to Hollywood in 1983 to become an actor. His enthusiasm for every aspect of filmmaking quickly forced him to broaden his horizons. He has worked alongside such Hollywood heavyweights as James Cameron, Rob Cohen, Kathryn Bigelow, John Badham, Penelope Spheeris, Jonathan Kaplan, David Fincher, and Jim Kouf. Williams produced William Shatner's GROOM LAKE, Jeff Burr's Universal Studios' STRAIGHT INTO DARKNESS, Robert Englund's KILLER PAD, and the first American lucha libre film, MIL MASCARAS VS. THE AZTEC MUMMY. Most recently he produced THE TELLING with Bridget Marquardt and appeared opposite Bruce Campbell in Don Coscarelli's BUBBA HO-TEP.

DRAVEN: *What is the best way for a low-budget filmmaker to finance a horror film?*

WILLIAMS: Rob a bank! Just kidding. Usually you first ask a family member to help get you started in the industry, and after you burn that bridge, you beg, borrow, and steal from investors, doctors, or anyone who owns a business. They'll usually take a chance on a low-budget film without getting hurt financially.

DRAVEN: *What are three of the biggest pitfalls you have encountered in making low-budget horror films?*

WILLIAMS: One pitfall is having no money, which adds stress in every department. The second pitfall is that most folks think just because they own a camcorder they are ready to be filmmakers; nothing could be further from the truth. They should go spend some time on a set and get hands-on training. The third pitfall is filmmakers who hire inexperienced friends to fill important positions. This is a major pitfall. I suggest at least looking for film students in the local area to fill those unpaid, merciless jobs. It seems to me that half the time when you hire

continued on the next page

continued from the previous page

friends you can't pay, it spells disaster for your friendship.

DRAVEN: *For a low-budget horror film, is it more beneficial to shoot in Los Angeles, or out of state, or possibly even out of the country?*

WILLIAMS: I love filming outside of Los Angeles—I find most places are very accommodating with free locations, permits, crews, and there is also a general excitement that you're shooting in their town. Actors also love to shoot on location, and this is a big plus when attracting talented actors for very low pay.

DRAVEN: *When you're producing a low-budget horror film, what is your interaction with the director like? Does a producer's own ideas and budget restrictions often clash with the director's vision?*

WILLIAMS: As a producer, you should never clash with a director. You are there to bring his vision to the screen. If not, you should have never hired him in the first place. Remember, all crew members in my book are artists. They all bring major talents to the table, and you should respect them. You should never spend time in breaking them down to feel they are not contributing. It's their film, too.

DRAVEN: *What are three tips you could share with new low-budget horror film producers to save money in the budget?*

WILLIAMS: Firstly, treat everyone like family; this will help to get better communication and focus on your set, resulting in saving money and keeping everything smooth. Secondly, I used to send everyone to Costco, but now you must shop at the dollar stores for your craft service and other disposable items. You must never

have a weak craft service table; your crew will start complaining, and mutiny will be right around the corner. You must feed them well with hot meals. Thirdly, you must negotiate every deal personally. Nobody is better at saving money than you. You must be hands on, not a loud-mouthed, chain-smoking, coffee-drinking producer calling the shots at arms length and completely annoying everyone.

DRAVEN: *What do you think are the three most important elements for a low-budget horror film to have to be sellable in the horror market?*

WILLIAMS: The most important, I think, are a great story, gore, and an awesome soundtrack! A name actor is also a plus.

DRAVEN: *What is the Chuck Williams secret to dealing with day-to-day problems on set?*

WILLIAMS: You should always be on set, never be cocky, and always listen to your crew. They know what is really happening, so you should treat them with respect. If you do that, I guarantee I'll be watching your movie on my HD 60-inch screen TV.

Danny Draven and Chuck Williams as the Darkwalker on set in 2002.

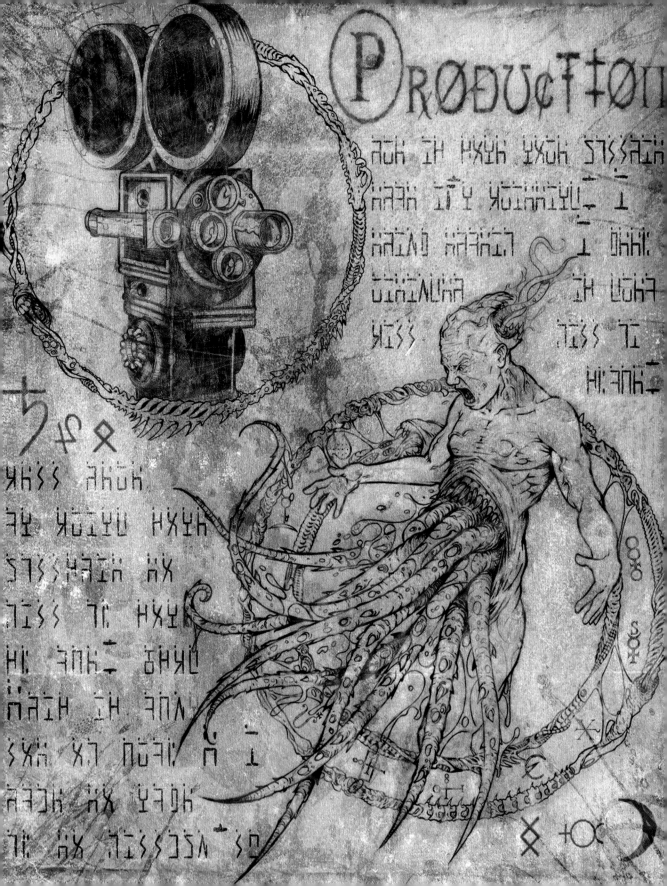

PART THREE

PRODUCTION

CHAPTER 6

PRODUCING A HORROR FILM

> **I aim to provide the public with beneficial shocks. Civilization has become so protective that we're no longer able to get our goose bumps instinctively. The only way to remove the numbness and revive our moral equilibrium is to use artificial means to bring about the shock. The best way to achieve that, it seems to me, is through a movie.**
>
> **—ALFRED HITCHCOCK**

If you are a new producer and considering making a horror film, the journey ahead is a long one that is filled with joy and heart-attack inducing fear. On my first producing job, I was a nervous wreck over every little detail. My mind was overwhelmed with questions like: What if the actor quits during production? What if the cash runs out? What if a crew member gets hurt? What if I get sued? These questions filled my mind day after day until the end of production. On one occasion, I had a serious nosebleed and heart palpitations from stress and almost had to put myself in a hospital because I was worried about so many details that fell on my lap at once. And after all that, I would do it all over again.

When producing an indie film, it's often the case that you can't afford to hire professional producers that know what they're doing. You rely on yourself and those who are helping you. I went to film classes, read books, watched videos, and went to conventions and seminars, but none of this research and schooling prepared me for life on the set. My producing school was very simple. I was given a tiny amount of money to make a genre-specific feature film in 6 days and deliver a final master in less than 3 months. In retrospect, this was the best thing that could have happened to me as a producer. The things you learn when you are under pressure are invaluable. Your character and determination will be tested, but ultimately this is what will shape you into a great producer.

A film production is a giant puzzle of details, schedules, and personalities, and all of these pieces must fit together to form a whole; otherwise disaster strikes. The heart of a smooth production is in its middle management— your line producer, unit production manager (UPM), and first assistant director (1st AD). These are the people that will keep the machine working. If you lose them, the engine will shut off. It's important to never overwhelm yourself with too many producing responsibilities in an effort to save money. You must know when and how to delegate your work flow.

WHAT IS A PRODUCER, ANYWAY?

In general, a producer is one who acquires material, hires key talent and crew, and essentially "produces" the film. The producer's talent lies in recognizing ideas that have merit creatively and commercially and bringing those ideas to fruition.

There are often several producing credits on a film, and sometimes it gets confusing to understand who does what. Here are the most common producer types and their definitions:

EXECUTIVE PRODUCER

The executive producer, sometimes known as the executive in charge of production, is the person who isn't directly involved in the technical operations of the production process. He or she, or often a group of people, is the one who provides funding for the entire film. Executive producers are also known as the investors. Sometimes this credit is also given to a person who doesn't directly participate in the technical process but who oversees the whole production (i.e., the writer or the creator of the film or script). In big-budget films, such as major studio productions, this title is often, but not always, given to the CEO of a major studio.

PRODUCER

The producer is essentially the one who makes certain the movie happens; this person produces the film. He or she oversees the entire process of filmmaking from conception to completion. On a low-budget film, because there isn't much money to go around, productions often eliminate the line producer position; therefore, the producer will also have to do the line producer's job.

COPRODUCER

A coproducer is generally the one who helps the producer on the film; the right-hand person, so to speak. He or she is directly involved in the day-to-day production activity. On low-budget productions, there is only a handful of crew members, and the producer is doing most of the work, therefore the presence of a coproducer helps tremendously.

LINE PRODUCER

The line producer is the one who does all of the grunt work of producing, especially during the preproduction process. This includes everything from negotiating rates with crew members, rental, and postproduction companies to working out the specifics of day-to-day production. The line producer also oversees the entire budget and makes sure the production is not going over, as well as supervises day-to-day activities during production.

The lonely life of an indie producer after everyone is sent home.

ASSOCIATE PRODUCER

An associate producer is usually a person who acts as a representative of the film's producer. A producer will often delegate some responsibilities to an associate producer. It's common that the producer and associate producer may share creative, financial, and administrative responsibilities. The responsibility is sometimes given to a person who consults on the film in a significant way or makes creative and financial contributions.

THE PRODUCER'S RESPONSIBILITIES

A producer is always the first one to arrive and the last one to leave on a production. But what does taking the "produced by" credit really mean? What do you need to do?

In an effort to help you understand what the produced by credit really means, I have chosen an excerpt from the Producer's Code of Credits for theatrical motion pictures as established by the Producers Guild of America. This is a great example of what a producer *does* during a movie to earn his or her credit. The following text is reprinted with permission of the Producers Guild of America.

JOB FUNCTIONS FOR "PRODUCED BY" (THEATRICAL MOTION PICTURES)

Subject to the control of the Owner, the "Produced by" in Theatrical Motion Pictures is expected to exercise decision-making authority over a majority of the following specific job functions:

DEVELOPMENT

Conceived of the underlying concept upon which the production is based or involved at its inception.

Selected the material upon which the production is based and secured necessary rights for development and production of the material.

Selected the writer(s).

Supervised and oversaw the development process.

Secured the initial financing.

Served as the primary point of contact for the studio and/or financing entity.

PREPRODUCTION

Selected the director, co-producer and unit production manager.

Selected the principal cast in consultation with the director.

In consultation with the director, selected the production designer, cinematographer, editor and visual effects company

Participated in location scouting in consultation with the director.

Supervised the preparation of the preliminary budget and approved and signed the final budget in consultation with the Co-Producer and UPM.

Creatively involved in the final shooting script in consultation with the director and the writer(s) and approved and signed the final shooting script.

Approved the final shooting schedule in consultation with the director.

PRODUCTION

Exercised final approval of the deals for the principal components of the production.

Provided continuous in-person consultation with the director and principal cast.

In collaboration with the director, provided in-person consultation with the production designer, art department, wardrobe, make-up and hair.

In collaboration with the director, provided in-person consultation with the stunt coordinator and on mechanical effects (if applicable).

Supervised "on-set" and on a continuous basis the day-to-day operation of the producing team and the entire shooting company.

Approved the weekly cost report.

Viewed the "dailies" and provided in-person consultation with the director, the editor, the studio and/or financial entity.

POST-PRODUCTION/MARKETING

Provided in-person participation on visual effects in consultation with the director, the studio or financial entity.

Selected the composer in consultation with the director, and participated in-person with the composer and the director in the scoring process.

Provided in-person consultation with the editor along with the director, the studio or financial entity, and participated on the final cut of the motion picture.

Consulted with the director and the editor during the preparation of the first cut that is shown to the studio/financial entity.

Selected the music supervisor in consultation with the director, and participated in-person during the music recording sessions.

Provided in-person consultation with the director on the re-recording stage.

Provided in-person consultation with the director on the titles and opticals.

Provided in-person consultation with the cinematographer, the director, the studio and/or financing entity on the answer print or edited master.

Consulted on the media plan and materials, and the marketing and distribution plans for the motion picture.

Consulted on the plans for exploitation of the motion picture in ancillary and foreign markets.

For more information and to see other codes of credits for producers, visit the Producers Guild of America web site at www.producersguild.org.

THE PRODUCER'S VISION

Just like a director's vision for a film, a producer also has a vision. You need to ask yourself: Why is this film being made? You need to know the direction of the film and where you are going with the finished product. It is the producer's job to create a film that is going to be marketable and sellable and protect the investors' money. This determines what kind of movie you want to make and which creative team to hire.

(L-R) Director of Photography Mac Ahlberg, Screenwriter John Strysik, Executive Producer Stuart Gordon, and Producer/Director Danny Draven during a meeting on the set of DEATHBED.

BE A JACK-OF-ALL-TRADES

Since I became involved in film productions, I have worn many hats. I've been everything from a runner and production assistant to gaffer and cinematographer, to name a few. I have accepted all those jobs for the experience, and not necessarily because I wanted to pursue a career in that particular job. If you want to be a great producer, it's your job to know everyone else's job and have the knowledge and experience to know when they are doing it right or wrong!

Danny Draven filling in for a camera operator who got sick.

THE IMPORTANCE OF THE FIRST DAY

I always take the first day of production very seriously. As the producer, I make sure I do my rounds—like a doctor—and talk to each and every crew and cast member in detail. Remember that you're the one that everyone looks to for answers, so you better have them. I make sure everyone knows what is happening for the duration of the shoot and answer any last-minute questions. This is also a key day to make sure everyone on the cast and crew understands that the production is a professional operation and no laziness or horseplay will be tolerated. They must understand that they are there to do a job, a lot of money is on the line, and the production is not fun time.

A GREAT PRODUCER IS...

1. Diplomatic, patient, and prepared to handle any situation.

2. Supportive of his or her director and crew.

3. Someone who understands that most problems. On set are usually related to money, ego, miscommunication, food, and sleep.

4. A great negotiator and people person.

5. Someone who is fantastic with people and a keen listener.

6. Someone who always makes sure the production funds are on the screen!

I also regularly check up on the technical side of production and make sure everyone is performing the job they were hired to do. This is very important because if I don't supervise people and their performance, no one else will.

DELIVERING ON TIME & BUDGET

I'm no stranger to overambitious indie filmmaking. What often seems impossible is usually just my lazy side unwilling to figure out a solution. I've spent a lot of time around filmmakers who shoot quickly and get the job done. There is no real secret. A well-planned and managed production and an efficient crew and director are the key. It's really as simple as that.

As the producer, you must understand that things do and will go over budget. You must always have a cushion to cover the overages.

Producer Chuck Williams working out details and wrangling crew while playing a monster.

Marina Resa, Danny Draven, and Rick Irvin during a camera rehearsal.

You can't micromanage every little penny; you can only prepare yourself for the worst. One word of advice on budget: *never* pull out your personal credit cards to pay for overages. Once I got stuck with thousands of dollars of debt because I wanted to keep buying extra items on my own to make the movie better. I kept telling myself that I would just pay for it myself and it wouldn't affect the budget. At the end of the day, it made no difference for the film, except to my credit card company who became an uncredited investor in the film. They made more money in high interest rates than I made on the film.

THE WAR OF THE SELF

When making indie films, it's always tempting to save money by trying to do everything yourself. I always seem to think I can take on more than I can really handle. I have done this on several films. The most difficult task yet is wearing the producer's hat while being a director at the same time. It's your producer side that seems to be at constant war with the director side, and sometimes this can cause problems.

On my film Stuart Gordon Presents DEATHBED, I was producing (on this film the job also meant being a line producer and unit production manager) and directing the film at the same time. As we were doing a take during a dramatic scene, a flag started to smoke in the corner. I was seated next to Stuart Gordon and was watching a perfect performance on the monitor when I noticed the flag burning. Suddenly, my producer side kicked in and my focus shifted to the smoking flag that was being destroyed from the heat of a 2k lamp. I was completely distracted and became overly concerned with how much I was going to be charged if that flag was destroyed. I stopped the take and had a grip fix the problem. Unfortunately, the take was cut short and a performance ruined. I'll never forget Stuart leaning over and telling me to keep my eyes on the monitor and the hell with the flag. I didn't even realize I did it until he pointed it out to me. It was then I realized that something in my head was at war—and something had to give.

If you decide to produce and direct at the same time, which is common in the independent film world, just know yourself and delegate as much responsibility as possible. Make sure you have at least one line producer or coproducer who can help you take over the tasks of a producer while you're directing.

INTERVIEW BOX

CHARLES BAND PRODUCER, DIRECTOR

FULL MOON FEATURES

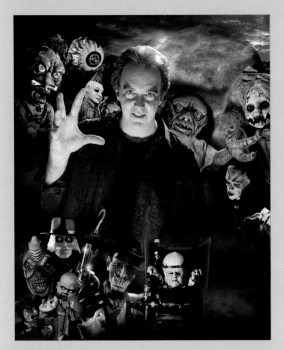

Charles Band

www.charlesband.com

www.fullmoondirect.com

CHARLES BAND is a leading producer of home video movies, with nearly 300 films under his belt and over 30 years in the business.

Charles learned how "the fantasies were put together" on the movie sets of his father, veteran director Albert Band. He produced his first film, MANSION OF THE DOOMED at age 21. In 1977, Band paved the way for the colossal home video boom by founding

Media Home Entertainment, one of the first independent video distributors. In the 1980s, he directed two 3-D features: METALSTORM (1983) and PARASITE (1982), which featured a young Demi Moore and special effects by future Oscar winner Stan Winston. His films—including the popular PUPPETMASTER, TRANCERS, and SUBSPECIES horror series—have been shown across the globe. In the decade since he founded Full Moon, Band's sci-fi/horror empire remains a mainstay in video stores and online across the United States.

Full Moon is now ready to explode with new franchise stories and characters like *Killjoy*, *The Gingerdead Man*, *Doll Graveyard*, and *Evil Bong*. More crossovers are coming, and infinite ideas and adventures abound in his never-ending Full Moon Universe!

DRAVEN: *In 1977, you helped pave the way for the home video market by founding Media Home Entertainment, one of the first indie video distributors. Over the years, how has the business changed for you and the way you sell your movies?*

BAND: Today we are in a transition period. DVDs will be somewhat of an antique some-day, like the VHS format. We live in digital times, and the distribution outlets are becoming more digital download oriented, with things like video on demand [VOD] and pay per view [PPV]. The days of renting vid-eos at stores and getting charged late fees are almost over, and with that, it's the art-work and title that will be the big ingredient for capturing people's attention.

In today's world, the title is becoming one of the most important elements for capturing your imagination. On most digital services today, your choice usually starts with the title first. There is no artwork attached unless you choose the title first, then you can choose the trailer, etc. On a movie selection list, all the choices will be by title, and there is a very long list, all in alphabetical order. With this scenario, you must have a unique and strong title to pop out. The closer it is to the letter A, the bet-ter, due to the attention span of someone zipping thru the menu.

In today's world, pay more attention to the title, artwork, marketing campaigns, and your first impressions. That is key.

DRAVEN: *As an indie producer, what is a day in your life like during a production?*

BAND: The day changes shape and color every 60 minutes. You have to break it down and be responsible to your budget. Everything in every category has a tendency of going over. People are always asking for more gear or money, and every one item that is added is death by a thousand blows. You just keep agreeing to things because you want to do the right thing. The day becomes a roller-coaster ride. There are hours when you say, Oh my God, how are we going to get thru this; how are we going to finish this; or this was the stupidest idea ever!

As the producer, you have different mood swings. You must always be making sure people are doing a good job and dealing with all the little problems that come up daily. A good producer always keeps a calm demeanor because freaking out doesn't help anyone or solve the problem. You need to keep your director, actors, and crew happy at all times. On some days, I sit back and feel like Cecil B. DeMille and think every-thing is awesome. On other days, it's back to thinking about the money, marketing, release dates, and other issues. You're not just building a house—you're marketing the house, too. It's a whole crazy experience.

BLOOD DOLLS (1999)   DOLLMAN (1991)   HEAD OF THE FAMILY (1996)   HIDEOUS! (1997)

continued on the next page

continued from the previous page

DRAVEN: *Full Moon has always had fantastic artwork. How important is the artwork and trailer when selling a film?*

BAND: Things are way different these days than 10, 20, or 30 years ago. Today, you can't really presell a movie. You need to actually make it first and then come up with the most clever campaign that may only rely on a title.

Today is different than in the early 80s when the video market was exploding. In my career, especially in the 80s and 90s when we were making 18–20 movies per year, many of those films at that time were exploding because we had a lot of creditability, because our films were doing well commercially. I could presell a movie with nothing more than some art and a synopsis, which is a pretty heavy stretch to be able to do that. That doesn't exist anymore as far as I know.

The market conditions have changed. I think that in the digital market, with outlets like pay per view and video on demand, they will be so hot in a few years that a great title for a low-budget movie could be presold again.

LASERBLAST (1978)

MERIDIAN (1990)

DRAVEN: *From BLADE and PINHEAD to MARVIN and EVIL BONG, Full Moon consistently gives the fans strange and bizarre characters. What is your creative process for dreaming up such bizarre characters and catchy titles?*

BAND: When it comes to creativity, whether you are writing a song, novel, or coming up with ideas for a movie, it's difficult to give a recipe. For me, ideas come in all shapes and forms.

I have a lot of artwork and scrap material I've put together through the years. I surround myself with this material and get inspired from it. It usually starts with what sort of genre or subgenre I'm working in, whether it's a killer doll movie—which I'm known for—or something new. I have a material bank of thousands of titles and images that I've had for many years. Sometimes, I'll just go through that and see what comes out and makes sense. Many times I will play around with words. Simply say the right word at dinner and I will go, "Oh my God, that's a perfect movie title!" Then the title idea will spawn the movie concept and story.

A big film that has the luxury of a $150 million ad budget will certainly educate the public as to what the title means or what kind of film it is. But when you have no money and you're at a video store or scrolling down the menu on iTunes or Apple TV, the title has to be understandable so people get it. If you can tell a story without even a log line, you've got a killer title. "Evil Bong" does it. No one has to wonder what that movie is about. The greatest title of all is the shortest title and one that absolutely tells the story.

DRAVEN: *As someone who pioneered early 3-D films like PARASITE and METALSTORM, what are your thoughts on seeing it reemerging in today's world with films like MY BLOODY VALENTINE 3-D? Do you think this is the future of the genre?*

BAND: From my experience, and having seen a lot of 3-D films and directed a few, it's a very different mindset. It's like a special effect that is there from start to finish, layered on to the story that you are trying to tell. Telling that story with your actors through a 3-D window is a gimmick. It depends on how it's used.

Would every horror movie benefit by being 3-D? I don't know. You have to think of the classic ones and wonder if they would have been better off done in 3-D, or if 3-D effects distract you from the storytelling. I like it for some films and look forward to doing some again in the future.

DRAVEN: *The PUPPETMASTER franchise is the most successful straight-to-video horror series ever. From a* producer's *perspective, what is it about these films that made them successful and spawn so many sequels?*

BAND: The first PUPPETMASTER film was shot in 1989 and released in 1990, and we were at the height of the exploding video market. At that time, a lot of money was spent at the video store to promote films.

With the first PUPPETMASTER films, we did our job well enough in the marketing campaigns to shape the way people perceived these movie before they were released. We would tease the video stores with media and run some ads. Some people would look at these ads and ask themselves, "Maybe I missed this movie when it was out in the theater." I think shaping their perception and thinking it was a theatrical release and something they might have missed was part of the success of PUPPETMASTER series.

First and foremost, it's the title that says it all, and the cool-looking evil

SUBSPECIES (1991)

THE CREEPS (1997)

METALSTORM: THE DESTRUCTION
OF JARED-SYN (1983)

continued on the next page

continued from the previous page

The PUPPETMASTER franchise.

puppets coming out of the case, which was pretty unique. A whole case of puppets, a theatrical-looking ad, with a great title and a lot of marketing made it a huge success. Not the #1 or #2 of the year, but people fell in love with the characters. The originality of the piece made all the sequels do well.

DRAVEN: *In your career, you've started out actors like Helen Hunt (TRANCERS), Demi Moore (PARASITE), Mariska Hargitay (GHOULIES), Julia Louis-Dreyfus (TROLL) and Viggo Mortensen (PRISON) to writers like David S. Goyer (DEMONIC TOYS) to directors like John Carl Buechler (TROLL), Scott Spiegel (INTRUDER), Stuart Gordon (RE-ANIMATOR) and Renny Harlin (PRISON). For aspiring actors, producers, and directors who want to break in to the film business, do you think starting out making a horror film is the right way to go?*

BAND: There are so many misconceptions of what people say that are actually opposite of the truth. You think, "I'm going to start my career and make a low budget horror movie." Or a director, who has no feature film experience but has done some documentaries and works in theater, says, "The only way I can get going is make a low-budget movie."

The trouble is, ironically, the people that are best suited to make a low-budget movie are the more experienced. The perfect director for doing this is the guy who's made 50 of them. He has tons of experience and knows how to get in there in 4–6 days and get the job done. That is the best director for a low-budget movie, not the novas with all the good intentions in the world who has no experience and makes all the mistakes that everyone makes. Then again, how else can you begin? I would say, you should start on an inexpensive product and make those mistakes either on your dime or someone else's.

Then there are those first-time directors like Stuart Gordon, who directed RE-ANIMATOR (1985) for me at Empire Pictures, who did an amazing job. He had my help, my father's, and a lot of others' who were pros. He is a very confident guy. Then you'd ask, what did he have that other people didn't have that made Stuart so good? Well, he had 20 years of experience in the theater and knew how to direct and tell a story.

Today, some people are too caught up in the technical side, but in my opinion it is almost meaningless. Of the thousands of people who can shoot a show well, edit well, and are good craftsmen, few know how to really tell a story with a camera and direct actors. Once you have that down, the rest is, well, you know...

I am much more interested in a movie that is shot straight up and a story that has wonderful acting because that's what you care about. No one walks away and says, "That acting really sucked, but what great camera work!"

DRAVEN: *Is horror dead?*

BAND: I think the horror genre will never be dead; it's completely evergreen. Some people think that every one of these movies has been so beat up. Every other month there is another horror film being released at the box office. Hundreds are made and dozens are released every week. Just when you think it's over, you have the remake of FRIDAY THE 13TH

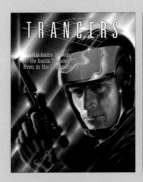

TRANCERS (1985)

TRANCERS II: The Return of Jack Deth (1991)

TRANCERS III: Deth Lives (1992)

TRANCERS4: Jack of Swords (1994)

continued on the next page

continued from the previous page

TRANCERS 5: Sudden Deth (1994)

(2009) come out grossing 30 million in one weekend, the biggest gross in theatrical history of any horror film. So, there is an appetite there for the right thing. Yes, it is oversaturated. So you have to judge that. People love horror films; they love a good roller-coaster ride. I think nothing can drive that home like successful theatrical horror films that have done really well.

Horror is evergreen. It's true that no matter what, people love horror films. If you have material that you are really close to, a story you want to tell, and you have a real affinity or passion for, than that's the movie to make—horror or not.

CHAPTER 7

DIRECTING A HORROR FILM

> **Horror is about making mental things physical.**
>
> —JOHN CARPENTER

It has been said that horror is one of the hardest genres to direct simply because the director is always walking a tight line between what is believable and what isn't. If there is one false step along the way, it all crumbles like a house of cards. It's very easy to underestimate and lose your audience or create something laughable and boring. As the director, you must choose your material and storytelling style wisely. This is key to everything that will follow.

Your primary job is to bring the script to life and oversee all creative aspects of the filmmaking process, from preproduction to final product. It's a tough world out there; when a movie fails, the director is usually blamed first.

THE DIRECTOR'S VISION

It's important for you as the director to have a clear, realistic vision and a plan to execute it. Before preproduction, I always have a notebook with my vision clearly identified and mapped out on the page. I break down all creative and technical elements of the story and what direction I will pursue (e.g., lighting, sound, set design, costume design, and so on) for each item. This notebook is invaluable during all aspects of filmmaking, and

Checking the notebook on set.

it also helps ensure that your vision stays on track until the final release date. When in doubt, check the book.

On my film GHOST MONTH, my vision was clear from the beginning: I wanted to make an Asian-influenced horror film set in America with an unknown cast of actors. I wanted to shoot it secluded and in the desert. I wanted the pacing to be a slow setup and let the story unfold to an intense climax with multiple twists. I wanted to shoot on film and I wanted the colors to be dark and have a lot of high contrast. I wanted the editing style to be nonintrusive and not too choppy. I wanted the music to be piano based with accents of Asian instrumentation. These are just a few items I wrote down in my original vision for the film. Because I established my vision for

Directing a scene during the film GHOST MONTH.

the film from the beginning—and wrote it down—I was able to stick to it for the entire production. I hope you will do the same for your film.

COMMUNICATING WITH ACTORS

When I first started directing actors in my earlier movies, I had the wrong approach. I thought that just telling them what to do and where to stand in a scene was enough. I was a director who had a lot of technical knowledge

Directing the undead.

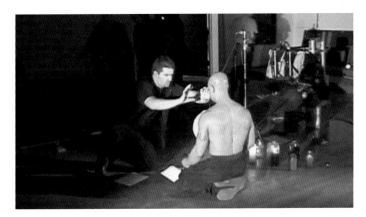

Draven working with actor Andre "Chyna" McCoy on the set of CRYPTZ.

but not much experience with actors. In fact, I was afraid of directing them. It took me several films to get over that fear and learn how to communicate in terms they could understand. I learned the hard way, but sometimes that's the only way.

If you want great performances in your horror film, start with hiring great actors. If you can get past this hurdle, the rest comes a little easier. The next stage is to understand the actors' language so you can communicate effectively on set. They do all the hard work, but they need you to bring it out of them and make sure their performance is serving the story. In a way, you're the stand-in audience for them. You're the only one they can trust, and if they don't trust you (the director!), you're in big trouble.

Here are some common things *not* to do when working with actors:

1. Don't overdirect or micromanage your actors.

2. Don't talk actors through a scene as if you are describing what is happening on the page. Remember, *directing is not narration!*

3. Do not give an actor a line reading. This means do not mimic or perform lines the way you want them to be spoken and expect the actor to repeat them back to you verbatim. Actors are not parrots.

If you want to understand actors and their language, I encourage you to take or audit an acting class. It's important for you to experience what it's like to play a character and be directed by someone else. This will give you a valuable insight and new respect for actors that can only help you as a director.

The actors block a scene on the set of CRYPTZ.

SHOT LISTS

I've directed with and without shot lists. On a few of my films, we shot so fast that the shot lists were thrown in the garbage and we just improvised. I work well on my feet, so this was never a problem for me. However, the director still needs a plan because the DP and AD usually want to see that you have one, even if it's one you know you may

Danny Draven and the actors blocking out a scene on the set of GHOST MONTH.

not follow exactly. When creating the list, it's best to be as detailed as possible.

BLOCKING

In preproduction, I usually create a blocking plan for each scene in the script based on the rehearsals. I know, however, that it will most likely change the day of shooting, but I feel more prepared if I at least do the work.

On set, there is usually an energy and magic that happens organically when you are running through the movements of a scene. It's important not to ignore this energy. If it works, do it. I always work with the actors to make sure the blocking of the scene feels right for them and technically right for the camera. In low-budget movies, we often see actors standing in place going through pages and pages of exposition. Don't be afraid to move the actors around in the frame.

NONUNION DIRECTOR CONTRACT (DOWNLOAD)

** web file: Director_Contract_NONUNION_SAMPLE.pdf

COMMUNICATING WITH YOUR CREW

Danny Draven explaining to the director of photography and gaffer what the next shot will be and how it will play out.

When I'm directing, I'm always in direct communication with my key crew, especially my director of photography and assistant director. I always need to be thinking ahead. What is the next setup? How much coverage do I plan on doing in this scene? What is the next scene? How long will it take, and how far am I behind? These questions are always on my mind, but they should never interfere with directing. As the director, everyone is looking to you for answers. It's vital that you always make the time, no matter how busy you may be, to answer questions. You should *always* have an answer.

A GREAT DIRECTOR IS:

1. Someone who has a unique voice and storytelling style.

2. A problem solver, both technically and creatively.

3. A leader.

4. Someone who can communicate his or her ideas and vision clearly.

5. A listener.

6. Diplomatic, patient, and prepared to handle *any* situation.

7. A collaborator.

STORYBOARDS

Whether or not to do storyboards is a decision for the individual film-maker. Everyone works differently. I have several director friends who never do them at all and others who swear by them and won't step on the set without them. I think storyboarding is a fantastic way for you to previsualize your film and communicate your ideas to other departments. If you're doing complex action or special FX sequences, I highly recommend that you storyboard. If you see it one way in your head, you need to communicate that vision to several other departments, and nothing does that better than detailed storyboards.

If you can draw, fantastic! If you aren't any good at it, like me, your storyboards don't need to be works of art. You can simply use stick figures and primitive renderings of objects to get your point across. Another inexpensive option is to use digital previsualization software. These software packages work great because they allow you to choose from a library of locations, sets, people, and objects, and you illustrate and animate the storyboard in the program. As long as everyone who is looking at your storyboards knows clearly what is going on, that is as good as they need to be.

I use PowerProduction Software's StoryBoard Artist Studio for all my storyboard work. It's a fantastic previsualization tool in my arsenal of film software. For more information, go to www.storyboardartist.com.

A storyboard frame from StoryBoard Artist Studio (www.storyboardartist.com).

A storyboard frame from StoryBoard Artist Studio (www.storyboardartist.com).

CREATIVE DIFFERENCES

We have all heard the horror stories of people in Hollywood that had "creative differences" with one another. If you want to direct, you must understand that so do most of the people you surround yourself with during a production. Actors, writers, cinematographers, and other people will throw ideas at you faster than you can say no. It's important to never discredit a person's idea because sometimes the person may catch a mistake or have an idea that is better than yours.

THERE IS NO ROOM FOR EGOS ON SET

I have been in several productions where the executive producer's creative contributions were in direct conflict with my vision. Sometimes I let it slide, other times I'm forced to take their notes for fear of losing my funding. If you are in that position, try to listen to the other person and, if needed, come to a compromise. It's important to pick your creative battles wisely.

JAMES WAN DIRECTOR, SCREENWRITER, PRODUCER

James Wan (2007)
Source: Wikipedia

JAMES WAN is the creator of the SAW series and director of SAW (2003), DEAD SILENCE (2007), DEATH SENTENCE (2007), and CASTLEVANIA (2011).

DRAVEN: *When directing a film, how do you prepare for the shoot? How do you visualize the film you want to make?*

WAN: For me, it's very important to know the script inside out and have a strong vision for the film. This way, you can answer whatever questions people throw at you, and more importantly, you know which direction to improvise in when roadblocks inevitably arise.

This was the only way I could deal with the short shooting schedule for SAW, which was 18 days, and a super-low shooting budget (for a movie with a mainstream cast) of $700,000. As debilitating as it was to never get the shots you want due to budget and time constraints, at least when I was improvising by the seat of my pants, I knew that the overall picture would still be intact and therefore, I could let certain things go.

DRAVEN: *Do you use storyboards to help visualize the scenes?*

WAN: Oddly enough, I'm not a big fan of storyboards even though my films tend to be very visual. Mainly, I use storyboards as a way to appease the producers/studio and to give them a peace of mind that I'm prepared for the shoot. If they feel confident in you, they'll support you more and stay off your back. But in terms of communicating with my crew, I sit down with my DP and production designer and we go through every single aspect of shots and sets, and I'll try to be as articulated as I can so that the filming can have a fighting chance at running smoothly.

DRAVEN: *What is the best way to approach directing actors in a horror film?*

WAN: This is no different to directing actors in any other genre. Once again, if you know your film really well, you would know your

continued on the next page

continued from the previous page

characters too, and therefore you could guide your actors. Remember, communication is important. Your actors are like your friends, and you speak differently to one friend than you would to another. The dumb-ass joke you crack to one friend might be hilarious, while another friend might think it's totally stupid. This is the same with actors, and each actor needs to be approached differently. If you get to know them, then you'll know the best way to talk to them.

DRAVEN: *What are the most important elements for a successful horror film to have, and why?*

WAN: I think it's important for a successful horror movie to not be afraid to break the convention. The horror genre is so established that when a scary movie comes along and breaks some of the conventions, it is perceived as groundbreaking. I think this is what makes horror films so much fun—the unpredictability. That's why indie horror films are the best, because you're not constrained by the studio system that wants everything to be homogenized.

DRAVEN: *How is editing a horror film different from other genres?*

WAN: Pacing and timing are very important. A good scare scene has the structure of telling a joke. You set up the gag, and then with the right timing, you throw in the punch line. That's how a scare works. You build up the tension (to a boiling point), and then you release the tension with a crescendo. This is usually a big "boo!" But stay away from fake scares. Nothing sucks more than the screeching cat that jumps out!

DRAVEN: *If you could pick one tip to give an aspiring horror filmmaker, what would it be?*

WAN: When I was in film school, I found that the best way for me to learn was to watch lots of movies that I admire and study them meticulously. And then I would just go off and put what I just learned into practice. Then over the years, from playing around making my short films, I found my own voice. Don't be afraid to just go out there and film something. And don't think it needs to be a masterpiece immediately, because ultimately, you'll learn more from your failures than your successes.

STUART GORDON DIRECTOR, WRITER, PRODUCER

Stuart Gordon (2007)
Source: Wikipedia

STUART GORDON is a legendary film director in the horror genre who started his film career in 1985 with the hit RE-ANIMATOR (1985) for Empire Pictures. He has since become a household name in the horror genre for his unique style and vision as a filmmaker.

Some of his credits include RE-ANIMATOR (1985), FROM BEYOND (1986), DOLLS (1987), ROBOT JOX (1990), THE PIT AND THE PENDULUM (1991), FORTRESS (1993), CASTLE FREAK (1995), SPACE TRUCKERS (1996), DAGON (2001), Stuart Gordon Presents DEATHBED (2002), KING OF THE ANTS (2003), EDMOND (2005), and STUCK (2007).

Gordon has also directed for Showtime's *Masters of Horror* series, including the episodes "H. P. Lovecraft's Dreams in the Witch-House" (2005) and "The Black Cat" (2007), and the episode "Eater" (2008) for the horror TV series *Fear Itself*.

DRAVEN: *How did your background in the theater help you as a director?*

GORDON: I had a lot of experience in theater working with actors, writers, and playwrights. All of that was very useful to me. We did a lot of plays that were fantasy or horror based, and we did all of the effects live on stage. A lot of those effects were used in RE-ANIMATOR (1985), which was my first film. I didn't know anything about filmmaking; not even the basic things like screen direction (or crossing the line). On the set of RE-ANIMATOR (1985), I was run over several times by the dolly because I didn't know where to stand. Luckily, I had a great director of photography, Mac Ahlberg, who I still call "The Professor," because he gave me a crash course in filmmaking.

DRAVEN: *Your film RE-ANIMATOR (1985) is a classic because of its combination of extreme gore, sexuality, and macabre humor. The film masterfully balances gross-out horror and macabre humor. Why is laughter an important element in horror films?*

GORDON: You will never find an audience that likes to laugh more than a horror movie audience. Laughter is the antidote to fear

continued on the next page

continued from the previous page

Mac Ahlberg and Stuart Gordon on the set of DEATHBED.

and helps them relieve the tension. People are always trying to find something to laugh at. I always thought it was a good idea to give them something that is not going to be at the expense of my movie. You don't want them to laugh at your monster thinking that the whole movie is ridiculous. It's great to have those moments when you can break the tension with a laugh and then crank up the suspense again. A good example is in the movie JAWS, when they are out on the water and they say, "we should have brought a bigger boat" after seeing a big shark's head coming out of the water. It gets a huge laugh and then you're right back into the danger.

The humor comes out of the characters; it's not winking at the audience. You have to be careful not to mix comedy with horror or they will cancel each other out. I think you have to take the movie seriously. Your audience wants you to do that. If they sense that the director thinks the whole movie is silly, or that he thinks he is slumming by doing a horror movie, they will have nothing to do with it. They want to know the people who made the movie are fans of the genre and take it seriously.

DRAVEN: *How important is sexuality in horror films?*

GORDON: I always felt that sex and horror go hand in hand. They are basically two sides of the same coin. You can go back to some of the old drawings in the middle ages and they have something called "Death and the Maiden." They would use the characters, "Death," as a picture of a skeleton caressing a beautiful naked woman. I think what it is, is life and death. Sex symbolizes life and procreating. Horror movies are really about death, and it's the conflict between the two. Even in the older horror movies there are scenes of the monster picking up the woman and carrying her off. They never used to show you what happened when they carried her off, but now we do.

I am sensing a backlash recently. Kids are getting more puritanical. In one of my movies I was looking at some of the comments about it on IMBD, and one of them wrote, "How bad is the nudity?" It was somebody who wanted to watch it with his girlfriend but was afraid if it was too sexually explicit she might think he was a pervert or something. It was just really weird. I think now, there is sort of an antisex feeling in horror movies as well.

I think things are changing. I feel if there is a reason for the nudity, in terms of the story, fine, then do it. If the audience feels that you are doing it just to add T & A to your movie, they tend to turn off to that.

DRAVEN: *What are the mechanics of a successful scare?*

GORDON: It depends on what you are calling a scare. Stephen King once said,
"The strongest emotion one can create
is horror, a sense of dread." The sense
that something awful is going to happen
is *true horror*. The next level he said was
"shock," when something jumps out at
you and goes "BOO!" The lowest level is
"gross out," something that is just plain
disgusting. Those are the ways he broke it
down. I think for me, in regards to scaring
the audience, is creating characters and a
story you care about. Once your audience
is involved, you can put your characters
in dangerous situations and they will get
scared for them.

DRAVEN: *What is the best way for a new director to communicate with an actor on set?*

GORDON: I think it's helpful if the director
knows what goes into acting. I always
advise new directors to do some acting
or theater classes. If you take an acting
class, you will know how to speak the
language of the actor. It's important for
the actor to know that the director understands what they are going through.

The thing I have learned over the years
is ask questions of the actors and let them
solve the problems, so it's coming from
them. You ask questions like, what would
you do if this were to happen? The actor
has to believe that this is all really happening to him and put himself in that situation.
Giving an actor a direction by saying "be
more scared" isn't helpful because you are
just asking him for results of what you are
looking for, as opposed to asking, "what
is it about the situation that would scare

you?" Something you can also do is the
what if situation. "What if you are being followed by somebody? Suppose you heard
the person breathing, not knowing if it was
human or animal." By this, you're putting
their imaginations to work, putting them in
that situation.

Good directors don't say a lot to the
actors, but they say just enough and encourage them. The director is kind of a surrogate
audience for the actor. So it's encouraging
to say "wow, you did great!" to the actor to
put them at ease. It's important for them
to be relaxed, to create a comfortable
environment on the set, even though you

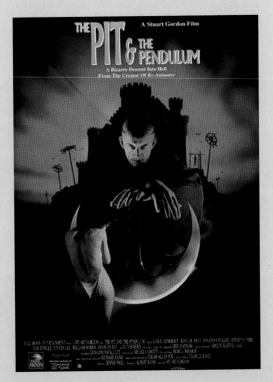

THE PIT AND THE PENDULUM (1991).

continued on the next page

continued from the previous page

are under a lot of pressure to work quickly. You should never rush the actor. You try to make them feel they have all the time in the world to do what they have to do.

I think in movie making the actors are the most important part of the process. It's all about the acting for me. The technical part is important, but movies are all about the actors, that's what makes them so powerful. Actors become like family to the audiences, and we care about them.

DRAVEN: *When directing horror films, what criteria do you use when determining where to put the camera?*

GORDON: The best answer I've heard came from Steven Spielberg, who said that he likes to put the camera where he sits to watch the rehearsals. I think that's a very practical way to look at it. I also recommend rehearsing with your actors before production to work out all the character motivation and other details.

For RE-ANIMATOR (1985), I was influenced by Roman Polanski's work. He shoots his movies by making his audiences feel they are a character in the film. One of my favorite shots is the over-the-shoulder shot. It gives the audience a real sense of being in the movie instead of watching it from a distance. Alfred Hitchcock had a great line, too. He said, "I want to be on the train, I don't want to be a cow in the pasture watching the train go by." What I like in movies is when you forget you are watching a movie. You're engaged and you're in it. As an audience you want to forget that these are actors and there is a script. When you start to say to yourself, "WOW, what a great shot!"

you're out of the movie. The positioning of the camera can really have an affect on how the audience takes in the scene.

One of the other things I've learned is that horror is slow. Horror is about anticipation. The longer it takes someone to walk up the stairs the better, because you know something is at the top waiting for them. You need to slow it down. I read somewhere that when David Cronenberg makes movies, his scripts are very short because he knows he will play things as slowly as he possibly can.

DRAVEN: *Do you storyboard?*

GORDON: Yes, I do storyboard, but not everything. I storyboard effect sequences and

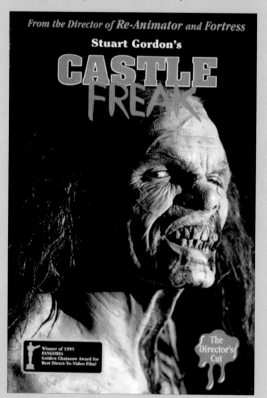

CASTLE FREAK (1995).

stunt scenes. I think it's important to show departments what you have in mind and how you are planning on shooting it. When dealing with special effects or mechanical prosthetics, they will know where the camera is going to be. This way they can hide the machinery or see how they can accomplish the shot.

In one of my earlier movies, we had an effect where we had a thing coming out of this guy's forehead [FROM BEYOND, 1986]. Sometimes we used a dummy and sometimes we used the actor, puppeting from the side of his face the camera couldn't see. So we had to have a drawing on how we planned on shooting it.

It's a good idea to sit down with the effects guy before you storyboard so you know what the effects are and how they are planning to accomplish them. I usually don't storyboard everything because I like to see what the actors are going to be doing. They may not want to come through the window and would prefer a door. Well, then your storyboard ends up in the trash can. That's why I think rehearsals are important. I don't even do my shot list until after I rehearse with the actors.

DRAVEN: *In today's digital revolution, there are more horror films than ever being made. What do you think are the biggest mistakes of new filmmakers when making their first horror film?*

GORDON: I see more movies concerned with the gore effects than the actors or the story. The most important thing— and this is true about all movies, not just horror movies—is the script. You really have to get your script right and

ROBOT JOX (1990)

create a story that is really captivating and that every scene flows into the next one. I've seen a lot of movies where the script is just nonexistent, but you can tell they spent a lot of time focusing on the makeup FX. This is not only true with little films, but big Hollywood blockbusters. No matter how wonderful your actors and effects are, if the script is bad, you're doomed.

DRAVEN: *In your experience, what do you think are the most vital elements a horror film must have to be successful with an audience?*

continued on the next page

continued from the previous page

GORDON: A story with characters that you care about, I think, is one of the most important. One of the things I see a lot are people that make movies about other movies. They borrow scenes from other films. You think you are seeing retreads from other movies and scenes you've seen a million times. What's important is to come up with something fresh and new. I also think you need to go beyond what has been done before in the past. I think good horror movies are transgressive and do things that are taboo. There are so many horror movies out there. You have to do something that separates your film from the rest of the pack, something that has people talking about how they can't believe what they just saw.

It's interesting how time has a way of dulling everything down. Amazingly, about 30 or 40 years ago, NIGHT OF THE LIVING DEAD (1968) was being shown at midnight screenings, with scenes of zombies eating flesh and intestines. No one had ever seen this before, and it was very disturbing. Audience members vomited and fainted. Now that movie is shown uncut, on television, at 3 p.m. in the afternoon.

In PSYCHO (1960) Hitchcock sets up the whole story with Janet Leigh stealing money from her company and being on the run. This whole story line builds up to her getting stabbed to death in the shower. The stabbing in the shower was a famous scene, but the scene would not be as powerful as it was had he not done all the setup for it, getting us involved with the character's predicament. This makes the audience feel as if they are getting stabbed in the shower. That's why it's so shocking.

The greatest tool that a filmmaker has is the audience's imagination. If he can manipulate, tease, and engage them, he will get their imagination spinning. With a great filmmaker, you feel you are in the hands of a guy who is not going to stop. He is going to go way beyond anything you have ever seen before. You get this weird feeling where you are excited and also terrified, wondering if you can handle this. I think that is the goal of the filmmaker. When you realize that the filmmaker is smart and talented and that you are under his spell, it's a great feeling.

In ALIEN (1979) you don't see the whole monster until one of the last shots in the movie. You see little pieces of it, a little mouth or pieces of a hand. You're not even sure what you are looking at half the time. It makes it mysterious. The idea is that once you show the monster, the

On the set of Stuart Gordon Presents DEATHBED (2002) Cinematographer Mac Ahlberg (far left standing), Producer/Director Danny Draven (center with camera), Stuart Gordon (far right standing), and screenwriter John Stysik (middle sitting down).
Photo Credit: Ward Boult (2002).

movie is over. It's the fear of the unknown that is the strongest fear. Once the unknown becomes known, then you can handle it.

DRAVEN: *In 2002, I produced and directed a film with you for Full Moon Pictures called Stuart Gordon Presents DEATHBED for a budget of only 35 thousand and shot in 8 days in Los Angeles. As someone who regularly works on larger projects, this was somewhat of a different world you entered into working under these constraints. What kinds of things did you learn from working on this ultralow budget level and fast-paced schedules?*

GORDON: I learned a tremendous amount! That was a really good experience for me. I felt like I was seeing the future of filmmaking. Seeing how you produced and directed DEATHBED was a revelation to me. It made me realize that the whole world that I had known was about to change in a big way. I remember you guys were making movies out of an apartment complex, which seemed to be a miniproduction studio. We did Foley and ADR in the bathroom, sound design in another apartment, and our commentary in your living room.

What I feel that will never change is the importance of story, strong performances, and imagination. That is what you need

no matter what the format is. It all comes down to the script, actors, and the director being able to tell that story.

I always tell my students that the problems are always the same no matter what the size of your budget. You never have enough time or enough movie. When James Cameron did TITANIC, he wanted to build the whole Titanic full size and couldn't do it. He had to build half of it. There was a scene where he had to show the other side, and he ended up just flipping the negative. He had all the signage written in mirror image because he knew he was going to flip it. The whole scene where the passengers were boarding the ship was all shot with a negative flipped because the ship was facing the wrong way. Amazing!

My mother used to always say, "There are two ways to solve a problem: one is to throw money at it; the other way is to be clever."

Stuart Gordon Presents DEATHBED (2002)

Danny Draven (left) and Stuart Gordon (right) going over the day's shooting schedule on the set of Stuart Gordon Presents DEATHBED.

CHAPTER 8

CINEMATOGRAPHY OF A HORROR FILM

> **I think of horror films as art, as films of confrontation, films that make you confront aspects of your own life that are difficult to face. Just because you're making a horror film doesn't mean you can't make an artful film.**
>
> —DAVID CRONENBERG

> **A widescreen just makes a bad film twice as bad.**
>
> —SAM GOLDWYN

When I was in film school, I read all the books I could find on cinematography. I understood the theory and technical process, but it wasn't until I was put into a professional situation with a seasoned cinematographer that everything made sense. Everything I learned early on about cinematography was through a Hollywood veteran, a director of photography named Mac Ahlberg (HOUSE, RE-ANIMATOR, INNOCENT BLOOD) who is now retired but shot several of my films. I remember the first day we worked together we got into a disagreement over how long it was taking him to light a scene. I was pressed for time and needed to plow through ten more pages. He pulled me aside and told me I was taking too long to block the scene, and he was right. It was at that moment I realized the DP would be my conduit to getting my vision on screen, and we must work in sync. Constant communication and mutual respect were the keys to getting the job done.

Danny Draven and Mac Ahlberg gather around the monitor to check a shot.

Mac Ahlberg and Danny Draven on set.

I once asked an old Hollywood cameraman what he thought was the best way to learn the craft. He simply smiled and told me to watch all the films I could get my hands on, good and bad, but watch them *without* the sound. He said this would force you to be more critical of the lighting, colors, and shot compositions. When you can dissect a film in this way, it all starts making sense and you'll discover how and why some things work and others do not. I have followed that advice ever since.

TIPS FOR WORKING WITH A CINEMATOGRAPHER

After you hire your director of photography, you should be in constant communication with him or her from the first day of production to the last day of post-production. Here are some tips from the trenches:

- Hire an indie-friendly director of photography with experience shooting quickly and efficiently. It's important that you creatively trust whom you hire.

- Communicate your vision and style clearly from day one. You should make sure the director of photography stays on track during the shoot.

- Storyboard scenes that require special effects or complicated camera moves or any other ones you feel best communicate your ideas to your director of photography.

Director of photography Michael King shooting a fight scene on the set of GHOST MONTH.

- Come to set prepared with shot lists, even if you end up not using them.

- Always do a blocking rehearsal with your director of photography present. He or she may offer great suggestions or point out potential problems.

- Invite your director of photography to all postproduction sessions so he or she can offer input. Don't leave them out!

HORROR FILM TECHNIQUES

In a horror film, there are many visual techniques you can use to manipulate the audience. The more you can disrupt their emotional stability in a scene, the more effective your cinematography will be. You should be encouraged to invent your own, but here are some common examples:

Concealment – Concealing information from the audience using the camera is a wonderful way to build suspense and instill fear. This can be as simple as shooting a killer through a rain-drenched windshield, blurring the focus, using fog and light to blind the audience, or even shooting a death scene through an aquarium.

Lens Distortion – This is a technique where you use the lens of the camera to distort the image for a desired effect. Examples are changing the focal length of the lens or using a special lens, such as a fish eye lens, to distort the visual interpretation of a scene, or using lens flares for a creative effect. The push-in and zoom-out effect pioneered in JAWS (1975) is a great example of lens/space distortion in a horror film.

Handheld – This is the process of the camera being used without a tripod to give the sense of uneasiness or a frantic feel. It's often used in action scenes or for atmospheric POV shots. The handheld camera has to be the most overused effect in all genres. It has its uses, especially in horror, but it should be used sparingly.

Voyeurism & the Killer POV – If your movie requires the camera to be a voyeur, then the handheld technique usually works. It has been done to death, but if used sparingly it still holds up. The killer POV shot is usually a staple of the slasher subgenre. Most of us have seen John Carpenter's HALLOWEEN (1978), so we know what can be achieved by putting the audience inside the killer's mask.

Camera Placement – Where you put the camera in a scene dramatically influences your audience's perception of the events taking place in front of them. In horror films, sometimes what you don't show the audience is scarier. For example, if you hear a scream from a room but the camera is in the hallway shooting a closed door the entire time, this produces different results than if you showed the entire murder on screen.

SHOOTING MULTIPLE CAMERAS

In my experience, shooting two cameras for an entire production is not worth the hassle and extra resources required of the production. It only makes sense in certain situations. It also introduces a lot of new problems that are unwelcome on a low-budget set. When I work as an editor, I too often receive footage from productions that have A and B cameras, and the majority of the time the B camera footage is not helpful. It seems to me that too many productions try to save time by shooting two cameras, and they overcover scenes instead of knowing ahead of time what the scene requires visually. I believe a director and DP should concentrate on one thing at a time. Unless you have a very good reason, use this only for shots where there is no second take (like blowing up a building!) or complicated action and death scenes. I have seen way too many indie filmmakers use two cameras because they believe they are saving time, but they're oftentimes just indecisive filmmakers overshooting the scene because they don't know what the scene requires visually.

Shooting a vampire scene on the set of CRYPTZ.

Lining up a shot on set.

INSERT SHOOTING

It's a great idea to always schedule a day of insert shooting for your film. This is fairly inexpensive to do because it usually requires only yourself, your DP, and an assistant. I schedule this after the first cut of the film is done because this is usually the point in time that you realize a close-up or insert of a knife blade is needed to help an important scene along.

(L–R) Danny Draven, Gaffer John Mays, and DP Michael King reviewing dailies from the lab on set. Checking your work at the end of the day is always a great idea.

COLOR CORRECTION

During the color correction stage of your film, it's always best to invite your director of photography to the session. They can offer advice and help communicate with the colorist in terms of hues, contrast, saturation, and so on. This is the stage where you can really give your horror film its final look. It's important for you as the filmmaker to understand the tools that are available to you in the color correction stage. For example, you can change the color of a person's clothes, skin tones, and even isolate areas such as the sky and pop out the clouds and darken the sky.

I always pick a look or color that fits the overall mood or atmosphere of my film. For example, if my film is about the undead and it's primarily a dark and rainy film, I may choose a blue, cold look for the entire film. I always choose colors and a look that psychologically reflects the subject matter and tone of the story.

SAM McCURDY, BSC, DIRECTOR OF PHOTOGRAPHY

Sam McCurdy on set.

www.sammccurdy.com

SAM McCURDY is a London-based cinematographer. He often shoots films in the horror genre and regularly works with director Neil Marshall. McCurdy's credits include shooting the British werewolf film DOG SOLDIERS (2002), THE DESCENT (2005), COLD AND DARK (2005), THE SICK HOUSE (2007), THE HILLS HAVE EYES II (2007), DOOMSDAY (2008), DREAD (2009), THE DESCENT: PART 2 (2009), and CENTURION (2009).

DRAVEN: *From the time you are hired to shoot a film, what is the director of photography's work flow on a film?*

McCURDY: For me personally, I always start with the script. I break it down into two parts: how the story is going to work visually and how best to achieve the results. The next step is we scout possible locations, sets, and studios. Based on what we find, I then begin designing the lighting plans. Because there is a lot of preplanning, shooting the movie always seems the easiest part!

DRAVEN: *As a director of photography, what are your responsibilities on set?*

McCURDY: On set, my main responsibilities are dealing with camera, lighting, and grips. How the film looks and feels is the responsibility of the director of photography.

DRAVEN: *Is lighting and photographing a horror film different from other genres?*

McCURDY: I was always told that the two hardest genres to get right were horror and comedy. Horror is very different from any other genre. I guess because if you make any mistakes, it just won't work. I love shooting horror films. It allows you to try things you would never have the opportunity to do in any other genre. And I love the dark! Shooting the darkness is a difficult task, I think. When you get it right and you only allow the audience to see what you want them to see then it feels great.

DRAVEN: *What are your thoughts on shooting digital versus film?*

McCURDY: Both formats have their place in filmmaking. The difference is in other people's attitudes towards them. As long as people put in the same amount of effort on a digital format as they would a film format they can both work. I recently shot a digital movie and found it very forgiving as a format, and I feel the look suits the movie, so the right format was chosen.

DRAVEN: *After you shoot a film, how much of its final look is done in post? Can you describe what the post process is for films like THE DESCENT (2005) and THE HILLS HAVE EYES II (2007)?*

McCURDY: A lot of movies spend a lot of time in postproduction these days, and this can be a good and a bad thing. The digital intermediate stage is now a director of photography's new tool and long may it continue. However, with the films THE DESCENT (2005) and THE HILLS HAVE EYES II (2007), a lot of the work is done in camera. The lighting, the coloring, all of these are talked about in the beginning, and hopefully this means you spend less time in postproduction.

DRAVEN: *In terms of cinematography, what are the biggest things that annoy you when you see a low-budget horror film?*

McCURDY: I guess the things that annoy me the most are the lack of respect to a script. Sometimes you can see that someone is just painting by numbers, so to speak.

DRAVEN: *What are a few of the biggest pitfalls you have encountered in shooting independent films, and what is your advice to help others avoid it happening to them?*

McCURDY: I guess the pitfalls are financial mainly. Independent cinema by its nature means you have to make do with what you have. My advice is to always prepare as much as you can beforehand. Even if you have no money, there is no excuse for not doing as good a job as possible. Always prepare before you shoot, think of all the things you want to do and work out how to do them before you're on set.

DRAVEN: *If you could pick one horror film that was influential to you in terms of having exceptional cinematography, what would it be and why?*

McCURDY: HALLOWEEN (1978) has always been, and will always be, my favorite movie. It is one of the reasons I'm a cinematographer today. For a low budget movie, it has everything such as great ideas beautifully executed (excuse the pun), exceptional photography, simple and thought-out camera moves, simple frames that allow a viewer to watch the screen, and an exquisite composition that makes you want to watch. I love this movie. HALLOWEEN isn't just a great *horror* movie—it's a great movie!

CHAPTER 9

WAR STORIES & ADVICE FROM THE TRENCHES

> ❝ A film is a boat which is always on the point of sinking—it always tends to break up as you go along and drag you under with it. ❞
>
> —FRANÇOIS TRUFFAUT

Independent filmmaking can be stressful. Typically, you are the one doing everything and trying to make everyone happy. When I make a film, I plan everything very meticulously, but I know from experience that what I'm planning will usually not work. However, this doesn't mean I shouldn't plan. I still must do the work and come to the set with a direction. Independent filmmaking is not a mechanical process you can map out on paper; there are too many variables. If one thing doesn't go as planned, other plans tumble like a house of cards. The key is to know how to deal with problems calmly and be quick on your feet.

Perhaps you can learn from my mistakes or laugh at my follies. Here are some anecdotes from my productions:

WEATHER PROBLEMS

I think Mother Nature hates filmmakers, or maybe just me, or perhaps doesn't like to work for free. If your production has a lot of exteriors, you need to seriously consider a backup plan if you suspect rain, snow, fog, or

After being caught in a nasty hail storm.

On this day, the blizzard came with no mercy.

overcast skies. Your location and geography determine a lot, but you need to keep up to date on the weather conditions in your area daily.

On GHOST MONTH, we shot entirely in the mountains of Nevada in the cold months of December. During the first half of the shoot we had beautiful weather and shot most of the exteriors, but about half-way through the shoot, I got word a snowstorm was imminent. I decided I had to shoot the rest of the exteriors while I still could, but we were losing light fast, and I could see a dark cloud of doom on the horizon. I didn't have a backup plan and decided to take a chance and shoot anyway. I had to rework the scenes, limit my coverage, and do no more than two takes. On the second take of the last shot, a blizzard blanketed the entire mountain within a matter of minutes. The gear was buried in white powder—most of which we found days later under the ice—and everyone scrambled to get inside where we continued to shoot the rest of the day. I felt a sense of relief that I beat Mother Nature…this time.

MORAL

Don't ignore Mother Nature.

GAS MONEY LEECHES

If you are shooting in town and the cast and crew is local, they pay for their own gas. If you are shooting out of town and they drive, usually as an incentive the production will reimburse gas expenses. It's a good idea to cap the amount and only allocate a reasonable *flat rate* for the duration of the shoot, or just make it clear that the production doesn't pay for gas. The problem is each person drives a different vehicle. They drive vans, SUVs, and monster trucks and other gas guzzlers, and some people even fill up with the most expensive premium gas they can find—and get a car wash too—then hand the producer the bill!

MORAL

Flat rates always work best.

THE COPS

It's funny how fast cast and crew disappear into dark corners when they see the boys in blue arrive. Los Angeles is one of the worst places to bring out a camera and crew without a permit. It seems no matter how small your crew is or how inconspicuous you are, the cops are always hiding in the corner somewhere looking for filmmakers. I have been shut down many times and almost arrested on one occasion.

A woman (Lunden De Leon) dressed like this, walking down a public street in Los Angeles is bound to draw attention!

On one of my films, we shot a scene on a major street in North Hollywood, complete with a scantily clad vampire stripper prowling the streets looking for fresh meat. I knew it was only a matter of time before the cops would arrive, and they eventually did. They were intimidating and interrogated us with questions. I was 23 at the time, so I told them a story about how I was a broke filmmaker trying to get into USC Film School by spending my life savings on this little horror film. One cop in particular became very interested in the film and wanted to meet the large-breasted actress. Later, he told me his wife was also an actress and he was interested in filmmaking, so I got his phone number and told him I would put his wife in the next one. They even volunteered to do a cameo on the next film.

MORAL

Some cops want to be directors or action stars.

MONEY PROBLEMS

If you are paying for the film yourself, great. If you have executive producers and you're being cash flowed the production money in pieces, that is cause for alarm. I have worked as a producer for hire and have been cash flowed on almost every production, and let me tell you, it's a nightmare. Nothing is more troublesome than making deals, booking locations and gear, all based on money you haven't received yet. I have been disappointed many times, so my rule now is to never go into production without the entire budget in my bank account. Never take it in payments. As the producer, your reputation is on the line. I take that very seriously and always look out for the people who work for me.

WORKING WITH ANIMALS

I dearly love animals, but when making a low-budget film you must be as practical as possible. As a producer, if I read a script that has any kind of animal, I have the writer remove it. Unless you really need the animal to move the story forward, you should stay away from animals of all kinds on low-budget films.

On one film we had a cockatoo bird in the script, so we hired a professional bird actor. The bird was animated around people and its handler, but it didn't always do what it was told when the camera was rolling. This so-called professional bird tended to go to sleep sporadically, usually mid-scene or after I called action. It was frustrating, expensive, and completely unnecessary. I remember during its close-up, the bird kept falling asleep and wouldn't react properly for the shot, and I spent way too much time trying to get any reaction so it didn't look like a stuffed animal. My assistant director, with his loud English accent, would shout out things like, "Can't we just poke it with a f&*%^$ stick to make it move?" or "Maybe a firecracker in his arse will jump-start it?" or "Let's pluck a feather and see what happens!" His humor upset the handler, and it was downhill from there. I even had to pay the narcoleptic bird overtime!

WORKING WITH FIRE

Working with fire, or *pyrotechnics*, usually requires a skilled technician, permit, and the fire department on set. It's expensive anytime you have this in your script. If you can, try to do without it. When I was starting out making movies, I had fire scenes in my script and we almost had several serious accidents, including burning down a location.

MOVING VEHICLES

If you can avoid driving scenes in your script, that is always best for low-budget films. I have almost been killed several times while shooting in a moving car on the open road. I have dangled out of many trucks holding a camera, sat on roofs and hoods at high speeds, all in an effort to get moving car shots.

In GHOST MONTH, the opening scene involves driving on public roads in a small minivan. Inside that van, we fit the director of photography, Mike King, sitting on an apple box with a Moviecam 35mm camera on his shoulder, along with one camera assistant, me directing from a corner, a monitor, the actress, and a driver who was also acting. We drove down a one-lane highway nicknamed "The Widowmaker" because so many people met their fate on that road. Fortunately, I lived to write this book.

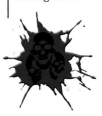

ANGRY NEIGHBORS

When shooting on location in the city or suburbs, you may have to deal with irate neighbors. Even if you have a permit, you may still be making too much noise or causing some other kind of disturbance. Sometimes a neighbor will politely come over and tell you what is bothering him or her and ask you to stop, or more commonly, the neighbors just call the cops. For example, we once parked a generator next to a house in Hollywood where we were shooting and ran the heavy cable up a telephone pole and hung it over a street alley and into a window so it would look like telephone wire. Yes, that was very stupid, but a great disguise. After a day of shooting undisturbed, an old man came over and told us the fumes from the generator were bothering him and his wife. Fortunately we moved it with no problems or cops (we had no permit!).

MORAL

Scout your locations and prescreen the neighborhoods.

In Los Angeles in particular, a popular scam for locals is to make noise until someone from the production asks them to be quiet. They usually demand money and then stop after they have been paid cash. I've been on productions where neighbors yell on the fence and demand money to be quiet, or mow their lawn for hours, or have a pool party with a radio blasting, or work on a backyard building project, or anything to make noise so you can't shoot sound. We once politely asked some neighbors to halt work for a short period of time while we shoot, and they responded by shooting BB guns from their roof at the crew!

NARCISSISTIC MONSTERS

I once hired an actor to simply be a slow-moving monster in a cloak. On the day of shooting, he arrived with his *fan club* (translation: family members) ready for his film premiere. After we put him through wardrobe and makeup, I explained to him that I wanted the hood pulled completely over his head. He then complained to me that we couldn't see his face. I explained that the scene was not about him and he was simply a background

A production assistant who got promoted to monster duties to replace a troublesome actor.

MORAL

Egos have no place on the set.

monster. On the first take, I saw he had removed his hood and proceeded to make strange monsterlike gesticulations. I told my assistant director to tell him to pull the hood back over his head, and he did. On the second take, I couldn't believe my eyes. He charged into the scene, front and center, with his hood down and his face contorted in a permanent growl, drooling, and moaning loudly like a George Romero zombie. On the third take, he was gone because I fired him. I then promoted my production assistant to monster duties.

ALCOHOLIC VAMPIRE

It was the last few hours of a long day. We were shooting at a new location in the morning and we needed to finish the last scene at the current location, no matter what. The scene was scripted as a complicated ritual with magic potions, blood, and mayhem. The actor, who spent hours in the makeup chair getting prosthetics, contact lenses, and vampire teeth applied, decided to get drunk before the scene. I don't know why, and I had no idea at the time. A few minutes before shooting, I went over the blocking with the actor and noticed she was somewhat comatose. Here I was with hours left at this location and I had a half-naked, drunk vampire staring at me. Her speech was slurred, her balance was off-kilter, and I knew she hadn't been drinking blood, but gin and juice. We were in big trouble!

MORAL

If there's a will, there's a way. No matter how bizarre.

I told everyone to take 10 and then I threw away the script and my plans. I sat there and asked myself: What do drunks like to do? After a few moments, and remembering my Uncle Bob, it hit me. They like to *fight*! I quickly called everyone back and improvised the entire ending of the movie as a fight scene. We shot it all and wrapped on time. I'll never forget that story, so cheers to drunk vampires everywhere…this Bud's for you!

STALKERS

I once had a crazy actor show up at my apartment unannounced at night. I don't know how he knew my address, but I guess that is a stalker's secret. He had an entourage of goofy friends with him and demanded to get prosthetic teeth that he claimed were promised to him by the makeup artist. I had no idea what nonsense he was talking about, but he wouldn't leave. I had to shoo them all away several times. Finally they left, but hours later, they were all hanging out on my stairs outside my apartment building. Email stalking followed.

MORAL

Never promise anyone anything that isn't in writing.

SNAPPED LEG

During a death scene in my film HELL ASYLUM, actor Tim Muskatell was having his innards ripped out through his mouth. Pleasant, I know. He was standing on a sheet of plastic and shaking profusely, but eventually he

Actress Ali Taylor and an unmasked Chuck Williams on the set of DARKWALKER after an accident during a death scene.

Actor Tim Muskatell staring at his heart moments before he snapped his leg.

MORAL

Make sure you always have insurance!

MORAL

Be careful whom you hire! It can haunt you.

slipped and dislocated his leg. The paramedics arrived and he was rushed to the hospital, but being a trouper, he shot out the rest of the film with a limp. Sometimes filmmaking can be painful, but film is forever!

NEO-NAZI EXTRAS

I once made a film in a remote farming town. We wanted to save money, so we contacted a local casting agency to provide us with locals for a few supporting roles and extra work. The producers on low-budget films don't screen people's backgrounds and usually just take anyone who is interested in helping out for free. However, on this particular film we had some locals who were involved in white supremacist activities (we had no idea at the time). What people do with their lives is their own business, but these people were very controversial in their beliefs. A few years after the film was released, we started seeing reviews, blogs, and web sites talking about these people and attaching their names to our film as if we hired them to support their activities. Our little low-budget film has been unfairly criticized and abused because of them. I certainly don't endorse any of this insanity, but it reflected back on the film and filmmakers in a bad light, thanks to a few local racists.

RATS!

The rats are everywhere!

I once shot at a run-down building in downtown Los Angeles for 8 days. At the end of each day, we were allowed to leave our gear and craft service food in a locked room to save time. All of our food was kept in a sealed plastic container. One day, we came to set and found that an army of voracious rats had chewed their way through the thick plastic bin and ate the food. Everything was contaminated and we had to rebuy all the food.

MORAL

Never leave anything edible on set.

GIRLFRIENDS

I once had an actress that was the girlfriend of an important money person. We had to stay after a 16-hour day to shoot a special, unrelated scene for her personal demo reel. Everyone on the crew had to stay and do it under quiet duress, and we wasted valuable production time and morale suffered.

MORAL

Never do favors that aren't part of your actual movie.

INTERVIEW BOX

TOM SAVINI SPECIAL MAKEUP FX ARTIST, ACTOR, DIRECTOR

Tom Savini

www.savini.com

TOM SAVINI is an actor, director, and makeup effects artist responsible for the creation of Jason in the FRIDAY THE 13TH movies, Leatherface in THE TEXAS CHAINSAW MASSACRE, and special effects and monsters in more than 37 horror movies. As an actor he played Sex Machine in the film FROM DUSK TIL' DAWN, the fingerless Tolo in GRINDHOUSE, has appeared on *The Simpsons* as himself, and was a villain in the TV series *Sheena: Queen of the Jungle*. He also directed the 1990 remake of NIGHT OF THE LIVING DEAD, THE CHILL FACTOR, and TALES FROM THE DARKSIDE. He currently owns the Tom Savini Special Make-Up Effects Program (www. douglas-school.com/savinisite/index.html) at

the Douglas Education Center in Pittsburgh, Pennsylvania.

DRAVEN: *When directing horror films, what is it that actors really want from a director?*

SAVINI: That depends on the actor. Some actors want you to leave them alone, and if you've hired good actors, you should leave them alone and sit back and enjoy their performance and make sure the camera gets the emotion they are trying so hard to feel. Other actors need guidance and someone to help them sculpt a performance, and know a little better what you want from them…what you want to see as the director. I think they all want to know if they're doing a good job or not, and as a director you may have to manipulate and be a bit of a psychologist to make them feel comfortable and that they are doing just fine.

DRAVEN: *What are two of the biggest pitfalls you have encountered in making independent films, and what is your advice to help others avoid the pitfalls from happening to them?*

SAVINI: When I first started directing I read every book I could get my hands on. I felt like I knew what I was doing, but I wanted to see what other successful directors had to say about the process. I yellow highlighted the stuff in the books I thought was important, and when I was finished I copied all the highlighted stuff onto a legal pad. The very first thing was "producers

and technicians will ruin your film...
IF YOU LET THEM." The important part
being "if you let them." Be always aware
that a good director listens to everyone.
I've seen it. They might not do everything
suggested, but if you're smart you realize
that one person can't think of everything
and there is a lot of value in brainstorming
ideas. But it's your vision and some things
are just instinct and from the heart and
don't let anyone interfere with that. Film is
forever.

DRAVEN: *In your experience, what makes a
great movie monster and why?*

SAVINI: To me, the great movie monsters
were Frankenstein, the Wolfman, The Crea-
ture from the Black Lagoon, Regan from
THE EXORCIST (1973), The Alien, Hannibal
Lecter, Jason, Leatherface, and many more.
They were great because they did what

they were supposed to do...scare the living
hell out of you.

DRAVEN: *When you are doing special makeup
FX on a horror film, what is your interaction
like with the director? Can give us some
insight on how this process works in the
professional world?*

SAVINI: The good directors let you do what
you do and just put the camera in the right
place for people to see it and give you the
freedom to do your magic. Sometimes you
have to educate a director that these are
magic tricks and require maybe a setup
shot to establish the weapon as lethal
before you use the rubber one, or that
moving the camera as the effect is happening might be detrimental to the effect
of the illusion. Eventually my contracts
included the clause that I direct the effect
in the scene, and that helped so much in

continued on the next page

continued from the previous page

creating the magic. You don't just walk on the set and say here's what I'm going to do. There is a lot of conversation between the time you get the script and break it down into a list of effects that need to be done. I always have a lengthy conversation with the director to see exactly what he wants to see and that is my goal, and by the time you get to the set there are no surprises and in my experience that's what makes things go smoothly and a lot of fun for me and the director.

DRAVEN: *For low-budget horror films, what do you think makes the most effective types of monsters? What should filmmakers with big ideas but microbudgets stay away from?*

SAVINI: I don't care what the budget is. Limitations always—*always*—make you more creative. It's your job to create what is required, and your mindset should be what do I need to see to make an audience believe what they are seeing is really happening. Then you create the pieces. Zombies are easy to do but hard to make scary; big hairy creatures might not be a good idea unless, like the shark in JAWS or the alien in ALIEN, you never see the whole thing until it matters. Once you see the monster your feeling is "oh is that it... well I can deal with that." So you postpone seeing it and build suspense, but of course the answer depends on the budget.

DRAVEN: *If you could choose three horror films that best demonstrate the use of simple, effective, low-budget FX, what would they be and why?*

SAVINI: THE HAUNTING (1963), there was not one makeup effect or monster and it scares the hell out of you. It was psychological and went deep into your insecurities.

THE TEXAS CHAINSAW MASSACRE (1974), there probably was not a budget for makeup effects and lots of blood, but you never saw anything and the effect was truly horrific as you had to imagine the effect of what you were hearing off camera.

THE LEOPARD MAN (1943), again what you didn't see stuck with you and haunted your mind in the way the horrible stuff was presented.

DRAVEN: *What do you think are the three most important elements for a low-budget horror film to have?*

SAVINI: A threat of some kind. A threat that makes you afraid of it and then the threat is placed in your vicinity.

Suspense, anyone can jump up and say "boo" and you can just about scare anyone with that, but the really true and deep jolting scares come from suspense. A buildup of an outcome, a plunge into the unknown and then an unexpected turn of events that is shocking.

DRAVEN: *What are your thoughts on people making homemade bullet squibs?*

SAVINI: I don't advocate making your own squibs. People email me about their films and they are putting firecrackers on their friend and I scream back... DON'T DO IT. Professional squibs bought after you've earned a license that are controlled is what I advocate and I do not want to talk about how I used to make them. Suffice it to say there was much experimenting to find a fine-grain, high-combustible black powder and a lot of thought going into making the explosion fire away from the subject safely. Firecrackers don't do that. I remained making them safe way before I got my license.

PART FOUR

POSTPRODUCTION

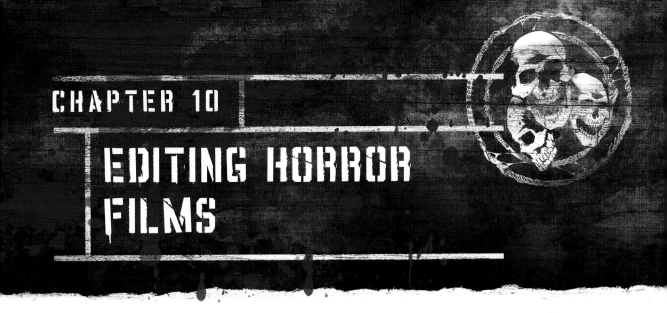

CHAPTER 10

EDITING HORROR FILMS

> **Evil is just a point of view.**
>
> —ANNE RICE

Now that production has wrapped, it's time to do the most important task of all: take an extended vacation. I'm serious. It's counterproductive to jump into postproduction without at least spending a week away from the material. I always take a break between production and postproduction; it really helps prepare you for the long haul ahead. After you've been at the beach for a week, it's now time to come into the studio with a fresh mind focused on seeing everything you've shot. The postproduction phase has officially begun.

THE EDITING WORK FLOW

Editing work flows vary from film to film and usually depend on what your final delivery requirements may be. It is vital to know this before editing begins. On my films, this is the work flow I use:

1. **Watch the raw footage** – The first thing you should do is review *all* the raw footage you shot during production, which is usually in the form of a master tape, DVD, or digital QuickTime files. At this stage, you can make any notes for yourself or the editor relating to performance, lighting, angles, or VFX shots. The worst thing you can do is start editing or hire an editor without *first* watching the raw footage from beginning to end. You must know what you've shot because this is vital in communicating with your editor and knowing your choices. I know this may seem obvious, but I've worked as a professional editor

for producers and directors who never watch their raw footage and rely on the editor to make it into a movie.

2. **Hire an editor** – On indie films, unless you are editing the film yourself, it's best to hire an editor who owns a professional-level nonlinear editing system. Make sure their equipment is of professional quality and can successfully handle your footage. This is also the stage in which the producer, director, and editor should meet to discuss the vision of the film, any special areas that may need attention, VFX scenes, and lay out the postproduction work flow specs.

3. **Delivery** – For the editor to get started, you need to deliver the raw footage (tapes, hard drive, and so on), a *lined script* from your script supervisor, storyboards, and any logos, credits, temp music, or other special items that need to be edited into the picture.

4. **The editing process** – After you have delivered your film to the editor, he or she usually logs and bins the footage first then starts by editing in a software package such as Apple's Final Cut Pro, Sony Vegas, Adobe Premiere, Media 100, or Avid, to name a few. You should be available if the editor has any questions, but do not bother the editor until he or she is ready for you. The editing stage usually goes through several cuts until a final director's cut is reached. Then it may require further changes depending upon who has *final cut*.

5. **The locked cut** – When the *final cut* is established, the picture is locked, and no further changes can be made. This is the point when the postproduction process moves forward to the sound mixing, music composing, VFX, and titles stages. All these people need to work off of a locked cut so it will sync with the final picture.

6. **Delivery of work materials** – Because everyone must work in sync, you must have the editor deliver the locked picture to the composer, sound mixer, and VFX artist. I always deliver a QuickTime movie with the following specs for each:

Composer – A QuickTime movie in the H.264 codec, 23.98fps, a visible timecode burn-in in the lower middle frame at 24fps (23.98), with a dialog-only guide track (no temp music). I also usually provide a second file with the temp music separate for the composer to use as a reference, if needed.

Sound mixer – A QuickTime movie in the H.264 codec, 23.98fps, a visible timecode burn-in in the lower middle frame at 24fps (23.98), with

GHOST MONTH editing session in Final Cut Pro.

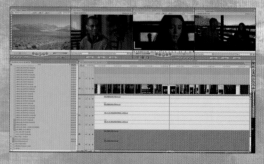
GHOST MONTH editing session in Final Cut Pro.

no sound track. An OMF 2.0 file is generated for the sound mixer with 3-second handles, usually in 24 bit/96k. You should also provide the sound mixer with all the raw sound masters or export them from your session to AIF or WAV files.

VFX artist – A QuickTime movie in the H.264 codec, 23.98fps, a visible timecode burn-in in the lower middle frame at 24fps (23.98), with a dialog guide track. The VFX artist can use this file as a movie reference. Each shot that is to have VFX needs to be exported from the highest quality source separately with at least a three-frame handle on both ends of the shot. An uncompressed Quicktime file or DPX/ CINEON image sequences are usually best for CGI work.

7. **Online** – If you have been working from a low-resolution source up to this point, also known as an *offline*, you will now need to *online* your footage. This involves recapturing the clips at the highest quality possible. Because hard drives are bigger these days, the online step is usually skipped because we tend to cut at online quality from the start. Eliminating the online stage will save you time and money.

8. **Titles** – The titles for your film can be done by an outside source or your editor. It's best to use a readable font, like Helvetica 16 point, white on black, for the end crawl. If any of your titles are over picture, make sure your editor pulls those sections out to include at the tail of your master. This is known as a *textless version* and is used for foreign delivery.

9. **Color correction** – This is the stage in which you take your final picture and color correct each scene shot by shot. The goal is to make sure the transitions from shot to shot within a scene are smooth by matching the color and brightness from shot to shot. If you don't do this step, your film will look unprofessional. If you go to a post-production house to have this done, it does get expensive, but they usually do the best work and their monitors are calibrated to industry-standard specs. Doing color correction with a trained colorist is a great experience, especially on a high-end system like the da Vinci 2k. It's also a good idea to involve your director of photography in this final process.

If you can't afford a colorist and a suite for your film, you can always do it yourself. This can be achieved using the color correction features of your editing program, or you can use a third-party application. To save money, I did all the HD color grading for my film GHOST MONTH using Apple's Color software, which gives you an amazing prolevel color-correction suite on

From SKULL HEADS (2009). Courtesy of Full Moon Features.

From SKULL HEADS (2009). Courtesy of Full Moon Features.

From EVIL BONG II: KING BONG (2009). Courtesy of Full Moon Features.

your desktop. If you do it yourself, make sure you calibrate your monitors properly and you are working in broadcast safe mode!

10. **Preparing for mastering** – After your visual and audio elements are done, it's time to make your master. To save money, I usually prepare the master files myself and hire a lab to layoff to a tape format, such as Digital Betacam or HDCAM SR.

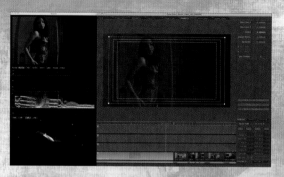

GHOST MONTH HD color grading in Apple Color.

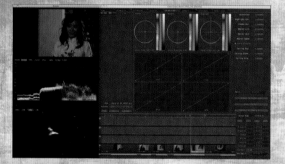

GHOST MONTH HD color grading in Apple Color.

GHOST MONTH HD color grading in Apple Color.

COMMUNICATION WITH YOUR EDITOR

An editor can make or break your film, so it's best to hire a talented one and keep your communication open. If you plan on editing the film yourself, I suggest you consider hiring someone else so you have an objective person involved. As an editor myself, I find it easy to miss things in my own films that may be obvious to others. A fresh perspective will really help your work, and you may see a scene in a new way.

Communication with your editor is key to getting what you want from your story. However, do not overwhelm the editor with your comments, or worse, become a backseat editor. It's best to first have a meeting and then give any notes or comments; after that just let your editor do the job: *edit!*

During the editorial phase, if you want to make changes in your cut it's usually more effective to communicate in terms of what dramatically is wrong with the scene, not exactly what shots to change. For example, here are some director comments an editor can work with:

- I don't know the killer is in the room until the end of the scene. I want the audience to know he's behind the curtain with the knife from the beginning to build tension.

- I don't feel I'm scared enough when she's walking around the house. Intensify the threat.

- I don't jump during the scare.

- I don't *see* her get sliced.

- I want to build more suspense when she is looking in the basement for her keys.

- Feature the victim more and don't cut as much to the monster.

- All I want in this scene is *more blood and teeth!*

There is no need to be a backseat editor.

HORROR FILM EDITING TECHNIQUES

When editing a horror film, it's the editor's job to become an objective, stand-in audience as he or she edits. The editor can control so much of the fantasy world. Here are a few editing techniques in the genre.

False Expectation Editing – This technique works great in horror films. The editor can steer the audience in one direction by intercutting with another scene leading up to a false expectation.

For example, in the film THE SILENCE OF THE LAMBS (1991), the FBI gets a hot tip on the trail of serial killer Buffalo Bill, who likes to skin his victims. Within moments, they're on the way to raid the house. Simultaneously, FBI agent Clarice Starling (Jodie Foster) is doing a routine investigation. The FBI surrounds the house as it's intercut with Buffalo Bill torturing his victim in the hole. An FBI agent rings the doorbell. There is a cut to Buffalo Bill's basement, and he hears the bell. He panics and goes upstairs to answer. He opens the door, and it's Clarice.

We cut back to the FBI raiding a house, but it's not the one we thought; it's vacant. The stakes just got higher for our hero because she's now on her own in the lair of the killer.

THE SILENCE OF THE LAMBS (1991)

THE SILENCE OF THE LAMBS (1991)

THE SILENCE OF THE LAMBS (1991)

THE SILENCE OF THE LAMBS (1991)

THE SILENCE OF THE LAMBS (1991)

THE SILENCE OF THE LAMBS (1991)

THE SILENCE OF THE LAMBS (1991)

The Shock Cut – The shock cut is a sudden, violent eruption or peak moment in a film narrative. It can also be a jarring juxtaposition of two shots. You know it works if your audience jumps, shouts, giggles, or you see popcorn fly into the air. For example, in Wes Craven's A NIGHT-MARE ON ELM STREET (1984), at the end of the film Freddy's hand bursts through the door window and pulls Nancy's mother through the opening.

A NIGHTMARE ON ELM STREET (1984)

A NIGHTMARE ON ELM STREET (1984)

Another example is in CHILDREN OF THE CORN (1984) when a young couple is driving down the road, and out of nowhere a boy appears in the middle of the road and they hit him.

CHILDREN OF THE CORN (1984)

CHILDREN OF THE CORN (1984)

CHILDREN OF THE CORN (1984)

CHILDREN OF THE CORN (1984)

CHILDREN OF THE CORN (1984)

In the ending scene of Brian De Palma's CARRIE (1976), a shock cut occurs when Carrie's hand bursts through the ground and grabs the arm of the sole survivor of the prom night massacre.

CARRIE (1976)

CARRIE (1976)

CARRIE (1976)

The Pursuit – If your film has a killer or monster pursuing a victim, your editing is vital to keeping the tension. It's best to build up to the capture or kill, rather than have it happen too soon.

The Flashcut – In today's world of MTV-style editing in horror films, you see much more use of the flashcut. It's a stylistic choice. Flashcutting is usually a sudden burst of imagery using white flashes or other glowing light bursts to jar the audience out of the narrative. It's meant for shock effects or flashbacks. If you use flashcutting, use it sparingly in your film.

PACING & TONE

The best place to start with pacing and tone for your horror film is in the script stage. A great script has a built-in pacing and tone. The director will take the script and interpret that onto the screen. In the editing room, the editor can further enhance the pacing by the manipulation of the images. Your editor must have good storytelling abilities and a good sense of timing.

EDITING WITH TEMP MUSIC

The use of temp music when editing is a common practice of a lot of editors. It's simply music you are temporarily using from another film during the editing process to help with the creation of scenes. It's usually up to the director whether or not they want to use it. I have worked with directors that say it's distracting and do not want any temp music, while others must have wall-to-wall temp music throughout.

A word of warning: don't rely too much on temp music. It's a good guide, but that's it. It's possible you may fall in love with the temp music you borrowed from a major Hollywood composer, but when it comes time to replace that music for your low-budget film, you may be disappointed. Don't expect your composer to mimic your temp music!

RUNNING TIME

It has been said that the way to time out your movie is by the 1-minute rule. That means that every page in your script equals 1 minute of screen time. That rule does work most of the time, but sometimes on low-budget films and with action scenes it doesn't quite add up and is usually less.

If you are making a feature film and you want to sell it, you must have enough running time. In general, 150 minutes is way too long and 65 minutes is too short. In my experience, the perfect length for a low-budget horror film is a minimum of 86 minutes and a maximum of 95 minutes. If your film comes up short, do everything you can without resorting to cheap fixes, such as padding with montages, 10-minute credit sequences, or extensive cast recaps.

FORMATS CHEAT SHEET

There are four quality levels in which to work in the motion picture industry: SD, HD, 2K, and 4K. This postproduction terminology is used to define and describe an image size and quality of data. Most video formats are described by the following characteristics: standard, image dimensions, aspect ratio, scanning method, and frame rate.

Standard Definition (SD) – This is the term used to differentiate traditional television broadcast resolutions from high-definition formats. There are a number of video standards in use today. These include NTSC, PAL, and SECAM, with each used in certain countries and regions of the world. Standard-definition broadcast resolutions are 720 × 486 (NTSC) or 720 × 576 (PAL).

STANDARD	SIZE	LINES PER FRAME	FRAME RATES	SCANNING METHOD
NTSC	720 × 486	525	29.97fps	Interlaced
PAL	720 × 579	625	25fps	Interlaced
SECAM			SECAM is not used in digital video editing. Work is usually done in PAL then converted to SECAM later.	

High Definition (HD) – This is the term used to define the high-definition formats. There are 36 broadcast HD formats in use today as defined by the Advanced Television Systems Committee (ATSC), so HD has a lot of variables. HD was created to increase the number of pixels/resolution of video images and also to solve many of the frame rate and cadence problems between film and video. An HD signal is a vertical line signal at 720 or 1080 and can be either interlaced (i) or progressive (p).

STANDARD	SIZE	FRAME RATES	SCANNING METHOD
720p	1280 × 720	23.98, 29.97, 59.94, 24, 30, 60, 25, 50	Progressive
1080p	1920 × 1080	23.98, 29.97, 24, 30, 25	Progressive
1080i	1920 × 1080	25 (50i), 29.97 (59.94i), 30 (60i)	Interlaced

2K – 2K data exceeds our preexisting television broadcast standards for both SD and HD. It is most commonly associated with traditional cinema and the emerging digital cinema initiative. This size refers to a film scan, which is 2048 × 1556 pixels.

4K – 4K is a very high-end and prohibitively expensive area in which to work. The size refers to a film transfer to data with a file size of 4,096 horizontal pixels and 3,112 vertical pixels.

HIGH-DEFINITION TAPE FORMATS

Some of the most common HD formats in use today are as follows:

HDCAM SR (Sony) – This format came about as an improvement on the HDCAM video recorder. The SR stands for superior recording and records onto 0.5-inch tape cassettes. HDCAM SR can record either 4:4:4 RGB or component 4:2:2 HD video at 440Mbps and 880Mbps. It is a fantastic high-end recording, editing, and mastering format.

HDCAM SR
Source: Wikipedia

D5-HD (Panasonic) – This is an HD version of the D5 half-inch digital VTR format and is widely used for HD mastering. D5 offers 4:4:4 and 4:2:2 at 360Mbps. There are eight discrete audio channels available, each at 24 bit/48k, which allows for 5.1 and stereo mixes.

HDCAM (Sony) – This format uses 4:2:2 sampling, 8-bit quantization, and a compression ratio of 7.7:1, with four audio channels (20 bit/48k).

DVCPRO HD (Panasonic) – This is based on the DVCPRO SD digital cassette format, also known as D7-HD and DVCPRO100. DVCPRO HD records

100Mbps to a 0.25-inch DV tape cassette. In the recording format, video sampling is 8 bit, 4:2:2 and 1080i, and 720p formats are supported. There are eight 16 bit/48k audio channels.

ProHD (JVC) – This format is JVC's adaptation of the HDV 720P recording mode that adds a 24-frame progressive scan. ProHD does not support the 1080-line format.

HDV (Sony/JVC) – This format uses tapes that are essentially the same as regular miniDV tapes and was designed as a low-cost system for shooting and recording HD. The recording format uses MPEG 2 compression (60:1), 8-bit sampling 4:2:0, 25Mbps tape data rate, and the audio is stereo 16 bit/48k.

STANDARD DEFINITION FORMATS

Digital Betacam (Sony) – This is also known as Digi Beta, a half-inch digital component system. This is a common broadcast format for NTSC (720 × 480) and PAL (720 × 576), offers runtimes up to 124 minutes, 4:2:2 sampling, 90Mbps bitrate, and offers four channels of uncompressed 48kHz PCM audio. There are other variations such as BETACAM SX and MPEG IMX.

DVCPRO25 and DVCPRO50 (Panasonic) – This format is identical to the DV format for recording and uses a 25Mbps recording stream. The video is sampled at 4:1:1, and it offers two tracks of 16-bit, 48kHz audio. DVCPRO50 has a 50Mbps recording stream that allows a reduction in the video compression. It uses a 4:2:2 sampling rate to give a much better image quality for professional productions. It also offers four 16-bit, 48kHz audio channels.

DVCAM (Sony) – The DVCAM format was originally geared toward wedding, corporate, and industrial videographers. This format is a professional variant of the DV standard and uses the same cassettes as miniDV

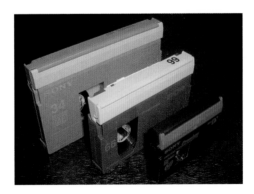

DVCAM, DVCPRO and MiniDV Tape stock.
source: Wikipedia

and the same compression scheme, but the transport moves 33 percent faster through the camera, allowing for wider data stripes across the tape. This makes it much stronger and reliable with fewer errors and dropouts. Larger sized tapes are also available.

miniDV – This format features an intraframe compression for easy editing, a FireWire (IEEE 1394) interface for easy transferring to editing systems, and excellent video quality compared to analog formats. MiniDV cassettes can store 60 or 90 minutes, depending on which tape speed you use, and the tapes are very compact.

FILE-BASED MEDIA FORMATS

The most common file-based media formats are solid state, hard disk, and optical disc media. A few examples are as follows.

P2 (Panasonic) – This is a solid-state recording system that records DV, DVCPRO, and DVCPRO HD video onto flash memory cards. By recording to flash memory, this format offers speed and reliability advantages over using tape, but there are shorter run times. This type of work flow would require you to data dump to a hard drive for storage and editing. It was designed to be used in Panasonic cameras, such as the HVX 200A or the Varicam 3700 (AJ-HPX3700).

XDCAM HD (Sony) – The XDCAM HD422, XDCAM HD and XDCAM SD lineup use an optical disc medium, called Professional Disc media, which offers large storage capacity of up to 50 GB at an affordable price. The XDCAM EX lineup uses a memory card, the SxS PRO™ card, having a highly compact design because the card itself is so slim, as well as offering data transfer rates of up to 800 Mb/s. The EX-1 and EX-3 cameras are becoming more popular on the indie filmmaking scene.

Sony Video Disk Unit/Hard Drive Recorders – This is simply a way of recording tapeless to a high-capacity hard drive. It's a very efficient way to work.

VIDEO CODECS FOR POSTPRODUCTION

A codec is a special algorithm for **co**mpressing and **dec**ompressing video signals. It's important when communicating with your editor or post house to have a general understanding of codecs.

The following is an overview of the most common codecs for editing.

Uncompressed – This is not really a codec, rather a way of storing a Quick-Time or AVI movie with no compression. This guarantees the highest video quality, but the file sizes are huge.

Apple ProRes 422 – This virtually lossless codec is a high-quality 10-bit 4:2:2 video codec designed for demanding postproduction work flows. Both SD and HD resolutions are supported at several quality levels: Pro-Res 422, ProRes 422 (HQ), ProRes (Proxy), ProRes (LT), and ProRes 4444. All standard frame rates are available: 23.98, 25, 29.97, and 59.94fps and you can use it with SD, HD and 2K source video. This is an excellent, space-saving codec; I recently used it for my film GHOST MONTH.

Avid DNxHD – This is a high-definition codec from Avid that was designed for video postproduction and to provide a high level of quality with small data sizes. It's a very common codec in the HD world.

REDcode RAW – The REDcode RAW codec samples the Super 35mm sized 4K sensor on the RED ONE camera. It then records compressed data using the REDcode RAW codec. This generates R3D files that may be resized to a variety of image formats, converted to DPX and TIFF files, and rendered to popular HD codecs like Apple ProRes HQ.

DV CODECS – This includes a wide ranges of DV codecs, such as DV NTSC, DV PAL, DVCPRO50, and DVCPRO HD. This codec allows you to natively capture, edit, and play back footage from DV camcorders without transcoding to another format.

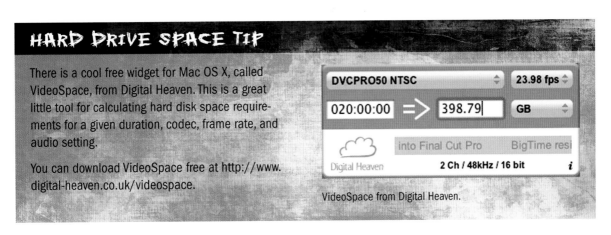

HARD DRIVE SPACE TIP

There is a cool free widget for Mac OS X, called VideoSpace, from Digital Heaven. This is a great little tool for calculating hard disk space requirements for a given duration, codec, frame rate, and audio setting.

You can download VideoSpace free at http://www. digital-heaven.co.uk/videospace.

VideoSpace from Digital Heaven.

FURTHER READING ON THE CRAFT OF EDITING

The Technique of Film & Video Editing by Ken Dancyger

In the Blink of an Eye by Walter Murch

CHAPTER 11

THE SOUND OF HORROR FILMS

❝ Listen to them, the children of the night. What sweet music they make. ❞
—DRACULA FROM BRAM STOKER'S DRACULA (1992)

Up to this point you have spent a considerable amount of effort on the visual aspects of your movie, but now it's time to shape the audio landscape and give the film a soundtrack worth listening to. On large-budget films, you may have a team of people working on the sound simultaneously for any given production; this includes dialog editors, sound effects editors, Foley artists, and mixing and recording engineers. On the indie level, there is usually one small company or a single person doing all the sound work. It doesn't matter if you have a team of people or not, the basic work that needs to get done is the same. So let's get to work.

COMMUNICATING WITH YOUR RE-RECORDING MIXER

When communicating with a re-recording mixer, you should always speak to him or her in terms of what you want to hear in a scene. This could be a room that needs an echo, a barn yard that needs more animal presence, or just louder music and more low end. If you speak in terms of audio, you and your re-recording mixer will get along just fine. It's a good idea to be familiar with terms such as EQ (low, mid, and high), dynamic range, reverb, gain, delay, compression, and general level requirements. The more you know about sound, the more control you can have over your vision for the soundtrack.

THE RE-RECORDING MIXER WORK FLOW

The key to great sound on an indie film always starts in the preproduction stage. If you hire a professional soundman with professional-grade gear, scout your locations for sound issues, record room tone, wild lines, and wild tracks as needed, and record at the highest quality possible at all times, your sound work will be a breeze. You must maintain a high technical quality from start to finish, and always capture sound at a high resolution on set and finish the same way during your final mix.

On my films, this is the postproduction sound work flow I use:

1. **HIRE A RE-RECORDING MIXER** – For indie films, you want to save as much money as possible by hiring a small company or a one-man operation for all your postproduction sound work. It's best to keep this process as an all-in-one package deal. If you decide to use more than one company to do the job, it can get very confusing and there are often compatibility issues going from one person to the next. Re-recording mixers generally use a variety of software and plug-ins for their work. Some popular applications for postproduction sound work are Digidesign's Pro Tools

HD and LE, Apple's Soundtrack Pro, and Apple's Logic Pro, to name a few.

2. **DELIVERY** – For the re-recording mixer to get started, you need to deliver the movie. I provide a QuickTime movie in the H.264 codec, 23.98fps, a visible timecode burn-in in the lower middle frame displaying at 24fps (23.98), with no sound. An OMF 2.0 file is generated for the sound mixer with 3-second handles by the editor (may vary), usually in 24 bit/96k. You should also provide the re-recording mixer with the production sound reports, a lined script, and all the raw sound masters (or have the editor export it from their session to AIF or WAV files).

3. **SPOT THE FILM** – When the re-recording mixer has your movie, you should set up a meeting to spot the entire film. The re-recording mixer will not know what you want unless you tell him or her, and this process saves a lot of time and money by getting it right the first time. During this session, you should come prepared with your notes and tell the re-recording mixer exactly what you are aiming for aurally in each and every scene.

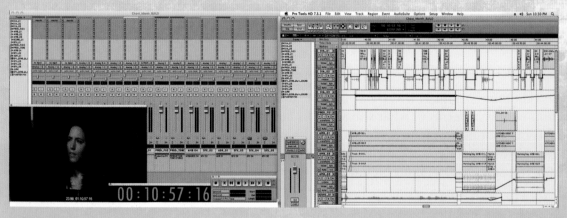

GHOST MONTH Pro Tools HD session.

This can include types of sound FX, special ambience, voice FX, monster noises, and so on.

4. THE EDITING PROCESS – During sound work, the film usually goes through a series of stages:

Dialog editing: This is the process of creating dialog-only tracks for your film. The dialog is cut, smoothed out, equalized, and then any problem areas can be addressed by using alternate takes from the production sound masters. The goal here is to have clean, high-quality dialog tracks isolated from the rest of the film. There should be no production sound FX on these tracks.

ADR: Automated dialog replacement, sometimes called "looping," is the point when you must bring actors into the studio to re-record lines of dialog that are not of an acceptable technical quality for the mix. After the dialog editing is completed, you will be able to generate a list of what actors and lines are needed.

The sound build: This is the stage when you build all of the sound FX and ambiences for the entire film. This can be anything from crickets and running streams, to doors opening, to someone being stabbed by a possessed doll. There are usually a lot of usable sound FX recorded on location. I usually replace them completely or just sweeten them by doubling the effect.

Foley: Foley is the process of re-creating sound FX on a sound stage to match what is happening on screen. This usually involves a professional Foley artist. If you want to save time or need more specialized sounds, you can buy Foley FX libraries, which are relatively inexpensive and have great high-quality prerecorded FX. You can also do your own Foley work to save money. On my films, I can be found banging on doors, running and jumping in small bins full of dirt and rock, banging pans on my floor, or making out with my own hand. It's all done in the name of cinematic art.

Music delivery: At this stage your composer will deliver the final cues to your re-recording mixer to be cut into the film. A music cue sheet is required with detailed timecode numbers so the editor knows where the cue's in point and out point are located. Always make sure your composer delivers you the highest quality music files (e.g., AIFF, WAV), which for my films are always a minimum of 24 bit/96k resolution.

The premix: This is the stage in which the re-recording mixer will reduce the number of tracks for fewer technical complications in the final mix. It's simply a way to prepare for the final mix. This can take several hours to a few days depending on length and complexity.

5. THE FINAL MIX – When the sound editing is completed and the re-recording mixer has done a general premix of your film, it's now time for the director to sit in and make all final adjustments. Always make sure you are mixing in an acoustically accurate mixing room. The talented folks that work in the sound profession are usually very auditory people; that is, they work with their ears. It's important that you work with someone who has a good ear and knows how to mix for feature films. It's a specialized skill, so a buddy who mixes music demos for a living does not necessarily have the same skills needed to mix a feature film.

6. FINAL MIX DELIVERY – After the mix is finalized, the re-recording mixer will be able to make masters. It's best to wait until you know your delivery requirements before you spend the money to make masters. It's more common, and cheaper, to have the mixer deliver digital files for everything, such as the stereo mix, stereo M&E, and the 5.1 surround sound files, and back up the master sound session to a hard drive in case you need anything in the future.

SOUND DESIGN TECHNIQUES FOR HORROR FILMS

The audio landscape of a horror film is an open and exciting field full of opportunities. In horror films, it's often what is happening off screen that can be the scariest—and great, well-planned sound design can take us there.

Spatial Relationships – You should always be very logical about spatial relationships on the screen and how that translates into the audio spectrum. The most effective 5.1 or surround mixing is when it doesn't draw attention to itself and serves the scene spatially. There are other high-end options, such as DTS and 6.1 and 7.1 surround sound, but these options are more complicated and expensive and may be overkill for your indie film.

Atmospheric Sounds – The atmospheric landscape of your film can be anything from birds chirping to a waterfall to a refrigerator hum. When choosing your atmospheric sounds, it's usually determined by what is happening on screen and what the location would logically sound like in the real world. It's catered to the particular tastes of the director and his vision. Other more artistic considerations are questions like:

- What is the emotional state of the character in the scene?

- Is there a mood you are trying to convey to the audience?

- What is the threat in the scene?

For example, if your terrified main character is walking slowly around a dingy basement looking for the light box, you can create the atmosphere in the sound design by using sounds such as dripping water with an echo, a low drone or rumble, occasional rat noises, or maybe a high-pitched breeze blowing through an open basement window creating a rhythmic sound of the wood frame crashing in and out. You can be very creative with these situations.

The Monster – When creating an onscreen monster, half the battle is giving it a life in the sound design stage. It's important to translate the imagery on-screen to something we can hear. When determining the sound design for your monster, here are some important questions to consider for making it realistic in the sound spectrum:

What does this vampire sound like?

What does this killer baby doll sound like?

- Is it human, human–hybrid, alien, or a creature no one has ever seen?

- What is the monster's texture and body like? Is it slimy and wet or dry and rough?

- What is the weight of the monster? Is it big or small?

- What does the monster's body sound like when it moves?

- Does your monster groan, squeal, roar, and so on?

Depending on how you answer these questions, this will determine the sound design for the monster. For example, a 40-pound creature with four legs and a slimy texture sounds different when it moves over a wooden floor than a 200-pound creature with six legs and a dry body texture. You can really bring these creatures to life in the sound design through understanding their basic characteristics and biology.

Sound Associations – When you can make an audience associate sounds of horror with a character or threat on-screen, this is a great scare tactic. This has its basis in psychology; it's the Pavlov's dog for horror filmmakers. It works by conditioning the audience's reflexes to a certain stimulus; in this case the stimulus is sound and the reflex is an emotional state, such as terror or dread. This unique sound could be anything you wish. It may be a knife scraping on a chalkboard or a wooden leg walking across a metal platform. For this sound association to work, it must be a shocking moment directly related to the threat or monster, and it must be established early in the film. For example, in HELLRAISER (1987), when we hear chains rattling we know the demonic Cenobites are coming. In POLTERGEIST (1982), when we hear TV static, we know *they're here.*

Silence – In horror films, one of the scariest things you can do is be silent. This is a psychological technique for making the audience anticipate what is about to happen. For example, if a young virgin runs into a closet and slams the door and the music stops, the audience will immediately become uneasy. The soundtrack is silent and any noise (including people sitting next to you) will disturb this moment of terror. Why did the music stop? Where is the killer? At this point you have the audience in your control, and it's up to you when you want to release the tension.

How would you make your death scenes sound?

THE SOUNDS OF GORE

If your horror film has a lot of violence and gore, it's a good idea to really pay attention to your sound effects quality. We have all heard those cheesy stock sound effects for knife stabs and blood splats, and when used on your film they can make the audience laugh at the cheesy sound job. It's always best to use the highest quality—and most recent—sound libraries available for all instances. If you can't find the right sound you're looking for, there is only one option: create it yourself! For example, if you need a good stabbing sound, take a knife and stab a watermelon a few times. If you need a disgusting gushy sound, take a handful of bananas and a few drops of honey, and slowly crush them in your hands. If you want to snap a few bones or necks, just break dry sticks or celery. There are hundreds of ways to create your own custom sound effects. Just make sure you record them with a high-quality condenser mic (like a Sennheiser MKH 416 or similar).

SOUND FX LIBRARIES FOR HORROR

There are sound effect libraries for all kinds of scenarios, but I thought it would be worth mentioning some horror-specific ones on the market. Besides, when making horror films, everyone could use an extra blood-curdling scream, blood splat, knife slash, or monster growl to sweeten things up a bit.

Image Courtesy of Sound Ideas (www.sound-ideas.com)

SOUND-IDEAS.com

The Darkside of Sound FX Collection (401 SFX)

Monsters & Creatures Sound FX Collection (675 SFX)

Thrillers, Fantasies, and Hauntings Sound FX Collection (574 SFX)

Jurassic Dinosaurs Sound FX Collection (665 SFX)—great for all kinds of monsters!

The Thunder Sound FX Series (111 SFX)—great for mood!

HOLLYWOODEDGE.com

Evil FX Sound FX Collection (588 SFX)

The Eerie Edition Sound FX Collection (297 SFX)

Hyperspace Sound FX Collection (641 SFX)

REMEMBER

Great sound starts in preproduction!

SOUNDDOGS.com

This is a unique web site that allows you to search for specific sound effects and download and pay per effect. This is a great resource if you only need a few effects and don't want to buy an expensive collection.

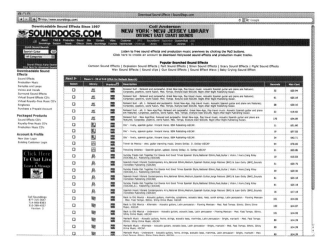

INTERVIEW BOX

REGGIE BANNISTER ACTOR, MUSICIAN, PRODUCER, ASSISTANT DIRECTOR

Reggie Bannister

www.ReggieBannister.com

REGGIE BANNISTER's film career began in the early 1970's through a chance meeting with Don Coscarelli, who asked Bannister to play a character in his first feature film, JIM THE WORLD'S GREATEST. A lasting friendship and working relationship was born, and Bannister went on to perform in 9 of the 12 productions Coscarelli has directed as of this writing. Bannister has appeared in more than 40 feature films, performed musically on television and film, has two solo albums, and owns and operates a production company with his wife, Gigi Fast Elk, in Southern California.

DRAVEN: *What is it that actors really want from their director?*

BANNISTER: I believe that every actor should want to know that they are moving in the right direction with their character. One begins to develop their character from the very first time they read the very first dialog line their character speaks in the script. As the character grows, the actor needs to have creative conversations with the director to make sure that they share the same vision. Once in production, the actor simply needs the director's guidance through creative collaboration.

DRAVEN: *The original PHANTASM (1979) is one of the great low-budget horror films and was directed by a young Don Coscarelli. It's horror film lore that Don Coscarelli rented all the film equipment on Fridays, shot all weekend, and returned it Monday and only paid a 1-day rental rate for the entire shoot. During the production, in what other ways did the production cut costs?*

BANNISTER: Well for one thing, they didn't pay the actors! Just kidding…sort of. They did "defer" actors' pay, and perhaps pay for a few others (though I do not recommend actors—or anyone else—agreeing to that since many times the deferment never

continued on the next page

continued from the previous page

comes). I must say, however, that some of the same solutions to cutting costs then are certainly true today—only on steroids. For example, Coscarelli didn't have a hard and fast shooting schedule, he took his time and shot as budget and actor availability would permit. I think that allowed him the opportunity to show his footage around to potential investors and grow his budget. Remember that he had two fairly successful films under his belt by 1976; both JIM THE WORLD'S GREATEST and KENNY & COMPANY had enjoyed theatrical releases. The biggest budget drawback for us, in those days, was that we had no option but to shoot on 35mm film. It's incredibly expensive between the cost of the film stock and then getting it processed. Today, we have all these wonderful HD cameras and software to give our footage that 35mm look, a film noir look, or even a comic book look. We can have it pretty much any way we want it now and it's cheap.

DRAVEN: *In PHANTASM (1979), what low-budget tricks did they use for the silver ball FX?*

BANNISTER: All the organic (in camera) tricks or sphere FX gags we used in the first picture we were still employing in the fourth picture with more finesse. As we moved from one film to the next, amazingly creative organic gags were used to make the spheres fly, wobble crazily, rotate, and kill. For example, to make the sphere fly into camera and hover menacingly in an actor's face we simply attached a sphere to a fishing pole with black line. The puppeteer works from a ladder off camera and swings the sphere into frame and stops in front of the actor's face.

Another simple gag to emulate the sphere flying at an actor from the actor's POV is to take a silver painted rubber ball and throw it down a mausoleum hall or other location while standing next to the camera. If it's a 35mm camera the DP overcranks the speed at which the film goes through the camera, then the shot is processed in reverse so that the ball looks as if it's screaming down on the actor at lightning speed. If you were to use an HD camera it's simply a matter of setting your frame speed higher and reversing the shot in editing. This reverse shot effect can be used for stabbing gags, beating gags as with a bat or some other instrument of death or any number of on-camera killings.

PHANTASM (1979)

PHANTASM (1979)

PHANTASM (1979)

DRAVEN: *When you are discussing a new character with a director, what questions do you usually ask and why are they important to you?*

BANNISTER: A character must be three-dimensional to be believable, so the actor must build the framework on which the character will exist. The actor needs to know why the character is behaving the way they are written in the script, so unless there are flashbacks of the character written in the script one must start from scratch to create a past that explains the behavior of the present. I always insist on reading the entire script, so I won't have a conversation with the director about my character until I have a pretty good idea of who I am and what my character means to the story. At that point, I will pitch the character to my director as I see it and ask if we're in agreement as to the direction I'm taking. I will ask questions regarding the foundation of my belief about why this character behaves and reacts the way they do. If we agree I begin detailing the character and the end result is what goes on the screen.

A warning to actors and actresses: The only time I didn't follow the protocol above I got blindsided on the first day of shooting by a director who had an absolutely *different* vision of my character than I presented...not good! I really had to scramble to give him what he wanted on the spot.

DRAVEN: *From an actor's perspective, what are the pros and cons of making low-budget horror films?*

BANNISTER: When you think about low-budget projects, you have to be aware that perhaps the cast, crew, producers, and the director may not have much experience at making a film—regardless of the remarkable talent they may possess. The negatives for an actor might be producers who don't understand the need to hire a professional stunt coordinator, in which case that actor could be injured performing a stunt. They might, for example, hire a makeup artist who has no experience with special effects makeup and actually use a product on the actor's face that causes a chemical burn. (This actually happened on a film I worked on.) An actor should resolve these kinds of issues with the producer/director before agreeing to participate in the project.

The actor must keep in mind that little money brings little or no amenities, such as no actors' trailers, low-budget dinner breaks (read pizza for every meal) or no dinner break at all. They may have to provide their own wardrobe and even find themselves outside shooting scenes in the middle of a blizzard...brrr!

The upside of indie film is the incredibly free and creative atmosphere of the film experience. There is a feeling of ownership shared by everyone on the project that's hard to beat and, might I add, that shooting in the middle of a blizzard adds a production value that would otherwise cost a large part of the budget.

DRAVEN: *What do you think are the three most important elements for a low-budget horror film to have to be sellable in the horror market?*

BANNISTER: First is the story. It has to be something that grabs you at the most primal essence of your human being.

continued on the next page

continued from the previous page

Second is well-written characters acted in a three-dimensional fashion on the screen. The actor has to make the audience value them whether they like them or hate them or no one will care if the character's life is in jeopardy or they are killed.

Third is production quality. It's difficult to sit through a picture—any picture—that is poorly shot, lit, or has a terrible soundtrack and Foley. No film will get picked up for theatrical distribution without decent production quality. I'm firmly convinced that at least 15 percent of a filmmaker's budget should be dedicated to postproduction.

DRAVEN: *For a low-budget producer, what are the advantages and disadvantages of using SAG (Screen Actors Guild) actors for their film?*

BANNISTER: SAG actors are professionals. This means they will deliver the performance you need to make your picture honest. There can be no drawback in hiring SAG actors.

With the new SAG low and ultralow budget agreements, a low-budget producer has the flexibility to hire SAG actors of various experience to fit their budget. They are constrained to pay the actors a certain minimum amount per day; however, that doesn't prevent them from making separate deals with actors whose names will help get distribution for the picture after postproduction.

Also, a growing number of SAG members have made the decision to take Financial Core with the union. Financial Core status allows a SAG actor to work union and nonunion films, which has greatly broadened the ability of the low-budget horror film industry to hire experienced name actors for their projects.

CHAPTER 12

THE MUSIC OF HORROR FILMS

> **Nobody goes to the movies to listen to the score. The score is simply assisting them in watching the film.**
>
> **—MICHAEL KAMEN**

Music is a vital accompaniment to the modern horror film. It assists in moving the story, creating excitement, and eliciting emotions. In horror films in particular, music is used to build an audience's anticipation and fear for a specific scene or sometimes just for mood and atmosphere. Talented directors and composers know how to weave the perfect music throughout a film and not draw attention to it. Some directors are known to score their own films. Horror maestro John Carpenter directed and scored HALLOWEEN (1978) and PRINCE OF DARK-NESS (1987) to name just a few, and Alejandro Amenábar directed and scored the fantastic ghost chiller THE OTHERS (2001). Even rock stars have started to venture into film scoring. Shock rocker Marilyn Manson partially scored RESIDENT EVIL (2002); former Nine Inch Nails band member Charlie Clouser scored all the SAW films and RESIDENT EVIL: EXTINCTION (2007); and rock star turned horror filmmaker Rob Zombie scored HOUSE OF 1000 CORPSES (2003) and THE DEVIL'S REJECTS (2005).

THE COMPOSER WORK FLOW

You should always check with the composer to see how he or she likes to work and what special specs the composer may require. On my films, this is the work flow I use:

1. **A director prepares** – Before you even start looking for a composer, you should spend time with your film. It is best to make a list of all areas where you want music cues and understand the functions for each. Consider things such as style, mood, and pacing. Nothing says low budget more than a constant bombardment of wall-to-wall music.

2. **Hire a composer** – Based on your preparation notes, it's now time to find that perfect composer. Choose this person wisely and make sure the composer has examples of his or her work to show you. Also make sure the composer scores films, not jingles or commercials. Film scoring has very different musical requirements than scoring a jingle or commercial for TV. Be honest about your budget and time frame. On independent films, a composer usually gets paid an up-front composer fee. He or she maintains the music and publishing rights, and if the film plays on TV the composer could collect royalties. I usually give a composer between 3 and 5 weeks to do an original score.

3. **Delivery** – At this point the editor needs to deliver the locked feature film with a timecode burn-in for reference. On some occasions, composers like to also get a version with the temp music the editor used when cutting the film. This sometimes helps the composer get a feel for what musical flavors the scene was cut to.

4. **Spot the music** – Your director should *spot* the entire film with the composer. It's important to stop and discuss each and every cue in as much detail as you see fit to express your vision.

5. **The work begins** – After you have delivered your film to a composer, he or she starts by composing, either by using traditional paper scores or in a software package such as Apple's Logic Studio Pro, Digital Performer, Cakewalk, or Cubase to name a few. On a big-budget studio film, a live orchestra is usually brought in and the score is recorded. In the independent world, film composers create and mix inside a computer using sound banks, and occasionally they add live instruments.

Logic Pro score session for GHOST MONTH.

Logic Pro score session for GHOST MONTH.

6. Final approval – You must approve every cue.

7. Final delivery – At this stage your composer will deliver the final cues to your sound editor to be cut into the film. A music cue sheet is required with detailed timecode references so the editor knows where the cue's in point and out point is located. Always make sure your composer delivers the highest quality music files (e.g., AIFF, WAV, SDII, etc.) to you, which for my films is always a minimum of 24 bit/96k resolution.

COMMUNICATING WITH COMPOSERS

Composers speak the language of music, and music is meant to make us feel emotions. It could be happy, sad, angry, or terrified, but good music makes us feel something. Film is the same way. At this point you have the visual elements together; now you need the composer to help enhance what we are feeling on screen.

I think the best way to communicate with a composer is with specific words that elicit emotions. For example, if you have a scene of a woman trapped in a basement with a killer upstairs sharpening the weapon he is going to kill her with, there are certainly intense emotions in this scene. The woman would no doubt be feeling complete terror and dread hearing the man upstairs sharpening his murder weapon. As the director, you could communicate with the composer with two words: *terror* and *dread*. A skilled composer will translate your emotional direction into the musical language.

When I spot a film with a composer, I give the composer an emotional direction for each cue. The following are the most common words I use (each one can be combined with others and has different levels of intensity over time):

- Fear
- Dread
- Suspense
- Terror
- Pain (emotional and physical)
- Confusion
- Panic
- Desperation

- Shock

- Curiosity

- Hunted

- Survival

- Isolation

- Surreal (dream state)

With these words and ones of your own, you will be more effective in communicating your vision. There is no need to hum, sing, dance, or hand a stack of Hollywood blockbuster soundtrack CDs to a composer and tell him or her to mimic someone else's work. In fact, asking a composer to do a sound-alike or mimic your favorite composer's work is an insult. You hired *this composer*, not someone else.

HORROR MUSIC TECHNIQUES

THE UNSEEN MONSTER

The unseen monster in horror film music is a music cue that identifies its presence. This is a very effective mental cue for the audience and adds more dimensionality to the score. When you establish the cue, which must be early in the film, the audience will identify it with the monster for the remainder of the film. The most famous example of the unseen monster concept in music can be heard in John Williams's famous score for JAWS (1975). When we hear that simple cue, we know the shark is swimming around somewhere and we grab our seats because we know something is about to happen. There is no need to see the shark, the music tells us it is present and hungry for all who trespass in its ocean.

VOICES

Adding human voices to your score can add a fresh dimension and make it seem more organic, for example, the lullaby that opens and closes ROSEMARY'S BABY (1968), or THE OMEN (1976), whose Oscar-winning score features male and female voices chanting Latin phrases such as "Ave Versus Cristus, Ave Satani," or "Hail the anti-Christ, hail Satan."

Children's voices can also be quite effective, especially because we generally associate children with innocence and purity. In the NIGHTMARE

ON ELM STREET films, the audience knows Freddy Krueger is around when they hear the creepy children chanting, "One, two, Freddy's coming for you. Three, four, better lock the door…Five, six, grab your crucifix…"

STINGERS

Stingers are short bursts of music designed to make the audience jump from their seats. They are very popular in slasher films. Horror director/composer John Carpenter uses them a lot in his films.

PREEXISTING MUSIC

Some horror filmmakers turn to preexisting music to get their vision across. This music could be a children's lullaby, an old jazz song, a modern song, or a classical composition. The music may not be scary when heard by itself, but when set in a horror film scenario the music becomes eerie. For example, THE EXORCIST (1973) and THE SHINING (1980) use modern classical compositions by Polish composer Krzysztof Penderecki, and those are two of the scariest films I've ever seen. In HALLOWEEN II (1981), the 1950s hit "Mr. Sandman" by the Chordettes is used, which made me never hear that song the same way again. There is something very creepy about taking everyday music and associating it with the macabre.

I think it is very important for an aspiring filmmaker to study in detail great horror scores and make notes on what works and what doesn't.

RECOMMENDED HORROR FILM SCORES TO STUDY

THE CHANGELING (1980) – Composer Rick Wilkins

THE HUNGER (1983) – Composers Denny Jaeger and Michel Rubini

THE OMEN (1976) – Composer Jerry Goldsmith

PSYCHO (1960) – Composer Bernard Herrmann

HALLOWEEN (1978) – Composer John Carpenter

STOCK MUSIC

I personally don't like to use music libraries. They have their uses for certain applications and media, but I think it's always best to do an original score. Indie filmmakers often want a quick, cheap solution for music, so they usually turn to royalty-free music libraries, also known as canned music, but as we all know anything that is sold in a can is never as good as something fresh. You want your movie to be unique and original, so when you start dipping into music libraries, you are recycling material that has been used in a lot of other productions.

There is a misconception among indie filmmakers that hiring a composer is costly. The truth is there are a lot of starving, talented composers out there willing to work and custom score your film.

USING SONGS

Every horror film has different requirements for music, but there are a lot of opportunities for songs (as opposed to a score). If your film needs rock music, metal, rap, industrial, techno, or even country, you should utilize the Internet and find the artist you want in your film. It's as simple as contacting the artist, telling him or her about your film and perhaps showing a trailer, then simply asking permission to use the artist's music in exchange for credit. There are many fantastic unknown bands out there that would love to have the opportunity and publicity that comes along with having their song used. I have had several bands volunteer to write original songs for my films. I have taken them up on it on several occasions, and one band even made a music video with the movie footage. They get the promotion, web site plugs and DVD copies, and we get a cool song to use. When indie filmmakers team with indie musicians, they can help one another.

Here's an example of a great indie band. www.trecherie.com

THE MUSIC CUE SHEET

This is a document the composer will provide you, detailing the particulars of all music cues contained in the film. This document includes the title of each composition, the names of composers, publishers, copyright owners, usages (e.g., instrumental, instrumental–visual, vocal, vocal–visual, and so on), performing rights society (e.g., ASCAP, BMI, SESAC, SOCAN), and detailed timecoded references and running times for each cue. It is important that the cue sheet is accurate and submitted on delivery to ensure the composer and publishing company will receive due royalties from their performing rights society if the film is broadcast on television.

MUSIC CUE SHEET SAMPLE (DOWNLOAD)

** Web file: WEB-Music_Cue_Sheet_Sample.pdf

INTERVIEW BOX

NATHAN BARR FILM COMPOSER

Nathan Barr

http://www.NathanBarr.com/

NATHAN BARR is a unique breed of composer. In addition to writing scores, he also performs all of the instruments in many of his compositions. Skilled in many styles and genres ranging from orchestral to rock, Barr is known for his collection and inclusion of rare and unusual instruments from around the world, such as human bone trumpets from Tibet, dismantled pianos, a rare glass armonica, and gourd cellos, among many others.

Barr began studying music in Tokyo, Japan at the age of four. He grew up surrounded by eclectic music ranging from Kabuki theater to the sounds of his mother performing on the koto and piano and his father playing the banjo, guitar, and shakuhachi. His interest

continued on the next page

continued from the previous page

in the art form was further influenced by extensive travels around the world, where he experienced music ranging from Bali's Kecak Orchestras to China's Beijing Opera. Barr went on to study at Skidmore College, and during the summer of 1993 he toured Italy and Switzerland with the Juilliard Cello Ensemble.

In 1996, Barr moved to Los Angeles to pursue a career composing for film. Shortly thereafter, he joined Media Ventures (now Remote Control Productions) and worked as assistant to world-renowned composer Hans Zimmer on films such as AS GOOD AS IT GETS (1997) and THE PRINCE OF EGYPT (1998). After just 8 months, Barr landed an agent and his first feature film (Lions Gate's romantic comedy TOO SMOOTH) and set out on his own.

Since then, Barr has scored more than 24 feature films, including Warner Bros.'s theatrical remake of the southern comedy series THE DUKES OF HAZZARD, the unconventional Broken Lizard comedies BEERFEST and CLUB DREAD, New Regency's hit supernatural thriller SHUTTER, Lions Gate's horrifying thriller HOSTEL and HOSTEL PART II directed by Eli Roth, and Universal Pictures's critically acclaimed documentary BEYOND THE MAT, among many others. Barr's most ambitious solo project to date has been scoring and performing all episodes of Alan Ball's award-winning HBO series *True Blood.* Barr is currently scoring the second season of *True Blood* and Strike Entertainment's film COTTON, produced by Eli Roth and Eric Newman.

DRAVEN: *What is your creative process in arriving at the concept for a horror film score?*

BARR: I'm not sure my creative process for a horror film is any different from my creative process in other genres. Generally speaking, my process first starts with digesting the film, figuring out who the characters are, what the ultimate point of the story is, where it's strengths and weaknesses lie, and what ultimately the vision of the director is for the film and its musical score. Once these elements have been established, then I sit down in my studio and begin plucking instruments off the wall, improvising to picture, and gradually (sometimes painfully) piecing together a palate of sounds and themes that seem to fit comfortably into the world of that particular film. Once the director reviews my work and we agree I am on the right track, then it becomes largely a technical exercise of placing themes in their appropriate scenes, creating tension or romance or drama wherever required, and hoping for those bits of inspiration or happy accidents that take the score from average to spectacular.

DRAVEN: *In the horror genre, what are the biggest mistakes you see in film scores in both low-budget and major studio films?*

BARR: The first problem I see with the horror genre in general is a lack of imagination on the part of many of the writers and directors working in the genre. The film industry seems to be inundated with the same old stories, the same old techniques, with only sporadic moments of inspiration which push the genre a bit further and into new and exciting places. Having said that, I love the genre enough to continue to go and see most horror films that are theatrically released, so maybe I'm a part of the problem since I'm still paying my 10 bucks for the same old song and dance!

Musically the problem is very much the same. It's very hard for composers to think outside the box and really go for something totally original and unique when the film doesn't achieve that end. This means that oftentimes the score is as dreary and boring and predictable as the film it accompanies. Composers tend to (and don't get me wrong—I consider myself a guilty party at times!) lean on drones and the same old orchestral effects that have been used for half a century now.

There is often way too much music, and this is more often than not because the film needs the help. The really good horror films don't need to overscore because they are well directed, acted, edited, etc.

Nathan Barr playing the glass armonica in his studio.

DRAVEN: *What is the best way for a director to communicate with the composer musically?*

BARR: Great question. Music can be such a difficult thing to discuss using words.

Imagine a director with little or no musical experience trying to speak about music! I find that the most successful communication I have with directors is working with those who are willing to admit that they do not know how to speak about music. We can talk in a general sense about what it is we hope to accomplish with the music in the film. Perhaps the director dislikes certain instruments or a particular composer's body of work, and this sort of information is very helpful to know at the outset. One director I worked with said "I don't like that flute part," but there was no flute part in the cue! Instead of making him feel like an idiot and telling him there was no flute part, I asked him to tell me what about the flute part he didn't like, and as he began to talk about what wasn't working for him, I was able to narrow down the real issue, which was that the cue reminded him of something else which he wasn't a fan of which did have a prominent flute part. I made some minor adjustments, he stopped hearing "the flute," and we were back on track.

DRAVEN: *In horror films, how do you determine a cue's dramatic function (e.g., fear, dread, suspense) and then execute your idea musically? Also, how do you know what to leave silent?*

BARR: A cue's dramatic function is very much determined by the director's intention in the way he shoots and directs any given scene. Sometimes the director is inexperienced or perhaps short on talent, and the intentions become muddled or confusing. At this point, I speak with the director and get them to explain to me what they are

continued on the next page

continued from the previous page

hoping for in the scene, and this gives me some guidance as to what direction to take. Once the direction has been determined, then I sit down and dig into my tool chest and begin to put together the music for the scene.

One of my greatest fears is overusing the tools in my toolbox or writing the same score over and over again—a problem that plagues some of the greatest composers in our business. So oftentimes I spend the first couple days or weeks coming up with stuff that works great but might sound too similar to other work I have done, or be a little too generic, and then I throw all that out and look for something more exciting.

DRAVEN: *Do you write on paper, or do you use software packages (e.g., Logic, Digital Performer)?*

BARR: I use Logic to write all my film scores. These days since directors expect to hear mock-ups that are very close to what the ultimate sound of the score will be once recorded, it is overkill to write everything out in pencil and paper and then go to the synths and mock everything up. I know of only a handful of older generation composers who still work with pencil and paper, and honestly I can't think of a single one of my peers today who works outside of some sort of sequencing program. The programs make life so much easier… particularly with our nasty deadlines!

DRAVEN: *In terms of style and technology, has the music for horror films evolved since you first started? If so, how and why?*

BARR: In terms of style I don't believe I have heard any real change in the music for horror films since I started in the business about 10 years ago. There have been a handful of really solid horror films made, but as they haven't necessarily initiated great change in the genre, so the music hasn't really either. In the past 30 years, a director like Dario Argento has really experimented with the genre and its music and pushed the limits of what is possible in horror. Using the bluesy, bell-infused music of Goblin in films like DEEP RED (1975) and SUSPERIA (1977) is super innovative and interesting. He really went for something totally different, and instead of high, eerie string parts as someone creeps down a hallway or approaches a house, he has a bluesy rock riff accompanying the scene.

DRAVEN: *In the low-budget horror films these days, there seems to be an epidemic of filmmakers using library music and recycling the same tired cues over and over again. I believe every film is unique and therefore the music should be original. What are your thoughts on filmmakers who try to save money by bypassing the composer and looking to libraries for their score?*

BARR: It's regrettable to see directors and producers recycling library cues in their original films. It's almost always about budget, so to some extent it's understandable, but still very regrettable. There are some exceptions though. Stanley Kubrick used previously recorded classical music to great effect in most if not all of his films. The famously terrifying score to THE SHINING (1980) is almost entirely assembled from previously existing modern classical music, and man does it work!

DRAVEN: *What do you think are the three most important musical elements for a score to have in the horror genre?*

BARR: From a story standpoint, horror movies are successful largely based on how well they create and release tension. How many times have we seen the knife-wielding teenager creeping down a hallway, tension building with every step they take, only to have one of their friends (or the killer) jump out from behind the refrigerator, releasing all the tension, giving the audience a false sense of security before the next big scare. So musically I would have to say the first important element is the score's ability to use tension and release in an effective way. Secondly, I think the score needs to establish the overall mood of the film through melody and texture. This instantly sets the tone for the journey the audience will be taking—we know it's going to be a scary or bizarre journey because we've paid our 10 bucks for a horror film, but what kind of scary journey? The very opening notes of the score should establish that. And thirdly, theme is generally very important, though there are exceptions, THE SHINING being one. I think having some sort of motif or melody or even texture that attaches to the audience's psyche when they leave the theater will help with the success of the film in its ability to really scare people. John Carpenter's theme in HALLOWEEN (1978) left the theater with every person that saw it and has since become a part of most everyone's sense of what horror film music is! PSYCHO (1960) would be another example. It is perhaps these two musical scores that people would hum before any others in the genre, and I think that shows how important theme can be.

DRAVEN: *In the horror genre, what are your favorite scores, and why?*

BARR: One of my very favorite horror scores is Wojciech Kilar's score to Francis Ford Coppola's DRACULA (1992) film. It's traditional orchestral in style, but the melodies and textures are first rate, thoroughly adding to the film's intensity, romanticism, and style. I do love Goblin's scores to DEEP RED and SUSPIRIA because the style of music was so unexpected at the time for the genre and they create such great mood for those films. And then of course I love John Carpenter's theme for HALLOWEEN, Bernard Herrmann's staccato strings in PSYCHO, Krzysztof Komeda's bizarre and beautiful score to ROSEMARY'S BABY (1968)—to name just a few.

JIM DOOLEY FILM COMPOSER

Jim Dooley

http://www.JimDooley.com

JIM DOOLEY, an Emmy Award–winning composer, is a graduate of New York University. Upon completion of his degree, he moved to Los Angeles to study the art of film composing with such prolific scoring legends as Christopher Young, Elmer Bernstein, and Leonard Rosenman. He joined Media Ventures (now Remote Control Productions) in 1999 and began collaboration with the world-renowned Hans Zimmer both as his chief technical engineer on GLADIATOR and as an additional composer, arranger and orchestrator on such notable features as THE DA VINCI CODE, PIRATES OF THE CARIBBEAN: THE CURSE OF THE BLACK PEARL, THE RING, TEARS OF THE SUN, KING ARTHUR,

and Ridley Scott's HANNIBAL and BLACK HAWK DOWN. Dooley also worked on several animated feature scores such as SPIRIT: STALLION OF THE CIMARRON, MADAGASCAR and MADAGASCAR 2, its spin-off short A CHRISTMAS CAPER, and the Academy Award–winning WALLACE & GROMIT IN THE CURSE OF THE WERE-RABBIT.

In terms of solo ventures, Dooley's most ambitious projects to date have been scoring all episodes of the critically-acclaimed ABC series *Pushing Daisies*, for which he received his first Emmy Award in 2008 for Best Original Music Composition for a Series. Dooley also recently completed the score for the upcoming film OBSESSED starring Beyoncé Knowles, and his first solo hit was the original score to Simon West's remake of the cult-classic thriller WHEN A STRANGER CALLS. Dooley's expertise in other mediums can be found in the complex, interactive scores for best-selling video game titles such as SOCOM 3: U.S. Navy Seals, U.S. Navy Seals: Combined Assault, and the upcoming anticipated game Infamous. He also fully scored the German animated release URMEL AUS DEM EIS (IMPY'S ISLAND), DreamWorks Animation's musically acclaimed short FIRST FLIGHT, and worked closely with director Fred Savage on the theatrical sequel DADDY DAY CAMP. Jim has also recently provided scores for episodes of the ABC television series *What About Brian*, Disney's video hit *LITTLE MERMAID 3: ARIEL'S BEGINNING*, a sequel to *Urmel aus dem*, and his first amusement park attraction score for the Simpsons ride at Universal Studios.

Dooley's music can be heard in the theatrical trailers for ELF, MAN ON FIRE, THE DA VINCI CODE, HARRY POTTER AND THE GOBLET OF FIRE, and SPIDER-MAN 3. Known for his interest and expertise in many mediums and genres, other projects include many well-known commercial spots, sports programming ventures, and the ground-breaking documentary THE MARS UNDERGROUND for which he donated proceeds to the Red Cross Disaster Relief Services. Dooley currently resides in Santa Monica, California.

DRAVEN: *From the time you are hired to the final delivery of your music, what is your technical and creative work flow like?*

DOOLEY: Horror films typically don't have pre-recorded songs or dance sequences, so normally composers are brought on fairly late. It was just like this when I did WHEN A STRANGER CALLS. The film was essentially done, with the exception of the score, when I was brought on.

On the technical side of scoring, just after being hired, the directors and producers will typically have a spotting session with the music editor. They will look at the music choices that have been made and see what I bring to the table. Then we all work together to blend the different ideas and tell the story. The scoring process normally takes between 4 and 8 weeks. Then I send the music and approved cues to the orchestrator. Then, about 2 weeks out, we are completing a reel a day plus

fixes and playbacks. All in all, it probably takes close to 2.5 months, if not 3 months to complete.

The creative side really begins in the spotting session. The director and producers that you are working with are responsible for guiding you through the scoring process. They inform you about their ideas and what types of music they used for the temp. Then you discuss your ideas with them and you find a common ground. The next set is to start executing the new idea. You start playing with themes during the early stages of scoring and save your car chases and fights for the end because they hurt your ears the most!

DRAVEN: *What is the best way for a director to communicate with the composer musically?*

DOOLEY: Use the tools you have! A director and a composer shouldn't be talking musically. That can be dangerous. For instance, I'm not a writer so I can't talk on that level about story structure. It's the same with directors; they can't speak music because it's almost medical. It's as if you were a doctor—except the difference between a doctor and a musician is the musician has had more training. Doctors start training much later in life. I started training in music when I was 5 years old. It's my job as a film composer to interpret the musical aspect of the film. If a director can speak that language they really don't need me!

DRAVEN: *In horror films, how do you determine a cue's dramatic function (e.g., fear, dread, suspense) and then execute your idea musically? Also, how do you know what to leave silent?*

continued on the next page

continued from the previous page

DOOLEY: A cue's dramatic function is usually clear based on the script and story. You're not going to score a chase scene as a love scene.

Many horror films these days are chaotic. Knowing when to leave things silent is a great thing. Music can sometimes let you know what's going to happen. If there's no music it can sometimes be more effective than having a score. There's the story of Hitchcock and Bernard Herrmann. Hitchcock was getting upset that the music was playing such a big part in his movies so he ripped a part of the score out of the picture and let it play totally dry. THE BIRDS, for example, has basically no score. It's one of the scariest movies I've seen. If you have a vision and an approach you can do whatever you want.

DRAVEN: *What is your creative process in arriving at the concept for a horror film score?*

DOOLEY: The creative process really depends on the film. Sometimes the movie tells you the approach. For instance, when I worked on THE RING (2002) with Hans Zimmer, we tapped into the music box that plays in her bedroom and that defined the theme. A lot of musical ideas come from the story. It's the best place to go for the theme, not somewhere outside. In THE RING (2002), I scored the horse chase on the ferry. I wrote the cue with sounds from the theme so it would be a constant through the movie.

DRAVEN: *In the horror genre, what are the biggest mistakes you see in film scores in both low-budget and major studio films?*

DOOLEY: I have a grudge against composers that make great sounds that cost a lot of money. If you care a lot, you can make great sounds cost-effectively. If you want the sound of a train, go and record a train. Go out and bang on some garbage cans, make a mess of things. Your limitations are your own—no one cares how much you spend. You can hear it in the music when a composer cares. Sometimes there is too much music in film. For studio films, I understand it, you need to create something to help people buy into a fantasy world. But for others...

DRAVEN: *Do you write on paper, or do you use software packages?*

DOOLEY: I write on a cue-based rig, but I keep staff paper in my drafting table at work. I've got staff paper in my bedroom, on my piano, and in most of the rooms in my house just in case I have to jot something down. Inspiration can happen anywhere, so I need to be able to express myself. I like writing things out by hand. It's an easy reference. I jot down what I need to know. It's like little keys into what I'm doing without being so elaborate.

DRAVEN: *In terms of style and technology, has the music for horror films evolved since you first started?*

DOOLEY: Music technology in film and television has changed incredibly. The majority of people's reactions to change is, "Oh my god. How is this new technology going to affect the community?" I say, in the same way it affects any other part of the industry.

As a composer these days you are as much a technician as a musician. You have to be able to produce the soundtrack using all the fancy programs. The technology for film editors used to be cutting and splicing. Now you have an Avid and you have to know imports and everything else. Technology has changed. We can put abstract things together because of it. We no longer have to do things that are linear-time based. Like with WHEN A STRANGER CALLS, the opening of the movie is a 50 case string drones playing at different speeds. I couldn't record that with a real orchestra. It's like a Picasso collage where you take macros and then put them next to each other. The juxtaposition creates the interest. I suppose technology has made things more easy but also more difficult. There's simply more to choose from.

DRAVEN: *What are your thoughts on filmmakers who try to save money by bypassing the composer and looking to stock music libraries for their score?*

DOOLEY: Horror movies can be done very low budget because they sell very well, traditionally, better than any genre of film. The best way to make money! If they skimped on the composer, they skimped on everything else, the acting, design, script, etc. At that point the film is inherently not great. I think it's rare when someone says, "Oh my god, everything in this film is great except for the score!"

If you give your heart to a project, you'll find a composer who will give it his all as well. There's no excuse. But if you're making sandwiches, you can make them elegantly or not, they might sell just as well.

DRAVEN: *How much time are you usually given to create a score?*

Jim Dooley at the 2008 Emmy Awards. He received his first Emmy for Outstanding Music Composition for a Series for *Pushing Daisies*.

DOOLEY: Usually, 2 months is the standard amount of time to create a score. For *Pushing Daisies* I scored about 8.5 minutes of music per day. For PIRATES OF THE CARIBBEAN, we had a team of 10 people working and had 2 weeks to complete it. It really depends on the film.

DRAVEN: *In the horror genre, what are your favorite scores, and why?*

DOOLEY: No one does it better than Bernard Herrmann. I don't think it's possible to beat him. I did my thesis paper at USC on the scores to VERTIGO and PSYCHO. But there's also the original *Twilight Zone* series! Unbeatable. But I also love CITIZEN KANE.

My paper about PSYCHO described how the film's music reflected the movement

continued on the next page

continued from the previous page

of the birds in the film rather than the knife. If you remember, there are many taxidermy birds in the scenes with Anthony Perkins.

The music of VERTIGO was all based around Spanish dance rhythms. All of these rhythms were slowed down, putting tension into the film, but also keeping it organic. In the plot of the film one of the main characters thinks she is the reincarnation of a Spanish woman who was murdered. This is where you find the great decisions; you find something organic and tell the story musically. That's how you do it.

CHAPTER 13

CGI

For a long time I was embarrassed to say I was a B movie actor, but now that I see what Hollywood's putting out, I realized B actually means better.

—BRUCE CAMPBELL

In today's digital world, computer-generated imagery, or CGI, is more commonplace in low-budget films. CGI can be anything that requires a computer to manipulate the image, such as rod and string removal, compositing, digital explosions, muzzle flashes for guns, spaceships, laser beams, or anything else you can imagine. On low-budget films, the visual effects (VFX) team is usually a small company, or more commonly, one very talented person doing all the visual effects.

I have edited and produced a lot of films with CGI involved. The VFX have been anything from killer satanic puppets to giant CGI spiders to digital underwear to cover private parts. It seems there is no end to producers on all budget levels who feel they must use CGI for any reason, even if it is just to add production value. Whether it's a fix or an enhancement, using CGI must have a function and must be used to move the story forward, not distract the audience with spectacle.

THE CGI WORK FLOW

Every film has different requirements, but usually the work flow is roughly the same with minor modifications to suit your needs. This is the work flow I use on every film when working with a VFX house and/or artist:

1. **Hire a VFX artist:** Choose this person wisely and make sure the artist has examples of his or her work to show you. You must be clear that you are working on a low-budget film, and don't be shy or vague about how much money you have to spend.

2. **Break down the script:** Your VFX artist can break down your shooting script to get an overview of what VFX will be involved in the production. This is the stage to be *practical* and change your VFX approach as needed to fit the time and budget restrictions. Also, this is usually the point where your VFX artist gives you a budget estimate or flat rate for the work they are about to do. I usually pay per shot, so it's best to wait until you have an exact shot count, which cannot be done until the film is edited and locked.

3. **VFX supervision:** During production, you want to make sure you have a VFX supervisor on set on the days you are shooting VFX shots. Don't make the mistake of thinking just because you've read a book or two about VFX that you don't need a VFX supervisor on set. Unless you are doing the visual effects yourself, you need the person who is actually doing the work—or someone he or she appoints—to supervise. This is your only insurance that the VFX will be shot and useable in postproduction, and believe me it will save you money and headaches in the long run.

4. **Communication during editing:** It is imperative that your director, editor, and VFX artist are in communication during the entire editing of the film. Your editor makes sure the cuts work, the VFX artist ensures he or she can execute the VFX shots with no issues, and your director makes sure his or her vision is intact. This is a great unison to have throughout the process. It's also a good idea to set up an FTP site or screen sharing session where you can interact with the VFX artist during editing. This provides a quick way to approve all VFX sequences.

5. **VFX shot count:** After the film is locked you can now start counting shots. You should determine an accurate VFX shot count for your film; this will help your VFX artist know what he or she is up against and estimate a time frame for working. I have worked on low-budget films with up to 400 VFX shots, usually with one guy doing it all!

6. **Spot the VFX shots:** Your director should *spot* each and every shot with your VFX artist so the artist is clear on what is required.

7. **Delivery:** At this point, the editor needs to deliver the plates to be worked on. Every project and artist is a bit different, but in general you need to export each shot individually at the highest uncompressed quality for the artist to work with. An uncompressed Quicktime file or DPX/CINEON image sequences are usually best for CGI work. It's also a good idea to give the artist a two to three frame handle on the head and tail of each shot.

8. **Final approval:** You must approve each shot.

9. **Final delivery:** At this stage, your VFX artist will deliver all the final shots to your editor, lab, or online editor, who will cut in the final shots for the film. Always make sure you deliver the final shots in the highest possible quality you can afford.

UNDERSTANDING VFX ARTISTS

The software tools to accomplish high-end VFX are now affordable for independent filmmakers. VFX software packages such as Apple's Shake, Adobe After Effects, 3D Studio Max, Nuke, LightWave 3D, and Autodesk Maya are some popular ones. VFX artists are very technical people and tend to go off on technical tangents where the average person may get lost very quickly. In my daily world working with VFX artists, almost every conversation I have involves a lot of tech talk. The following terms are the most basic CGI-speak I encounter when discussing projects:

Background Plates – A background plate is a live-action shot with the intention of adding actors or other CGI elements later.

Compositing – This is the process of combining visual elements from separate sources into a single shot or sequence. The goal is to give the illusion that all the elements are part of the same scene. This is usually accomplished using elements shot with a blue or green screen.

Rotoscoping – This is the technique of manually creating a matte for an element on a live-action plate so it may be composited over another background of some kind. Although some software can help speed up this process, it is usually a tedious, time-consuming process.

Digital Matte Paintings – When a location or set is too expensive to shoot or build, we usually turn to a digital matte painting. This is a computer-generated representation of a set, exotic locale, or other setting that is used to trick the audience's eye. This computer-generated illusion is a fantastic tool to add more production value to your low-budget film. I see it being used more and more on low-budget horror films.

Rendering – This is the process of generating a final rendered VFX shot for use in your film. The effect is created with software but needs to be rendered out to a useable format, such as a QuickTime movie, image sequences, or 2K files. You may hear a VFX artist talk about render time; this is because it takes a lot of computer processing power to generate a final shot, and you should allow for that in your schedule.

REMEMBER

The key to a smooth CGI experience on your film is to always communicate with your VFX artist during all phases of production.

DIGITAL GORE FX

Digital gore, or using CGI to create or enhance a violent and bloody effect, is one way for horror filmmakers to *sell* an effect on-screen. Big Hollywood productions do this a lot, and if used with discretion it can add a level of realism to your film. This could be VFX such as digital gunshot wounds, blood splatter enhancements, decapitations, and so on. I like to use this sparingly and believe the best approach is to have fantastic practical makeup FX done on set and only use digital gore VFX to enhance it in postproduction.

Original unaltered shot.
VFX by BFX Imageworks.

First, BFX Imageworks swelled up the cheek that took the impact. After all, it would be all messed up.
VFX by BFX Imageworks.

A CGI gash.
VFX by BFX Imageworks.

Final shot.
VFX by BFX Imageworks.

DIGITAL MAKEUP

Digital makeup, a phrase used to describe enhancing practical makeup FX that were done on-set with CGI in postproduction, is a new technique for filmmakers to add to their box of tricks. Imagine repainting your creature to enhance what you've shot. I've done this with faces, skin, and eyes with stunning results.

On my film GHOST MONTH (2009), my original concept for the ghosts in the film was to be practical makeup FX only. I was trying to save costs and time by doing everything practical. However, on my first day shooting the ghost scenes, I realized the makeup was too campy and needed to be hidden more in shadows. I knew it needed to be enhanced in postproduction, so I turned to digital makeup FX for help. Here are some examples of how I was able to enhance the practical makeup FX with digital makeup. The results were a much scarier and effective ghost.

The Crawling Ghost (before).

The Crawling Ghost (after). Digital makeup by John Lechago

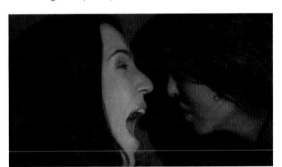

Mei-Ling Ghost (before).

Mei-Ling Ghost (after). Digital makeup by John Lechago

Mei-Ling Ghost (before).

Mei-Ling Ghost (after). Digital makeup by John Lechago

Mirror Ghost (before).

Mirror Ghost (after). Digital makeup by John Lechago

INTERVIEW BOX

STEVEN M. BLASINI VFX SUPERVISOR
BFX IMAGEWORKS

Steven M. Blasini

www.bfximageworks.com

BFX IMAGEWORKS, located in Los Angeles, California and founded in 2001, has produced high-end visual effects for independent studios throughout the United States and Europe. Our strength lies in our core business engine and strategies. By keeping our overhead low, we can provide very high-end work that is obtainable even within the modest budgets afforded independent film productions. Our work can be seen on Sci Fi Channel, ABC Family, HBO, Starz, MTZ, VH1, and more.

DRAVEN: *What does a VFX supervisor do? Can you describe your work flow and responsibilities during a film production?*

BLASINI: I believe that can vary from shop to shop, but I can tell you what I do. Generally (if the process is done correctly) I'll get early copies of the script, perhaps even just the three- or four-page treatment, and I let the producers know if there are any VFX items that may cause difficulties or be too costly. Once the script is locked, I then produce a VFX Breakdown that isolates all the scenes in the film that will be either completely VFX or VFX enhanced. I then create a budget based on those shots so that the total cost of the VFX can be known. Once principle photography starts (and if the production has enough money to cover the costs) I go on set and work closely with the director on all the shots requiring VFX. It is not uncommon that I then take on the role of second unit director for the shots that will require VFX, taking a small crew out and shooting background plates or specific talent performances that will involve VFX.

If the production doesn't have enough money to cover the costs of my being there, we usually keep phone contact with the director. This, however, is almost always dangerous, since shooting schedules don't always allow for calm phone interaction. I've seen many shots ruined using this method...but if that's all you can afford then we accommodate you.

Once the film is shot I am involved in the editing process, making sure that any shots/performances that are selected are indeed the best ones for the post job ahead. A lot of times a director/editor will just select a shot based on performance, but there may be a glitch in the setup of the shot that will make the VFX difficult, if not impossible, to complete.

Once the film is locked, we then order all the background plates from the lab and begin work at our studio creating all required elements and completing shots. We go through an approval process with the director then the producers until everyone is happy with the work. After approval, all shots are rendered in their final resolutions (usually Film 2K or HD) and delivered to the postproduction lab where it is usually color corrected, then sound/Foley/music are added.

DRAVEN: *What is the best way for a director to communicate his vision to the VFX artist?*

BLASINI: In our experience, the best way for a director to communicate his vision is via storyboards. However, it is unfortunate that usually at the budgets afforded to the average independent feature, there is not enough money for this. So it comes down to having as many preproduction meetings with the director and crew prior to principle photography as possible. Then location surprises or script rewrites have to be taken into consideration. For that reason, easy communication between the director and the VFX supervisor for on-the-spot decisions is a must.

With the exception of the background, this shot is entirely CGI. The spider, the torn body, and the pool of blood he's laying in are all computer generated. It's a POV shot, our heroes are trapped in a stairwell, and as they look outside to see if they can escape, they see this gory sight, it pretty much establishes that they are trapped where they are.

This shot is an example of good collaboration between practical and CGI techniques. The ravaged body is practical,

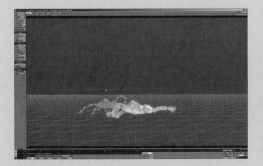

3-D model.
Figure Credit: From the Sci Fi Channel film ICE SPIDERS (2007) VFX by BFX Imageworks.

Final shot.
Figure Credit: From the Sci Fi Channel film ICE SPIDERS (2007) VFX by BFX Imageworks.

continued on the next page

continued from the previous page

3-D model.
Figure Credit: From the Sci Fi Channel film ICE SPIDERS
(2007) VFX by BFX Imageworks.

Final shot.
Figure Credit: From the Sci Fi Channel film ICE SPIDERS
(2007) VFX by BFX Imageworks.

as is the piece of intestine the CGI spider is slurping up into his mouth. The intestine was tied with fishing wire and pulled off to the left, while we removed the wire and placed our CGI spider where he could be slurping it up into his mouth.

DRAVEN: *Do you think CGI characters such as spiders, snakes, etc., are out of reach for independent filmmakers? Or can it be done on a low budget?*

BLASINI: It is definitely within reach of the independent filmmaker. The core of our very business has helped to establish that. Our design was structured so that most of the costs associated with having a VFX studio are *low* so we don't have to recover the many operating costs. The result is an obvious and immediate savings to the producers. The bulk of all our clients are independent filmmakers.

DRAVEN: *What types of CGI techniques are available to filmmakers in the horror genre (e.g., digital gore, digital makeup, etc.)?*

BLASINI: With us, the entire gamut of CGI techniques is available. This includes

digital gore and digital makeup as well as set extensions, matte paintings, wire and rig removal, and mood establishers (fog, smoke, fire). We've even had to do a shot where the dead victim flickered his shut eyes and we had to add steady digital eyelids!

DRAVEN: *Do you do a lot of digital gore FX, and how can a filmmaker prepare for this during production?*

BLASINI: The most important factor when shooting something that will need digital enhancement or replacement is the use of some kind of tracking marks that can then facilitate the frame-by-frame task ahead. Contrary to popular belief, it doesn't always have to be something specifically painted on for the process. As an example, we were called upon to create a digital eye morph on moving actors. Their eyes were to change from normal human to reptilian eyes. So I asked the director to make sure that he lit the talent in such a way that would produce a specular light reflection on the surface of the eyes that we could then use to track the motion. It worked

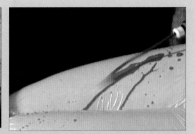

Original unaltered shot.
VFX by BFX Imageworks.

The severed ends were made to pulsate to make it look like they are spewing blood.
VFX by BFX Imageworks.

This is our matching of the angle of the victim in the car at our studio, her legs specifically, and we covered our model with *white* plastic so when we squirted her with Karo syrup in the positions of the arm stumps, the blood would drip and seep correctly over the victim's thighs. The white plastic also allowed a proper *key* so we could then extract only the blood and then composite it into the actual final shot.
VFX by BFX Imageworks.

Bloody squirts.
VFX by BFX Imageworks.

Final shot.
VFX by BFX Imageworks.

flawlessly and didn't require anything on the person directly.

DRAVEN: *What are the biggest mistakes you see new filmmakers make when doing VFX on low-budget films?*

BLASINI: They underestimate how complex a shot can really be. It's amazing how many directors and producers think that something can be just painted out or painted in. They forget that in order for a VFX artist to paint something out, there has to be some sort of palette to draw from that contains what is *behind* the item that has to be painted out. The less film shooters think ahead and provide to the VFX artist, the more expensive the shot becomes.

DRAVEN: *For filmmakers who can't afford a VFX artist, what tools/software do you suggest for them to do it themselves, and why?*

BLASINI: There are many VFX software packages out there that are accessible to anybody. The real way to answer this question is: go out and try them all yourself. What works for me doesn't necessarily work for you and vice versa. Before we established that we would use NewTek LightWave 3D as our main 3-D software

continued on the next page

continued from the previous page

and Adobe After Effects for our 2-D and compositing software, we spent many hours with *all* the packages available and decided which ones we felt comfortable with, not only in learning curve but ease of use and cost.

Original unaltered shot. VFX by BFX Imageworks.

Goopy throat and stream elements. VFX by BFX Imageworks.

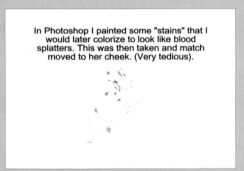

In Photoshop, we painted stains that would later be colorized to look like blood splatters. This was then taken and match-moved to her cheek. It was a very tedious process. VFX by BFX Imageworks.

Final shot. VFX by BFX Imageworks.

CHAPTER 14

THE PITFALLS OF POSTPRODUCTION

> **I see horror as part of legitimate film. I don't see it as an independent genre that has nothing to do with the rest of cinema.**
>
> —GUILLERMO DEL TORO

For many years, I have owned a small postproduction company called Darkworld Post. We specialize in postproduction services for independent producers of all budget levels. Besides doing all the post on my own films, we regularly post up to 20 features a year among other duties. We spend much of the day fixing post problems. In the hustle-and-bustle of production, some issues that will cause problems in post cannot be avoided, but I would say 95 percent of the problems we encounter could have been avoided. If your production has low standards, it will actually take more time to complete postproduction.

The following are the most common mistakes my company encounters with low-budget film productions:

REMEMBER

A competent and professional crew during production is key to a smooth post job.

BAD CAMERA AUDIO

Problem – Poorly recorded audio on camera, usually with noise or excessive amounts of peaking.

Solution – When shooting on digital, you are most likely recording audio directly into the camera. You must make sure your soundman is competent and monitoring the levels that are being recorded in the camera, not the levels from his production mixer only. It's a good idea to record one channel slightly lower than the other on camera to compensate for any peaks or distortion that may occur during a scene. At the end of every take, you should always communicate with your sound department and check if it was good for sound, and never shrug off any comments or suggestions they may have to improve it.

For example, my company recently posted an ultralow-budget film shot in HD with two cameras. They recorded audio directly into the A camera only and to a DEVA 5 recorder as a backup. However, by the time it got into our hands and we started editing, the entire film had an audio buzz on all camera tape masters because of faulty cables. The producers were furious with the soundman because he wasn't monitoring what was going into the camera; he was only monitoring his levels on his DEVA 5. Fortunately, his DEVA 5 audio was pristine. We had to manually resync

BEST SOUND ADVICE

Your soundman's gear quality and a little technical communication are paramount to getting the best sound possible on a production. There is no need to tell the soundman how to do his or her job; just specify what you want technically and follow-up on set to make sure they are doing it.

When shooting on film, your audio work flow is always *double system* sound. This means the audio is recorded on a stand-alone recorder during production and will be synced with the picture in post. The syncing is usually done at the film lab, or to save a few bucks you can do it yourself in your editing software.

When shooting on digital, I highly recommend recording double system sound to get the maximum quality from your production sound. I always let the camera record audio as a guide track, but

my main audio is being mixed to a separate audio recorder that I will sync later. I suggest using a digital recorder like a DEVA 5 hard disk recorder, or even directly to a laptop hard drive with multiple channels. I always record my production sound at a *minimum* of 24 bit/96k resolution.

Recording double system sound also makes your director of photography and soundman very happy because they are no longer tethered together with cables. This makes them more mobile, and camera setups are usually much quicker.

Never record MOS![1] Just because people are not talking in a scene does not mean the scene should be shot MOS. It's best to get the sounds of people breathing, walking, and handling props on set so you don't have to re-create it in the mix. Always record sound with postproduction in mind.

[1] MOS is motion picture lingo that means no synchronous audio track is being recorded. It's said this abbreviation is from the 1920s German directors who would say "Mit Out Sprechen" or "Mit Out Sound." It's a broken-English abbreviation meaning "Without sound," but it stuck ever since thanks to bad German accents.

the show from the DEVA 5 masters, and it was a very expensive fix. In this case, there was no communication between the producers, the camera department, and the sound department, and this is what happens as a result.

IMPROPER SLATING

Problem – The slating during production is unprofessional and unreadable. I have seen crew members use their fingers to slate take numbers, or use a slate with no backlit display or flashlight in a dark room, or no voice slate, or incomplete camera reports. These are all big problems.

Solution – No matter how low-budget your film may be, there is no excuse for poor slating. Your picture editor and/or telecine operator can waste a lot of time in post dealing with these issues. Your camera assistant should always voice slate each and every take and call out "Marker!" while slating. The slate should be visible and readable in frame and in focus, and the clapper should be visible when the sticks meet completely. Your camera assistants should never use the letters I, O, Q, S, and Z because they are too easily confused with numbers.

Can you read that slate? I can't either.

This is a good example of a proper slate.

NO ROOM TONE

Problem – No room tone was recorded during production.

Solution – Room tone is used to match the production soundtrack so that it may be intercut with the track and provide a continuous-sounding background and help smooth out edits. It's the location's aural fingerprint. It only takes a few seconds to record on set, and you should make sure your soundman knows you require it.

FOCUS PROBLEMS

Problem – Shots are out of focus or soft focus when using zoom lenses and primes.

Solution – This responsibility lies with your camera department, either the first AC or your focus puller. I take this job on my set very seriously. A bad focus puller can cost you a lot of money and time, especially when shooting film. In postproduction, there is no magic fix for focus issues. I have had many wonderful performances ruined by focus problems!

Man's best friend can also be man's best camera assistant and protect your expensive 35mm gear 24/7.

UNDEREXPOSED FILM

Problem – The film negative is improperly exposed.

Solution – Hire an experienced director of photography who regularly shoots film and understands its characteristics. There have been amazing developments in film technology over the past few years. The newer film stocks, like Kodak Vision 3 500T (5219/7219), are amazing in low-lighting conditions and have incredible latitude, which gives you a lot of flexibility in post. I have done tests with Kodak reps with this stock, and the results are stunning.

BLUE & GREEN SCREENS

Problem – Blue and green screen shots are improperly lit and executed for CGI work.

Solution – I have witnessed many productions that put white, blue, and green colored paper from Wal-Mart behind actors and expect that to be satisfactory for compositing work. This half-assed way of working always ends up costing the producer more money and time in post. Always have your visual FX artist, or someone the artist appoints, on set the day you are shooting to collaborate with the director of photography on lighting and approve all VFX shots.

CGI PLATES

Problem – The CGI plate shots have not been locked off properly.

Solution – If you are shooting a CGI plate, you must make sure it's locked off. That means there is absolutely no movement of the camera or tripod whatsoever while shooting your plate.

MULTIPLE CAMERA SHOOTS

Problem – There are excessive amounts of coverage for no reason.

Solution – It is my opinion that unless you are shooting a large action sequence or an expensive one-take shot (e.g., blowing up a building), there is no reason to have multiple cameras during a production on any budget level. It just ends up taking more time and crew than it is worth. A director should focus on *one shot at a time*, and having multiple cameras is a cheap solution for indecisive filmmakers to feel they got it covered.

TITLE SAFE

Problem – Opening or end titles were not properly formatted to fit into title safe specifications.

Solution – Whoever is doing your title work should know to keep it in title safe. If not, remind the person and check his or her work, or find someone else. All editing applications have guides that will show you the title safe areas of a frame.

CREDITS

Problem – There are misspellings and name corrections needed in the opening or end credits.

Solution – I know this may seem obvious, but this is very common, and usually the fixes happen *after* the final masters have been made, which costs a lot more money. It's usually a word or a name that's spelled wrong, or the producer forgot to credit a person who worked on the film. Make sure you check, double check, then check again before you sign off on your opening and end titles. I once had a producer spell his girlfriend's name wrong, and it got released on DVD before she noticed.

REMEMBER

Don't fix problems in post—fix problems on set!

WORDS OF WISDOM

It is imperative that you understand the postproduction process enough to make sure your crew is doing an acceptable job during production to ensure a smooth work flow in post. If you don't constantly monitor your crew, no one else will, and you won't know if they did their job right until it's too late.

J. R. BOOKWALTER PRODUCER, DIRECTOR

TEMPE ENTERTAINMENT

J. R. Bookwalter poses between shots of the Jason (Michael Todd) meltdown in THE DEAD NEXT DOOR (1989).

www.jrbookwalter.com

www.tempevideo.com

J. R. BOOKWALTER began his career in 1985 at age 19 with THE DEAD NEXT DOOR, an ambitious zombie epic financed by a now legendary Hollywood director. After learning the ropes with a series of work-for-hire features, Bookwalter chose Tempe Entertainment as an outlet to make and self-distribute such films as OZONE and POLYMORPH. In 1997,

Bookwalter relocated to Hollywood, where he produced 12 features for Full Moon Pictures in just 3 years and directed two popular WITCHOUSE sequels.

The Akron, Ohio native went back on his own in 2003 with Tempe DVD, releasing deluxe special editions of his past work as well as creating a new home for some not so classics with the comedy series BAD MOVIE POLICE. Considered by many to be a pioneer in the wildly popular shot-on-video movement, in 2005 Bookwalter celebrated his 20th year in the business, marked by Anchor Bay's release of THE DEAD NEXT DOOR Special Edition DVD, bringing his career full circle.

DRAVEN: *What were the most important things you learned making THE DEAD NEXT DOOR (1989), and what advice do you have for others who want to make their debut in the horror genre?*

BOOKWALTER: The business was in a very different place when I started that film back in 1985…there was no Internet, no YouTube, and few places for budding filmmakers to collaborate! It was amazing to me that people found the movie at all, especially considering how long it took to make and get released. But, I think the movie had an interesting take on the zombie genre, and it certainly had a unique behind-the-scenes story as far as how it

continued on the next page

continued from the previous page

got made, and those two things helped create enough interest for people to seek it out. And they still are…every year the movie seems to get more popular instead of disappearing, as I've often wished it would. [Laughs] So, I would say the first piece of advice would be, try to bring something unique to the table…that's easier said than done, but believe me, I'm not the most talented guy in the world. Sometimes, with a lot of patience and persistence, you can be resourceful enough to overcome your own limitations. And you better have patience, because you'll need it in this business.

As far as what I learned…I was barely 19 years old when I started THE DEAD NEXT DOOR, and by the time it was released I was almost 25 and married for the first time! So I did a lot of growing up over those years. I can't say that I learned as much from the movie itself, mostly because I had the luxury of time and an ever-evolving budget to play with, so there wasn't a lot of discipline there. But during the downtime, when nothing was happening with the movie, I shot weddings and music videos and even recorded and mixed a lot of music for myself and others—so I learned how to be resourceful and find other ways to survive. [Laughs]

DRAVEN: *What are the five most important things for an indie producer to do during production to save money?*

BOOKWALTER: It sounds terrible, but the real secret to making low-budget movies is simple: don't pay for anything! And if you have to pay for something, pay as little as possible. [Laughs] Seriously, it's not rocket science, folks. Spend your money wisely, and make sure every dime of it is on the screen…and then some! You have to be somewhat of a dictator with the dollars that you do have and not squander it on things that don't make a better production. That said, you want to treat your cast and crew right…feeding them a decent meal goes a long way toward keeping them happy, and if they're happy, they'll work those long, grueling hours and perform better for you.

The biggest thing is to stay connected to people, places, and things, or know reliable people who are well connected. You'd be amazed what you can get from asking the right person, and remember, the worst thing that can happen is that somebody might say "no," so why not give it a try?

DRAVEN: *When scheduling an indie horror film, what are some tricks you learned, and how has it helped the production be more efficient?*

BOOKWALTER: Man, when I started on THE DEAD NEXT DOOR, we used those old-school, expensive production boards with the cardboard strips. It was a nightmare, especially because the schedule changed so frequently! Now they have great software to do the same thing, but filmmakers shouldn't feel pressured into spending the dough on that stuff. Some of the better schedules I've done over the years were on tiny projects like OZONE, where I just printed out some calendars from my computer (for free!) and scribbled on them until things made sense. To me, the scheduling is much easier if you have a production-ready, production-friendly script to start with. That means write what you can pull off efficiently, yet effectively. I've seen too many writers scribble all these big ideas on paper, and more often than not, that stuff gets whittled down to a shadow of its former self on location. Get the script in tip-top shape for shooting, and the schedule will fall into place easily.

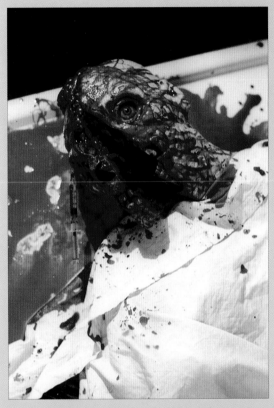

An experiment in Dr. Moulsson's lab, affectionately dubbed by its creators as the "Spazo" zombie in THE DEAD NEXT DOOR (1989).

DRAVEN: *What is the key to shooting quickly during a production?*

BOOKWALTER: A lot of filmmakers think that pages of dialog will help them speed through a shoot, but in my experience, that's rarely the case. Sure, if your actors have their lines memorized and you know what you want them to do (and they can actually *do* it), it can be done. But let's face it, with low-budget movies, you're often dealing with actors of questionable talent, and many times they might have no other on-set experience!

More than anything else, it falls on the shoulder of the director (and almost as equally on the cinematographer)...have the shooting day mapped out in your head, know what you want and have some good ideas how to get it, and for God's sake, be prepared for things to not work out the way you planned, because they seldom do.

DRAVEN: *What are the advantages and disadvantages to guerilla-style filmmaking, and why?*

BOOKWALTER: The biggest advantage is the freedom to do whatever you want, within your means. On a movie like OZONE, we had a great home base that doubled as our main location...it was an abandoned building on this large property belonging to the adjoining rehabilitation center. I was able to store all of the gear there and shoot probably 75 percent of the movie in and around that building. It was really like a studio playground for such a small movie! I think we were holed up there for almost a year until they said, "You guys have to get out now." [Laughs]

That said, the biggest disadvantage is you wear too many hats and you'll burn yourself out quickly. Trust me on that, I've done it time and time again! When

continued on the next page

continued from the previous page

I started out, I wanted to be writer, director, producer, camera operator, editor, cameo actor, squib guy, makeup effects guy… you name it. After awhile, it gets to be too much, so I gradually scaled back to mostly producing, directing, and editing.

DRAVEN: *Tempe Video is your indie distribution company and has been in business since 1991. When you release a film, what are the most important things you look for in a film for it to be sellable in the marketplace?*

BOOKWALTER: I get asked that question a lot by producers: "What kind of movies are you looking for?" And I always tell them the same thing: "Make whatever you want!" My reason for that is simple…you're stuck with these things for life! They're your children, even if sometimes they're of the redheaded stepchild variety. [Laughs] Better to make something that *you* want to see, rather than make something you think will appeal to a distributor. If you make what you *think* the market wants, very often that trend will have shifted by the time you're ready to sell the movie, and then you're stuck with something that nobody wants to see. Today there are plenty of ways to get your movie seen, and even with a distributor, there's no guarantee you'll see any money, let alone recoup on what the thing cost you to begin with.

Now the flip side of that advice is, try to put stuff in the movie that will *appeal* to an audience! While it's true that there's an audience for everything, you'll probably have a better shot at seeing a profit making a ballsy, gory zombie flick than some costume drama that's a hard sell. You have to decide up front what your intentions are and have the fortitude to stick to your convictions when all of the distributors pass or you can only sell 10 copies at some convention.

DRAVEN: *During production, how do you deal with day-to-day problems that arise on set?*

BOOKWALTER: The movie business is a veritable cesspool of insecure, neurotic artist types. It's a good idea to stay grounded and even tempered. Go in knowing that things can go wrong, and take them with a grain of salt. I've often compared being on set to a military operation, because no matter how well you plan it, you can't always control the outcome…you've gotta be prepared to follow another course of action rather than throw up your hands, pitch a fit, and give up just because your vision isn't being realized. I'd venture to say that few films ever turn out 100 percent the way their creators intended, regardless of budget, and your odds go down dramatically if you don't keep a cool head.

DRAVEN: *If you could pick one tip to give an aspiring horror filmmaker, what would it be and why is it important?*

BOOKWALTER: That's an easy one: don't be an ass! [Laughs] Seriously, so much of this so-called business revolves around pandering to egos and dealing with a lot of BS, and people can make the crappiest movies and still have a swelled head about it. I'm not saying don't be proud of your accomplishments, I'm just saying to temper it with a dose of humility. Yeah, I know, we've all seen bad behavior rewarded in our society, but trust me, people are more likely to want to work with you if you leave the chip on your shoulder at home.

And don't believe everything you read in reviews, especially the good stuff—the higher you fly, the farther you have to fall. [Laughs]

A whopping 1,500 area locals came out to play zombie extras in J. R. Bookwalter's THE DEAD NEXT DOOR (1989).

THE DEAD NEXT DOOR photos Copyright © 2005 Tempe Entertainment.

PART FIVE

DISTRIBUTION AND MARKETING

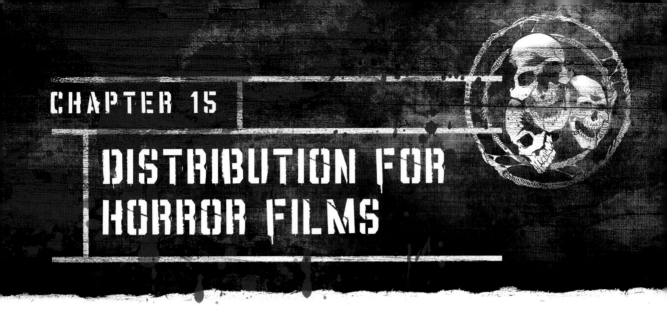

CHAPTER 15

DISTRIBUTION FOR HORROR FILMS

> ❝ Motion pictures are the art form of the 20th century, and one of the reasons is the fact that films are a slightly corrupted art form. They fit this century—they combine art and business! ❞
>
> —ROGER CORMAN

Horror films are a proven seller in the home video marketplace, so you are already on the right track by choosing this genre. The genre has a built-in audience. However, with more affordable means of making films and the advent of the digital revolution, there are more films being made than ever. Your film that costs $500 could be in the same pile as a film that cost $1.5 million or more. The indie horror genre is without a doubt over-saturated with product, most of which is in need of distribution. There is also a shift in the way people are consuming media content, and this is forcing filmmakers—both big and small—to evolve with the times.

PLANNING FOR DISTRIBUTION

A successful distribution strategy starts in the preproduction stage. It's a big mistake for filmmakers to go into production without first under-standing how they will be selling their film. If it's an art film you are mak-ing, that's perfectly fine, do whatever you want. If you want to *sell* your film and make your investors' money back, you need to shoot your movie with distribution in mind and make certain it is deliverable.

MARKET RESEARCH

When doing market research for the film you are about to make or distribute, it is always best to start by reading the trades (e.g., *Variety, Hollywood Reporter, Video Business*, etc.) and get all the details for films similar to yours. You should try to project a year ahead and write down all upcoming projects from major studios and small indie labels that are releasing horror films. I usually create a calendar and write in all the horror film release dates. It's always best to be ahead of the game and know the playing field. You should try to find out what is being made, what scripts were sold and to whom, and what companies are releasing what horror films in what month and in what format (e.g., theatrical, DVD, Blu-ray, video on demand [VOD], etc.). This is an important stage when planning your distribution strategy. For example, you don't want to release your indie vampire film the same week a big Hollywood feature with similar content is released. You will get smashed. It's interesting to note that a big Hollywood horror movie that sucks may taint the consumer's opinion of that content—at least temporarily.

REMEMBER

Information and planning is key!

THE TRADES OF THE BUSINESS

Variety: www.variety.com

Video Business: www.videobusiness.com

Hollywood Reporter: www.hollywoodreporter.com

SHOOTING FORMAT

If you want to sell your film, you must shoot on film (35mm or Super 16mm) or HD. Do not shoot in standard definition or on any DV format. If you are considering HD, you should always use the highest quality camera you can afford. There are lots of HD cameras and formats on the market, each with different specs and levels of quality (e.g., HDV, DVCPRO HD, XDCAM, RED ONE, and so on). I have several producer friends who shoot test footage with a new HD camera and have a lab QC the footage to ensure the camera footage will pass a tedious QC process. They understand the importance of choosing the right camera so they can sell the film.

It's also wise to shoot all your planned extra features in HD. This ensures a high technical quality and is a bonus if your film is to be released on Blu-ray. I shot and mastered all the extra features for my film GHOST MONTH in HD, and it received a Blu-ray release. The distributors were very happy, and it gives the movie a long shelf life.

PLANNING AHEAD

Here is a list of things you can do in preproduction, production, and post-production to prepare your film for distribution.

Preproduction Stage

1. Hire a professional sound crew. Nothing causes more problems than bad sound.

2. Hire a professional director of photography and camera crew who are all experienced on the camera of choice. This is vital. You need a great looking movie visually, or you'll be dead in the water when you try to sell it.

Production Stage

1. Shoot cover shots. If your film has excessive nudity or violence, or anything that may be obscene, you should always shoot alternates. This helps protect your film if there is a ratings issue.

2. Shoot professional on-set stills of the actors in action.

Postproduction Stage

1. Create a 1080psf, 23.98, closed-captioned universal master for your film in a popular HD format, such as D5 or HDCAM SR. From this master, all others can be made for distribution. This master must pass QC with flying colors.

2. Follow all deliverables I detail in Chapter 16.

DISTRIBUTION PATHS

As a filmmaker, it's easy to get frustrated and lost after your movie is completed. After all, you're an artist, not a salesman. When it comes to distribution it's important to understand the business side. Every film I've made has had worldwide distribution, and I've been very lucky to have always been involved in the selling side and interact directly with the sales people. Our ideas often, if not always, seem to clash. It's the creative side versus the bottom line; the latter always seems to win. It's important to understand that distributors are not art critics. They want a product they can *sell*, and that's the bottom line.

There are two possible paths for you at this stage: self-distribution or studio distribution.

SELF-DISTRIBUTION

Self-distribution is the process of you acting as the sole distributor and supplier of your film to the world through all distribution channels. You make all the deals. This is not a quick and easy way to do things and can often be very discouraging. It involves you doing everything a studio or sales agent would normally do on your behalf. You must be prepared to roll up your sleeves and do a lot of research, promoting, phone calls, following up, and order fulfillment duties. It's a full-time business.

When you've committed to the self-distribution path, the next step is to know where and how to sell your film.

Self-Distribution: The Rental Outlets

It's important to know who the major buyers are for rental. It's usually very difficult, but not impossible, to just pick up the phone and tell a major rental outlet why they should buy your amazing movie. In my experience, these companies tend to buy from producers or companies with whom they already have a buying relationship. The following are several of the top rental outlets for indies:

- Blockbuster Video

- Hollywood Video

- Netflix.com

- Redbox.com

- Moviecube.com

One way to track all rental and retail activity for your film is through Rentrak (www.rentrak.com). They can measure and report all forms of content performance. This is also a great way to do market research and see how other titles are performing in a variety of mediums.

Self-Distribution on the Internet

New technologies continue to offer unprecedented distribution opportunities, but the biggest outlet for the self-distributor is online. Your worldwide audience is at your fingertips.

- CreateSpace.com

- IndieFlix.com

- UndergroundFilm.com
- HULU.com
- FlickRocket.com
- Babelgum.com
- Vuze.com
- BigStar.tv
- Openfilm.com

Here are some popular VOD web sites for your film:

- Indemand.com
- DownloadHorror.com
- Cinedoo.com
- Netflix.com
- CinemaNow.com
- FilmBaby.com
- HDonlineCinema.com
- GreenCine.com
- EZTakes.com

Studio Distribution

If you want to solicit the studios to release your film, then you should do your homework. It's best to find similar movies to yours and make a list of all companies that release that type of genre product. I always put the companies in order of who I would like to release the film and end the list with who I would settle with in case I don't get what I want. If you are attempting to approach a major or mini-major studio, don't be surprised if you don't get a response. It's nothing personal. There are a lot of companies who provide content, or have output deals with the studios, and they may be your key to getting the release you want.

If you are contacting a company for the first time, you need to get your materials to the acquisitions department. If they are interested, believe me, you will hear back from them, and they will request a screener for review. It's best to follow-up with an email or phone call every week until you get a definitive answer.

REMEMBER

Always start at the top and work your way down.

LIST OF HORROR DISTRIBUTORS (DOWNLOAD)

** web file: Horror_Distributors_Listing.pdf

Here is a partial list of some popular studio labels that specialize in horror content:

Ghost House Underground: www.ghosthousepictures.com/

Dimension Extreme: www.dimensionextreme.com/

Lionsgate: www.lionsgate.com/

Magnet Releasing: www.magnetreleasing.com/

Anchor Bay Entertainment: www.anchorbayentertainment.com/

A sell sheet/sales ad for
CRYPTZ (2002).
Figure Credit: Courtesy of
Full Moon Pictures.

A sell sheet/sales ad for INTRUDER (1996 edition).
Figure Credit: Courtesy of Wizard Entertainment.

A sell sheet/sales ad for the U.S. DVD/Blu-ray release of GHOST MONTH (2009).
Figure Credit: Courtesy of North American Motion Pictures (www.noamp.com).

SELLING A HORROR FILM

It's important to understand how low-budget horror films are sold and packaged from a business perspective. Because you don't have the multi-million dollar marketing campaigns of the major studios behind your film, you need to work a bit harder to get it recognized in the world. It goes without saying that movie elements such as story, acting quality, direction, technical quality, and production value are important to selling a movie. These are usually reflected in the trailer.

Trailer – A slickly produced trailer is key to selling your film or at least getting someone to request a screener. You only have a minute or so to present this to a buyer, and you want to impress, so you should be encouraged to do your own unique vision. Don't put too much in the trailer, but don't put too little either; it's best to find a balance that works and tells the story without giving it all away. If someone watches your trailer and no longer needs to rent the movie because the trailer featured all the highlights, then you're in trouble. In the trailer you should feature any production value shots and any notable cast members.

REMEMBER

The most important elements for an indie horror film to focus on for sales are trailer, artwork, title, cast, *and* hook.

A COLLECTION OF INDIE HORROR TRAILERS (DOWNLOAD)

Visit the book companion website at http://booksite.focalpress.com/companion/Draven/.

Artwork – Horror films—and indie films in general—live and die by their packaging. The artwork is vital to capture a person's eye. Imagine yourself in a video store or browsing online through hundreds or thousands of titles. What will make yours stand out? Is it visually appealing enough for a consumer to pick it up and read the back? Maybe you have a sex and guns approach, or maybe it's the monster, or a funny and shocking photo. Regardless, it must pop from the shelf if you want it to be seen.

I once interviewed for a well-known independent movie studio, and the guy told me that they don't make movies. They make artwork. The movies are all filler for the great box art. What he meant, of course, is that the company's core business is selling art, not good movies. I don't agree with that approach, but that was my first encounter with a

TIP

If you want to see some fantastic horror movie trailers complete with critical commentary, go to www. trailersfromhell.com.

GHOST MONTH art variation 1.

GHOST MONTH art variation 2.

GHOST MONTH art variation 3.

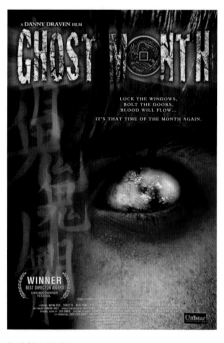

GHOST MONTH art variation 4.

company that releases product out into the world based on art and not content.

It's interesting to note that some of my earlier films that were released at Blockbuster would get special artwork versions just for them. It just goes to show you how serious rental companies are about the artwork. Every film I've made has several versions of artwork created throughout the sales process. This is usually because everyone thinks of him- or herself as an artwork expert, so it gets changed a lot. Here are a few from my last movie; you can see the evolution from one to another.

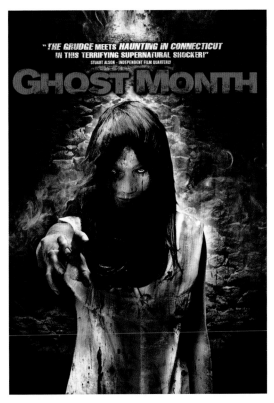

GHOST MONTH final North American DVD artwork (2009).
Figure Credit: Courtesy of North American Motion Pictures.

Title – A great movie title is what will make your indie horror film stand out. The best movie titles for horror films are ones that best describe the story in the fewest words. It's also very important to remember the searchability value of the title. The best way to choose your title is to imagine yourself at home hooked up to your satellite or Apple TV. When you want to watch a film you usually think of a genre then scroll down a list of titles. What would you click on? If a horror movie is called A BUMBLEBEE IN THE SHADOWS, you may pass it by, but if a movie is called DEMON TREE or KILLBILLY MASSACRE, you know what to expect from the title and may rent it.

Cast – Movies are about the characters, so casting your film should not be something you take lightly. You must always consider the needs of the story and character first. Acting ability and look is important. It's a big plus if you hire a star actor in your film, even if the actor is a B-level star. It seems to be harder these days to sell movies without some sort of name value. I personally like to hire unknown, quality actors. There are a lot of them out there eager for an opportunity. Because they are new and fresh faces, it makes the story seem more real.

A good-looking cast is also an important sales tool. How you determine who is beautiful and who is not so beautiful is certainly a matter

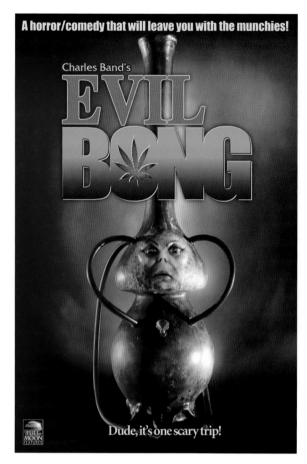

EVIL BONG (2006 original teaser artwork.
Figure Credit: Courtesy of Full Moon Features.

THE GINGERDEAD MAN (2005) original artwork.
Figure Credit: Courtesy of Full Moon Features.

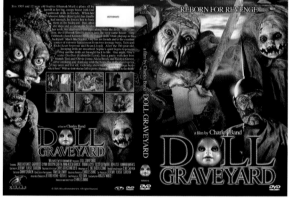

DOLL GRAVEYARD (2005) original artwork.
Figure Credit: Courtesy of Full Moon Features.

of personal taste and not a fair way to judge a person. It's important to mention this—whether it's fair or not—because it does seem to be a factor in selling a movie. I've been involved in a lot of films that have beautiful people on the cover art; sometimes it makes no difference if they can act or not. On one of my films, the distributor digitally replaced a character's face on the box art with another model!

Hook – A sales hook is something that is designed to catch people's attention. It's a concept or situation that grabs people's attention and interest right away; for example, zombies on an airplane, a person stranded on a lifeboat with a devilish mermaid, or a military squadron trapped in a wrecked submarine with a killer. It's just like fishing: when you have them on the hook you need to reel them in and deliver the scares as promised. A fisherman wants to reel in a big catch, not an old tire.

THE FILM MARKETS

It's important to understand where deals are made. Film markets are nothing more than trade events meant to promote a film to the distribution channels, and they are usually open to the public (for a fee). More business is conducted at a film market than at a film festival. Here is a list of the major markets for selling films. You can go as an attendee or get a seller booth. If you are represented by a producer representative or sales agent, make sure he or she attends all or the majority of these major markets—or find a new agent!

This is the Blockbuster double-feature artwork for Stuart Gordon Presents DEATHBED (2002).

NATIONAL ASSOCIATION OF TELEVISION PROGRAM EXECUTIVES (NATPE)

Time: January

Location: Las Vegas, Nevada

Web site: www.natpe.org

BERLINALE EUROPEAN FILM MARKET (EFM)

Time: February

Location: Berlin, Germany

Web site: www.berlinale.de

HONG KONG INTERNATIONAL FILM & TV MARKET (FILMART)

Time: March

Location: Hong Kong

Web site: www.hkfilmart.com

MIPTV/MIPDOC

Time: April

Location: Cannes, France

Web site: www.miptv.com

MARCHÉ DU FILM AT THE CANNES FILM FESTIVAL

Time: May

Location: Cannes, France

Web site: www.marchedufilm.com

DISCOP EAST

Time: June

Location: Budapest, Hungary

Web site: www.discop.com

HOME MEDIA EXPO (HME)

Time: June

Location: Las Vegas, Nevada

Web site: www.homemediaexpo.com

TORONTO INTERNATIONAL FILM FESTIVAL

Time: September

Location: Toronto, Canada

Web site: www.tiffg.ca

MIPCOM: INTERNATIONAL TV & VIDEO MARKET

Time: October

Location: Cannes, France

Web site: www.mipcom.com

TIFFCOM: MARKETPLACE FOR FILM & TV IN ASIA

Time: October

Location: Tokyo, Japan

Web site: www.tiffcom.jp

AMERICAN FILM MARKET (AFM)

Time: November

Location: Santa Monica, California

Web site: www.ifta-online.org/afm

ASIA TELEVISION FORUM (ATF)

Time: December

Location: Suntec, Singapore

Web site: www.asiatvforum.com

SALES REPRESENTATION

If you are like me and prefer to just make films and leave selling it up to the people with office jobs, then you need a representative. In most cases, distributors would rather deal with experienced salespeople and not filmmakers who are inexperienced in sales. Selling movies is a specialized skill.

What is the difference between a sales representative, producer's representative, and an entertainment attorney? There really is no difference. They are all doing the same thing: getting paid to approach distributors and sell your film. They can call themselves whatever they like, but their

ONLINE FILM MARKETS

The New Frontier

In the digital age, it was just a matter of time before someone created an online film market. I believe that just having a web site for your film online puts it out into the market. I've been contacted by people more often through my web site for distribution than any other way. There are several online markets out there, and I think they will become more popular over the years. I don't think they will replace the traditional markets, but it does seem to be a nice way to browse and find content a buyer may need. Here are two that are popular.

GMX–The Global Media Exhange: www.gmxmarket.com

reelport: www.reelport.com

GMX - The Global Media Exhange Website

Reelport web site (2009).

end goal is the same. Some may charge more than others or even be more connected, but don't let the fancy titles fool you.

These people or companies work on a percentage basis. Keep in mind that if you go with a sales agent or rep you will make less money because you now have another party dipping their hand in the cookie jar. For example, if you made a deal with an agent/rep for 15 percent of sales, and the agent/rep makes a deal with a distributor for 25 percent of sales, then 40 percent of the money is already claimed, minus expenses and any other odds and ends. They always get their money first, minus expenses, and then it goes to the filmmaker or investor. You will always be last unless you self-distribute.

One way to keep costs down is to do as many things as you can for your agent as possible. This could include DVD authoring or making masters, screeners, art, trailers, or any other items they may have to pay another party to do for the film. Because I own a postproduction company, I am able to keep these costs to a minimum by doing a lot of the work myself. When your sales agent has to go to a lab, the bill is usually staggering.

There are plenty of names you can pull out of a hat to represent your film. The trick is…whom do you trust? You should think of hiring a rep the same way you would if you were hiring a key crew person or house-keeper. This person must have experience in the film business and be able to give you a list of other films he or she represents, markets he or she attends, and an honest assessment of how he or she intends to sell the film on your behalf. If the rep can't pass those requirements, politely shake his or her hand with a California smile and leave. Remember, the rep works for you, not the other way around!

FILM RIGHTS

UNDERSTANDING WHAT IS FOR SALE

I often talk to filmmakers who don't understand what exactly they have to sell in the first place. The following is what is for sale:

- Theatrical rights

- North American DVD rights (United States and Canada)

- Worldwide and foreign territories

- U.S. broadcast and television rights

- Pay per view (PPV)

- Video on demand and subscription video on demand (VOD and SVOD)

THE ALL-RIGHTS DEAL

If you have been offered an all-rights distribution deal, and you get a large advance, and you are satisfied with your deal, go for it. A buyout/negative pickup deal is when a studio pays you a bunch of money to go away. This is not common these days, but it does still happen for indies.

SPLITTING UP THE RIGHTS FOR MAXIMUM REVENUE

Whether you are using a producer's rep, sales agent, or are self-distributing, you can always make more revenue out of a film by splitting up the rights. When you are offered a distribution deal, it's very easy in all the excitement and starry-eyed imaginings of what your DVD cover will look like to sign on the dotted line and give away all rights in an all-rights deal. That means what it says: *all rights!* Instead of giving it all away to one distributor, you can split up rights for DVD, cable, theatrical, digital downloads, and so on. This way you have your eggs in more than one basket, so to speak.

DISTRIBUTION CONTRACTS

There are plenty of fantastic books that break down contracts in detail, and this is not one of them. If you are seriously considering signing a distribution deal, you should always consult with an entertainment attorney, but make sure it's an *entertainment* attorney that works in a major city (Los Angeles or New York) and not your Uncle James who is a tax attorney in Ohio, or your brother in law school. A good entertainment attorney can give you advice and point out any loopholes or negotiate and close the entire deal on your behalf.

When you or your sales agent is in negotiations with a distributor, don't be afraid to ask for what you want. When I sign deals for my films, I have a list of items I want added to the contracts. Here are a few important ones.

Retail Copies of the Film – I always make sure to get enough for me and the cast and crew. Don't be greedy—I once asked for 1,000 retail copies and got them all as part of my deal, and I still can't get rid of them!

Final Approval of Credits & Art – To avoid any errors or misspellings, I like to add to my contract that I have final approval of the credit block and all text on the artwork. It helps ensure that all the hard-working people on the film have their names spelled right and jobs listed correctly.

No Changing Picture or Title Without Approval – Whatever you do, do not let the distributor change a frame of the picture without your approval. I have plenty of horror stories and do not want to see you be the victim of a recut. I let them cut any trailer they think will sell the film, but I never let them touch the feature without approval.

Performance Clause – A performance clause is a way of ensuring that the distributor or sales agent will perform. If the distributor or agent does not live up to the numbers and dates set forth, you have the right to take the film somewhere else. I usually give them 2 years, but I see a lot of contracts from distributors that want your film for no money for 10 to 15 years!

Audit Clause – It's important to have set dates for the audit. An audit clause without dates is useless.

Can you get screwed by a distributor? *Yes*. It happens all the time, especially to inexperienced independent filmmakers who think they know it all. It really is in your best interest to take the distribution contract to an entertainment attorney and have him or her either give you advice and look for errors or loopholes or have the attorney negotiate the contract on your behalf.

RECOMMENDED READING

The Movie Business by Kelly Charles Crabb.
The Insider's Guide to Independent Film Distribution by Stacey Parks.

REMEMBER

Always get money up front. It may be the only money you'll ever see.

SCREENERS

When your movie is ready to be sent out for sales or review copies, you should have a stack of screeners ready to go. You can burn your own copies as needed or go to a professional replicator for a reasonable price. You should always present your screener in the most professional way possible with all appropriate contact information in a visible place. I always have a full DVD sleeve designed and label it clearly as a copyrighted screener copy. On the DVD surface you should also print the information and clearly label it with things like aspect ratio, running time, and any special features you've included. On the feature film, you should make sure you *watermark* the video for the entire film in the bottom third of the frame. This is to deter piracy, but it doesn't always work. You should make sure the watermark is big enough that it can't be matted out. I know of several countries that steal the screeners and sell them. If you are ultraparanoid, you can number each copy and keep a database of each name and number, so if you ever see it on the streets of Bahrain, you know how it got there and who to sue. Do not hand out your screeners to just anyone, especially when they are not yet copy protected.

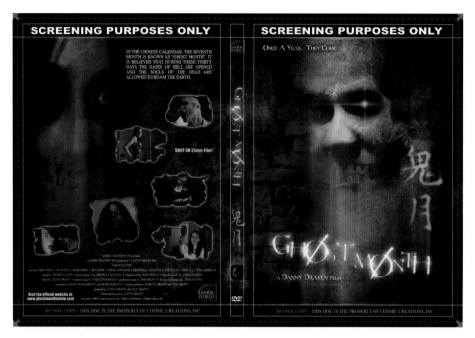

An early GHOST MONTH screener DVD sleeve.

DIGITAL SCREENERS

With today's fast broadband connections, it's now a reality that you can start doing digital screeners. You can be creative with this and even include the artwork (as a still) before the start of the film along with chapter stops.

A GHOST MONTH screener watermarked with a logo.

A GHOST MONTH screener watermarked with a text warning and the opacity set at 50 percent.

A screen grab from the QuickTime digital screener for GHOST MONTH.

The file size of the movie depends on the length and compression you use. I usually do digital screeners at 16 × 9 (480 × 270), 23.98, stereo 48 Khz audio, in the H.264 codec as a QuickTime movie. The file size is usually less than 400 MB, but it all depends on your settings. When you've completed your digital screener, you just send the person a link to a password-protected FTP site. You should make it as simple as possible because not everyone is a computer whiz. You can also send it through large file delivery services like YouSendIt.com or DropSend.com. You should take the same watermarking precautions on the digital files as well. Digital screeners are a fantastic way to save money for you and your sales reps.

PIRACY & YOUR MOVIE

Any time you release a product to the marketplace, it has the possibility of being stolen in one form or another, and DVDs are always easy targets for piracy. It really doesn't do you much good to be overly paranoid that some-one may pirate your film, but you should take all the precautions you can. All of my films have been released all over the world, and sometimes I find

little treasures when I travel. Every movie I've made has been pirated in one form or another; in fact, so many times that I have a little collection. For example, here is an Asian bootleg I found in a remote Indonesian mall while shopping there. I paid the equivalent of one U.S. dollar for it.

The criminal remains at large.

HORRORVISION (2001), VCD bootleg.

An Asian bootleg of my film GHOST MONTH selling for the equivalent of 60 cents (U.S.) before the U.S. release date!

Complete with Indonesian subtitles!

Still has the screener watermark!

FUTURE TECH & THE SMALL SCREEN

DVD won't be around forever and will one day share the fate of VHS and Betamax. The Blu-ray disc won the format wars, and I was always rooting for it. When it comes to distribution, there seems to be a new technology appearing every year that provides a new distribution channel for your work. The small screen channels include iPhone, iPod, and the plethora of other hand-held devices that people are using in their daily lives. I often hear skeptics ask the question, Why would anyone want to watch a film on a small screen? The answer is simple: portability and convenience. When I went to college in Boston, I spent most of my days on the subway going back and forth to school at Emerson College. I usually read books because those were pre-iPod days. If I could have watched movies on the way to film school, I could have saved some study time for sure. When you think of all the people in major cities who commute on subways, buses, airplanes, or folks just waiting in a doctor's office, you can start to see the need for portable entertainment.

Lloyd Kaufman

INTERVIEW BOX

LLOYD KAUFMAN DIRECTOR, PRODUCER

TROMA ENTERTAINMENT

www.troma.com

www.lloydkaufman.com

LLOYD KAUFMAN, entertainment industry veteran, is president of the New York-based production and distribution company Troma Entertainment, the longest-running indie film studio in history, which he and partner Michael Herz founded in 1974 shortly after they graduated from Yale University. In 35 years, Kaufman and Herz have built Troma up to legendary status as a bastion of true independence and a strong consumer

continued on the next page

continued from the previous page

brand through a visionary body of work that has had a huge impact on pop culture and today's mainstream filmmaking. *New York Post* film critic Lou Lumenick recently wrote that Kaufman "has been cited as a major influence by Peter Jackson, Quentin Tarantino and Takashi Miike, among others." Other writers and directors who have cited Kaufman as a major influence include Sam Raimi, James Gunn, Kevin Smith, and Eli Roth, to name a few. In addition, Kaufman has mentored many young independent filmmakers, and Troma movies or releases have given numerous now-famous talent their first start in the film industry, including Trey Parker and Matt Stone, Samuel L. Jackson, Kevin Costner, Oliver Stone, Marisa Tomei, Vincent D'Onofrio, and Jenna Fischer. Other major figures whose first work appears in a Troma film include Robert De Niro, Dustin Hoffman, and Carmen Electra.

Kaufman and Herz created Troma Entertainment with a series of highly original comedies, such as SQUEEZE PLAY!, WAITRESS!, and other titles that served as independent precursors to such later smash hits as NATIONAL LAMPOON'S ANIMAL HOUSE and PORKY'S. In 1984, Kaufman achieved new levels of success with his breakthrough movie THE TOXIC AVENGER, which led to the animated spin-off television series *Toxic Crusaders*, several different comic book titles published by Marvel and Troma's own independent comic book imprint, and three sequels. Its multiplatform success was followed by a string of commercial and artistic triumphs that blended fantasy, heavy action, and comedy in a style that the Cinémathèque Française described as

"Tromatic," including the CLASS OF NUKE 'EM HIGH trilogy, SGT. KABUKIMAN N.Y.P.D., and TROMA'S WAR. Kaufman most recently wrote and directed POULTRYGEIST: NIGHT OF THE CHICKEN DEAD. Kaufman's TROMEO AND JULIET, written with James Gunn, became a theatrical and critical hit, earning the grand prize at the Fanta Festival in Rome and the audience award at Raindance in London, among others.

In 1999, Kaufman founded TromaDance Film Festival in Park City, Utah, now in its 10th year (www.tromadance.com). His popular Make Your Own Damn Movie master classes have been given at universities and venues throughout the world.

In addition, Kaufman has been honored by various international film festivals and Troma retrospectives across the globe, including the San Sebastian Film Festival, the British Film Institute, the Cinémathèque Française, the American Cinematheque, the Chicago International Film Festival, and the UCLA Film Archives. Fluent in French and able to "get around" in Mandarin, he has also served on the boards of Trinity School and

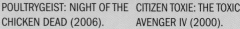

POULTRYGEIST: NIGHT OF THE CHICKEN DEAD (2006).

CITIZEN TOXIE: THE TOXIC AVENGER IV (2000).

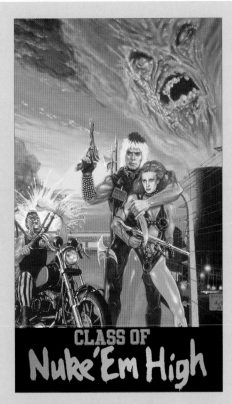

CLASS OF NUKE 'EM HIGH (1986).

Lloyd Kaufman directing on set

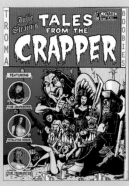

TALES FROM THE CRAPPER (2004)

ECO, the environmental foundation. Kaufman has also made films pro bono for his Yale University class and for Jacques d'Amboise's National Dance Institute. The author of three books, with two additional books in the making, Kaufman is married to Patricia Swinney Kaufman, the New York State Film Commissioner. He is also the elected chairman of the Independent Film & Television Alliance (IFTA), the global trade association of independent distributors and producers of motion picture and television programming.

DRAVEN: *Troma Entertainment is one of the longest-running independent film companies in the* world and has distributed hundreds of films. As a distributor, what do you look for in a film you are considering for distribution?

KAUFMAN: It has to be something that when people go to the movie theater and they know in advance that they may love THE TOXIC AVENGER (1984), or they may hate POULTRYGEIST: NIGHT OF THE CHICKEN DEAD (2006), or they may never forget TROMEO & JULIET (1996), that they will have been on an adventure in the cinema. They feel challenged that they've seen something they've never seen before. They won't be getting baby food or fast food movies. Ninety-nine percent of the films made are formulated baby food, and it's very boring. If it's not baby food, then you have fast food films like SPEED RACER (2008), which like fast food that tastes good going down, but then you immediately get diarrhea. So, we are making movies that people can chew on and have flavor. Our movies are like the jalapeño peppers of the cultural pizza.

DRAVEN: *You have been making films for over 35 years and are among the most influential*

continued on the next page

continued from the previous page

THE TOXIC AVENGER (1984)

independent filmmakers of our time. In retrospect, what are the biggest pitfalls you see new filmmakers make when trying to sell their finished movie?

KAUFMAN: You should do what you believe in and what is in your heart, "To thine own self be true." The mistake most filmmakers encounter is not abiding by the "To thine own self be true" maxim, which as you know was coined by the great William Shakespeare who wrote the best selling book, *101 Money-Making Screenplay Ideas*, otherwise known as *Hamlet.*

Another mistake is that when the movie is finished, some filmmakers feel it's beneath their dignity to go out and whore for their art. They're willing to compromise, and they are willing to copy other filmmakers, or try to make the next TOXIC AVENGER (1984) or the next Quentin Tarantino movie, but then they feel selling is dirty. They don't want to get their hands dirty by getting out there and selling the film.

Picasso was a genius, but he was also a great salesman, promoter, and merchandiser, whereas van Gogh, who was equally brilliant, didn't get involved in promotion. Charlie Chaplin sure as hell promoted and he died a rich man. Buster Keaton didn't get involved in that stuff and he went bankrupt. They both were equally brilliant.

DRAVEN: *What is the best way for a low-budget filmmaker to finance a film?*

KAUFMAN: The best way to get the money to make your own damn movie is to get your own damn script, and one that is really good. I never had the money to hire top-quality writers, so I write my own scripts. A good script equals power and is probably the best way to get mainstream financing.

You must speak to everybody. Tell everybody you know about your movie, even your bus driver. A perfect example is when I was making my first feature called BATTLE OF LOVES RETURN (1971). I was coming out of a movie theater—I think I was seeing STRAP-ON SALLY: PART 6—and I ran into one of my Yale classmates. Instead of exchanging just platitudes, he asked me how I was doing and *what* I was doing. I told him I was making a movie and I need someone to finance it, and bingo, he became my executive producer. If I would have been embarrassed to ask, BATTLE OF LOVES RETURN (1971) would not have happened, which was Oliver Stone's first film as an actor.

My wife and I put up 80 percent of the money for POULTRYGEIST: NIGHT OF THE CHICKEN DEAD (2006). Her retirement money is in that film, but I told her she was investing in TRANSFORMERS: PART 6. Don't tell her.

It's tough for independent filmmakers. I have always been upfront with investors. I have never tried to hoodwink anyone, and I've always told investors that they must be prepared to lose every dime. If you don't say that, then you may get your movie made, but may not get another one made after. So right now a $500,000 movie that is totally independent and distributed independent is very, very questionable whether it will turn a profit. This is because the industry is so consolidated.

DRAVEN: *In our modern times, the tools for making a film—such as affordable digital cameras and post-production on your desktop—has given just about anyone the ability to shoot their own movie. It has also caused a glut in the marketplace. What are some of the things a filmmaker should do before shooting to ensure their film will stand out above the rest?*

KAUFMAN: There is economic blacklisting in the mainstream industry because the media is consolidated and controlled by five or six devil worshiping, international media conglomerates. As a result, the independents are economically blacklisted. We cannot get our films on television in America, unless we come in through one of the vessels of the majors.

There is a trade association—which I was elected chairman of—for independent movie companies called THE INDEPENDENT FILM & TELEVISION MOVIE ALLIANCE. We are the equivalent of MPAA for independents. I ran for chairmanship because the consolidation of the industry has gone too far.

It is very important to maintain neutrality on the Internet. The Internet has to be kept open and free democratically because it's the last democratic medium. The phone companies and major studios are against Net neutrality because they want to get rid of it and want to control the pipes that go into your home. We have to preserve Net neutrality. If that goes, then we have a problem.

DRAVEN: *After reading an article that claimed horror films were dead, you had the idea to combine horror and comedy and THE TOXIC AVENGER (1984) was born. This genre combination has become a popular one. In your experience, what are the key components to have in a horror–comedy?*

KAUFMAN: Peter Jackson and James Gunn and a few others suggested we invent the slapstick–gore movie. This is not a very smart way to go because both horror and comedy ride the back of the bus, and certainly comedy is very subjective. What is funny in New York may not be funny in Hungary, or even Arkansas. You'll reach a much wider audience by *not* combining slapstick satire with horror and gore.

In the case of TROMEO AND JULIET (1996), we mixed eroticism and Shakespeare, horror and slapstick satire. In POULTRYGEIST: NIGHT OF THE CHICKEN DEAD (2006), we took it a bit further. We had singing and dancing along with horror, slapstick, and erotic scenes. What we do is comedy, and comedy is probably the most difficult economically from a distributor's point of view. I don't think there are rules to this game. What you do is what you believe in and what interests you!

DRAVEN: *Is it necessary to have a star in the film for it to be sellable, or are there certain nonactor*

continued on the next page

continued from the previous page

related elements that can be just as valuable to a distributor?

KAUFMAN: Personally, I don't care for stars unless you have three or four who can actually produce ticket sales, and there are very few of them. Stars are useless. In fact, they are a determent. With THE TOXIC AVENGER (1984), we created our own star. Today, without any advertising, he is more famous than probably 99 percent of the young actors who were heavily promoted or started in 1984.

The smart way to make a low-budget independent movie is to aim at some kind of audience. If you put a gun in the movie then people will look at the screen. If it is a monster, then someone will buy a ticket. If you have a vampire, there is an audience for every vampire movie, and they will go to see, buy, or rent it no matter what. So that might be a better backstop than having Stanley Tucci in your film.

The only kind of formulaic advice I would give is to try to have something in your movie that ensures someone will buy tickets.

DRAVEN: *Are film festivals a scam or a necessity?*

KAUFMAN: We setup Tromadance (www.tromadance.com) in 1999 as a reaction against Sundance. We felt that Sundance was exploiting independent filmmakers into sending in their money. A lot have paid entry fees and never even got a "F&%$ You" letter. That is what inspired us for Tromadance. Everything is free. You can submit your movie for free and watch them for free, and there is no VIP policy. It is also during Sundance, so you may see some celebrities and studio executives walking the streets of Park City, Utah. The big film festivals like Sundance, in my opinion, are fixed.

When POLTERGEIST played, the theater was packed. We had one screen in a theater in Manhattan. The week we opened we had the second highest gross in the country on that screen, and the third week, we were replaced by a studio blockbuster that took all the screens in the country. Luckily we found another movie screen, but all your momentum is destroyed if you have to change screens.

RECOMMENDED BOOKS

If you want some more great info on indie moviemaking, read Uncle Lloydie's books. I love them. They are TROMALICIOUS!!

Direct Your Own Damn Movie! Focal Press.
Produce Your Own Damn Movie! Focal Press.

CHAPTER 16
GENERAL DELIVERY REQUIREMENTS

> **Don't give me any money, don't give me any people, but give freedom, and I'll give you a movie that looks gigantic.**
>
> **—ROBERT RODRIGUEZ**

After you've signed a distribution deal, you will be required to deliver the film, which is essentially turning over all materials needed to release and exploit the picture worldwide. In a standard distribution contract, there is a section called a delivery schedule; this is a detailed list of everything you are contractually obligated to deliver to your distributor upon signing, usually within a very short amount of time. It's a big mistake to wait until you sign to begin collecting elements needed to deliver.

It is imperative *before you start shooting* to prepare for future delivery at industry-standard specifications. In the preproduction stage, plan on delivering your film in the highest quality standard you can afford, and never believe the old axiom: "We'll fix it in post." I have delivered many films, both as a filmmaker and also as the owner of a small postproduction company, and the majority of problems I encounter could have been avoided by a more competent crew and production team.

When I was starting out, I knew nothing about delivery and solely focused on getting the movie in the can. I learned through trial and error of battling with distributors. I have compiled a general delivery requirement list based on distribution contracts I've signed and delivery specs for feature films that my postproduction company regularly delivers for independent producers and studios. If you are like most filmmakers and are unsure of who will distribute your film, use the delivery items and specifications I've laid out in this chapter as a guide, and you'll be ahead of the game. However, if you know who will distribute your film, or at least who has a strong interest, you can ask for a sample contract and see all the required delivery items beforehand.

PICTURE & SOUND ITEMS

VIDEO ITEMS

This section details what video masters must be delivered and what specifications are required by the distributor. Keep in mind not all distributors require the same items and specs. There are two types of videotape masters: standard definition (SD) and high definition (HD). For maximum shelf life and to protect your investment, you should always master in HD (e.g., D5, HDCAM, HDCAM SR). By doing so, you will create a universal master, and from this source tape *all* other masters can be created with ease by downconverting[1]. It has also been my experience that having an HD master puts a higher sales value on your film, and it becomes more attractive to a distributor or sales agent.

There are three main video broadcast standards in use around the world: NTSC (National Television System Committee), PAL (Phase Alternating Line), and SECAM (Séquentiel Couleur à Mémoire, or Sequential Color with Memory); the others are small variations of these three. The standard used in North America and many Asian countries, such as Japan, is NTSC. The PAL standard covers most European countries, Australia, and eastern South America. The SECAM standard is mainly used in France for broadcasting, but their DVDs and VHS tapes are PAL. A television or DVD player can only read and display a video designed to support the system standard of that country, otherwise it must be converted.

High Definition (HD) Master

You should deliver one high-definition (HD) master of the feature film and trailer (if available) in the 16×9, 1.78, 1.85, or 2.40 aspect ratio. This master should be scene-to-scene color corrected and conform in all respects to broadcast television standards throughout the world. If the film contains text over action or title sequences, you must include

---

[1] Downconverting is a postproduction process of taking higher resolution source material, such as a high-definition (HD) master, and converting to lower resolution source material, such as a standard definition (SD) master.

a textless version at the tail (the end) of the master. You may, in most cases, also include your trailer at the tail of this master.

The HD master should have the following minimum stereo audio configuration:

Channel 1: LEFT composite mix

Channel 2: RIGHT composite mix

Channel 3: LEFT M&E mix

Channel 4: RIGHT M&E mix

If you are mastering to the HDCAM SR format, you have 12 audio channels, and you can add additional materials to your master, such as a 5.1 mix, audio commentary, or foreign language tracks. For example, this is what I did with the extra channels on my film GHOST MONTH:

Channel 5: Left (L) channel of 5.1 mix

Channel 6: Right (R) channel of 5.1 mix

Channel 7: Center (C) channel of 5.1 mix

Channel 8: Left surround (Ls) channel of 5.1 mix

Channel 9: Right surround (Rs) channel of 5.1 mix

Channel 10: Subwoofer (LFE) channel of 5.1 mix

Channel 11: Left cast commentary mix

Channel 12: Right cast commentary mix

HDCAM SR Mastering Specs There are a variety of HD formats to choose from, but for my film GHOST MONTH, I mastered it to HDCAM SR, 16 × 9, 1.78 aspect ratio, 4:4:4 color space, 1920 × 1080psf, 23.98. All other masters were created from this universal master.

NTSC & PAL Standard Definition Digi Beta Masters (16 × 9)
These masters should be created as a first-generation downconversion from your HD master, if available.

16 × 9 Anamorphic Widescreen (SD 16 × 9 Anamorphic) This master is a standard definition, 16 × 9 anamorphic or squeezed horizontal image, which maintains its full vertical resolution and aspect ratio. It is usually

DELIVERY TIP

Do not make your NTSC and PAL down-conversions until you have passed quality control (QC).

unsqueezed on a 16×9 monitor or DVD player. For standard definition, this is your best tape mastering option.

NTSC & PAL Standard Definition Digi Beta Masters (4×3 Full Frame & 4×3 Letterboxed)

These masters should be created as a first-generation downconversion from your HD master, if available. Your full-frame master should be a pan-and-scan version, or more common for indie producers is a center cut option or letterboxed version. You should check with your distributor to see what is acceptable to them.

Pan & Scan Version (SD 4×3 Full Frame) Pan and scan is a digital process of fitting a widescreen image within the proportions of a standard definition 4:3 (full frame) aspect ratio television screen, often cropping off the sides of the original 16×9 image, and following action to focus on the composition's most important areas to propel the story and still be pleasing to the eye. There are homemade ways of doing this if you are inventive, or you can use Apple's Color software.

Center Cut Version (SD 4×3 Full Frame) This is a process of simply centering the frame to a 4×3 and cutting off the left and right sides. It is important you understand that this is essentially cutting off the ears of your frame. This can be very unattractive if you have not properly composed your shots. If you do this, pay close attention to your shot compositions and titles, both the opening and the end crawl, and make sure they fit into the frame properly.

Letterboxed (SD 4×3 Matted) A letterboxed master is a way of playing a widescreen image inside a 4×3 image area. The resulting image has black bars, or mattes, at the top and bottom of the image.

SOUND ITEMS

Stereo Printmaster
You must deliver a DA88, or timecoded DAT, two-track printmaster. This is simply the final stereo, two-channel mix for the feature film and trailer.

5.1 Surround Sound Printmaster
You must deliver a DA88, six-track (5.1) printmaster. You should configure it in the following format, unless noted otherwise:

Channel 1: Left (L)

Channel 2: Center (C)

DELIVERY TIP

It's important to check with your distributor regarding running time, and make sure your film is not too short or too long. Having a solid 86 to 95 minutes seems to be popular for indie horror films. If your film is too short, don't be a chucklehead and add a 10-minute end credit crawl or other padding. Buyers will notice.

Channel 3: Right (R)

Channel 4: Left surround (Ls)

Channel 5: Right surround (Rs)

Channel 6: Subwoofer (LFE) (Note: The subwoofer channel, or LFE [low frequency effects] is the ".1" in "5.1," which makes up six channels total.)

Channel 7: MOS

Channel 8: MOS

DA88 specs: Master film speed, 23.98, timecode 29.97 nondrop frame (NDF), with a minimum sample rate of 48 Khz, 16 bit resolution, with no noise reduction.

Music & Effects (M&E) Printmaster

You must deliver a DA88, or timecoded DAT, two-track printmaster. This is simply the final stereo M&E, two-channel mix for the feature film and trailer.

This is your entire film and trailer without any dialog or narration, just music and effects. It's imperative you make sure the sound FX and Foley[2] are fully filled. That means in all areas where there is no longer dialog, the sound must not drop out; those areas must be filled with the appropriate Foley or sound effects, and it must be mixed and in perfect sync with the picture. *Do not take this lightly*; your foreign sales depend on it!

5.1 Surround Sound Music & Effects

You must deliver a DA88, six track (5.1) printmaster for the M&E. You should configure it in the following format, unless noted otherwise:

Channel 1: Left (L)

Channel 2: Center (C)

Channel 3: Right (R)

Channel 4: Left surround (Ls)

TIP

Depending on your distributor's requirements, you may be able to do a digital delivery and provide the distributor with the audio printmaster files on a DVD-R in AIF or WAV format. This can save you a bunch of money in mastering costs!

---

[2] Foley is the technical process of replacing sound effects using props to match actors' on-screen movements and actions (e.g., footsteps, clothing moves, fist fights, and so on), usually done by a professional Foley artist on a Foley stage with special floors and props. Or, you can do it yourself!

Channel 5: Right surround (Rs)

Channel 6: Subwoofer (LFE)

Channel 7: Blank

Channel 8: Dialog guide track

DA88 specs: Master film speed, 23.98, timecode 29.97 nondrop frame (NDF), with a minimum sample rate of 48 Khz, 16 bit resolution, with no noise reduction.

Split Tracks Master

This is delivered on a DA88 master. This is usually used for cutdowns, recuts, and, more commonly, trailers. Different types of films have configurations according to their needs, but here is an example from one of my films:

Channel 1: Dialog (left)

Channel 2: Dialog (right)

Channel 3: Effects (left)

Channel 4: Effects (right)

Channel 5: Music (left)

Channel 6: Music (right)

Channel 7: MOS

Channel 8: MOS

TIP

This can also be done as a digital delivery; providing AIF or WAV files is usually acceptable and can save you money!

TRAILER ITEMS

It's a great idea to do your own trailer first, but your distributor will usually do their own trailer with the materials you provide. For example, my film GHOST MONTH had four trailers: a teaser, a trailer I produced, a trailer the sales agent produced, and a final trailer the distributor produced. However, if you have a trailer already you can make a separate trailer master or just put it at the tail of your HD or SD master. You *must* provide your distributor with clean dialog tracks (separate from the mix) so they can cut a new trailer if needed!

EXTRA FEATURES

How many extra features you choose to create is at your discretion, but I can tell you from firsthand experience that the more you have, the better. It's best to create the features yourself instead of letting the distributor have the source materials, and you can maintain your creative freedom this way. You must maintain a high level of quality, so it's best if you shoot all behind-the-scenes footage in HD, especially with affordable HD cameras on the market.

There are many other extra features you can invent, especially with the advent of Blu-ray. Always check with your distributor to coordinate what will be on the disc; there are space limitations. I've never had a distributor complain that I've given them too many extra features.

Behind the Scenes Featurette

A behind-the-scenes featurette is usually a 10- to 20-minute insider's look into the production of the film. It's usually intercut with interviews, still photos, and sometimes has narration. Do not shoot your behind-the-scenes footage with an old camera. There is no excuse these days for not having high quality video footage!

BEHIND THE SCENES VIDEOS (DOWNLOAD)

Visit the book companion website at http://booksite.focalpress.com/companion/Draven/.

Commentary Track

A commentary track is a separate audio track or tracks on a DVD or Blu-ray disc. This is usually with the director, lead cast members, producers, and key crew members. If you record this yourself—which you can easily—make sure you are using professional equipment in a quiet room. If you want your audience to sit through your film with you talking, show the courtesy of recording in a soundproof room with professional equipment. Nothing says amateur like traffic noise, dogs barking, phones ringing, and low audio levels in the commentary tracks. If you have the resources, you should mix the commentary with the film's soundtrack.

TIP

I usually deliver the commentary as a 96k/24 bit high-resolution AIF or WAV digital file that syncs to the start of my master.

Deleted Scenes

This is any deleted scene from your final cut of the picture. A deleted scene could have been cut by the director, producer, distributor, or for rating reasons. They do make great extras if they are interesting and relevant. A word of advice: scenes are usually deleted for a reason, so unless it is a good scene and you have a reason for adding it to the extra features, don't include scenes that are bad just to fill out your extra features list.

Blooper/Gag Reel

When I'm in the editing room, I always keep a bin open for bloopers. These are fun, usually 5- to 10-minute clip reels, and make great extras.

PUBLICITY & ADVERTISING ITEMS

WARNING
Never use frame grabs, which are still images extracted from your raw footage, in place of professionally-shot photos. Frame grabs do not count as color photography stills.

Color Photography – This can be digital or 35mm still photography. It is important to hire a professional photographer to come to the set for photos. You must not hire a friend or family member unless he or she is a professional! Make sure you have a minimum of 200 high-resolution images (at a minimum of 300dpi resolution and usually in TIFF or JPG graphics format) that you can provide on a data disc, CD-R, DVD-R, USB flash drive, or hard drive.

Textless & Texted Artwork – Distributors usually do their own artwork, but if you have existing artwork you should provide it to them for use. This should be provided on a data disc (in a layered .psd Photoshop file) at least 300dpi resolution.

Credit Block – The credit block is a list of all contractual screen and artwork credit obligations as agreed upon with all involved in the production. It is very important you triple check all credits and name spellings and make sure the distributor doesn't release your movie without you approving the credits.

Biographies/Filmographies – You should include a biography and filmography of the principal cast members (I also include head shots), writers, director, producers, and key technical personnel.

Stories/Articles – Provide any relevant stories or articles (e.g., film reviews) that may be useful in marketing the film.

Production Notes/Awards – This is a Microsoft Word document containing any special notes on the production of the picture and special awards the picture has won at film festivals.

Synopsis – This is a summary of the story for your film. You need one brief synopsis, which is usually one paragraph in length, and one long synopsis, which is usually one page in length. It should be a Word document.

Advertising Materials – This consists of all materials available to help the distributor advertise and exploit the film. In the past, I've provided items such as predesigned DVD menus and music, EPKs, and graphic elements (e.g., Photoshop source files) for posters. Sometimes the distributor uses what I give them, sometimes they don't.

DOCUMENTATION

I've met too many producers who can't find their ass with both hands and a roadmap, and they always scramble at the last minute in an attempt to meet a delivery deadline. The film business is not a place to be disorganized or absent minded, and having all your documentation in place is essential. You must be extremely meticulous, and never forget to dot your I's and cross your T's.

There are many things a distributor may ask for that are not on this list, but this is a great place to start.

Combined Continuity & Spotting List (CCSL) – This is a very detailed final dialog, action continuity, and spotting list for the entire film. It usually

CCSL & DIALOG LIST SAMPLES (DOWNLOAD)

You can find the following samples on this book's web site (http://booksite.focalpress.com/companion/Draven/):

Comprehensive CCSL sample (PDF Download)
Simple CCSL sample (PDF Download)
Simple combined continuity sample (PDF Download)
Comprehensive dialog list sample (PDF Download)

Simple dialog list sample (PDF Download)
Comprehensive spotting list sample (PDF Download)

Samples courtesy of:
Line 21 Media Services Ltd.
www.line21cc.com
Da Vinci City Hall provided the original script, and it was produced by Haddock Entertainment, Inc.
www.haddockentertainment.com

contains word-accurate dialog, narration, song vocals, and a timecoded, cut-by-cut description of the film's action conformed exactly to the finished film.

Dialog List – This is simply all the dialog in the film that is conformed to the final picture. There should be no other scene description or exposition included, just the character's name and his or her dialog exactly as spoken, word for word, in the edited film. This is used for translating your film into other languages. This should be delivered as a Word document.

Literary Materials – Include a printed and digital copy of the screenplay (Final Draft file, Word or PDF formats) and a paper copy of the final lined shooting script of the picture, if available.

Music Cue Sheet – This is a document the composer will provide you detailing the particulars of all music cues contained in the film. This document includes the title of each composition, the names of composers, publishers, copyright owners, usages (e.g., instrumental, instrumental–visual, vocal, vocal–visual, etc.), performing rights society (e.g., ASCAP,

MUSIC CUE SHEET SAMPLE (DOWNLOAD)

** Web file: WEB-Music_Cue_Sheet_Sample.pdf

BMI, SESAC), and detailed timecoded references and running times for each cue. It is important that this is accurate and submitted on delivery to ensure the composer and publishing company will receive due royalties if the film is broadcast on television.

Composer Agreement & Sync License – This is a fully-executed contract for services of the film composer and the sync license from the publisher.

Credit Statement – This is a statement of credits you are contractually obligated to accord on screen.

Screen Credit Requirements – This is a list of the main and end credits of the film.

Cast List & Crew List – This is a list indicating the name of the character portrayed by each cast member and the cast members' contact information. The crew list includes all technical personnel, job titles, and contact information.

MPAA Rating Certificate – Include a certificate from the Motion Picture Association of America (MPAA). I usually have the distributor pay for this because it is expensive. Horror films are mostly rated R, so if your film is very extreme you may find yourself editing out any obscene material to get the rating. This isn't always required, and sometimes the unrated versions are more marketable on DVD.

MPAA Title Registration – You must provide evidence that the title of the film has been registered under the rules of the MPAA Title Registration Bureau.

Certificate of Origin – This is a document that states where you made the film, the production company's name, the running time, and the director's name. This document usually needs to be notarized, and you will need multiple original copies.

Copyright Registration – You should register your original screenplay (before shooting!) and your final finished feature film with the Library of Congress (before sending it out!).

Short Form Assignment – This document contains the minimum amount of information necessary to transfer the distribution rights.

Chain of Title – This is a document evidencing your right to produce, distribute, and exploit the film. It's proof that you own the film.

Errors & Omissions Insurance (E&O) – E&O insurance will cover the film against copyright infringement. This is usually a prerequisite for film distribution, and it is usually best to purchase this insurance before principal photography. I usually have the distributor pay for this because it is very expensive. It can cost $5,000 or more!

Copyright Report – The is a report on the copyright for the film and helps identify the legal ownership. It's a common requirement for E&O insurance.

Title Report – This report is a thorough search of prior uses of your title as well as other similar or closely related titles. It helps to alert you to any possible legal problems with the title you've chosen. It's a common requirement for E&O insurance.

Title Opinion – The title opinion document is done by a lawyer. They offer their legal opinion based on the title report information. It is usually required for E&O insurance.

Script Clearance Report – This is a report done with the goal of identifying all elements in a script that may expose a production to legal disputes, such as character names, business names, product names, trademarks, and so on. It is required for E&O insurance to minimize risk of legal claims.

Laboratory Access Letter – This is simply a letter granting access to the lab for masters and elements relating to your film.

Quality Control (QC) Report – Provide a recent and approved QC report from an experienced lab that does QC on a regular basis.

QUALITY CONTROL (QC): THE FINAL HURDLE

Quality control, or QC, is the postproduction process of putting your master through a stringent check to make sure you meet broadcast and quality standards. A QC operator, who has a reputation of being the enemy of low-budget filmmakers, watches and listens to your entire film and scrutinizes it, so this process is very subjective. What may be okay for one operator may not be for another. It is the operator's job to find problems and grade them based on severity, usually on a scale of 1 to 5. There are a lot of things that can flag your QC report, such as boom mics in the shot, film dirt and scratches, digital artifacts, audio peaks and hissing, lip sync, crushed whites and blacks, excessive grain, and even misspellings in the credits.

After QC is completed, you are given a very detailed QC report from the lab for your specific HD or SD master. There are only two possible outcomes for QC reports: pass or fail. I see a lot of independent filmmakers fail, and fail badly, usually due to amateur equipment and production methods. An HD QC session is even more demanding because everything is now bigger and cleaner, and these labs love to justify their paycheck. I had an experience recently where my film passed an HD QC at one reputable lab in Burbank, California with flying colors—a post job well done. However, when the film sold to a territory, the buyer wanted the film re-QCed at *a lab of their choice.* Well, we failed. I tried to fight it, but we had to make the fixes to complete the sale. Fortunately, the fixes were minor, but it cost us another $2,000.

I can tell you there are a lot of distributors out there who will not touch your movie without a passed QC report. The reason is because it's hard to sell a product that is faulty or not up to standards. Unless you are planning on self-distribution and free handouts, this is a *serious*

WARNING
Germany is the toughest country for QC. Watch out!

hurdle to overcome on your way to worldwide sales and distribution. You should keep your standards high starting in the preproduction stage, and use a top lab to get it done right the first time. QC fixes are very expensive!

NEGOTIATING WITH DISTRIBUTORS ON DELIVERY

Distributors will ask a lot from you, but remember: before you sign the dotted line, you must be certain you can deliver each element required on the delivery schedule portion of the contract. After you sign, you are contractually obligated to deliver, and if you don't know what you promised and how much it costs, you will find yourself at the bank asking for a loan (I see this happen way too much!). I always negotiate. Remember, just because they ask for it doesn't mean you must deliver it, or at least in the way they ask for it. You can save money by doing a digital delivery for some items on a hard drive or data disc, but you need to work this out first with your distributor.

WATCH OUT FOR HIGH LAB COSTS ON DELIVERY

In most cases you will be responsible for all the delivery costs for items in the contract, and believe me they quickly add up to thousands of dollars. If a distributor needs additional materials that are not listed, they may pay for the costs and retain the amount spent against the film's eventual profits. I recommend paying for as many items as you can upfront to avoid distributors' high lab costs. This way you can negotiate the best deal with the lab yourself, and you know exactly how much everything costs. The more things you can do yourself, the more you will save on delivery and the less the distributor can withhold from your profits.

REMEMBER
If you want to sell *your film it must be* deliverable!

CREATE AN ATTRACTIVE PRODUCT

If you have all these elements ready, it's attractive to distributors and sales agents. It shows you are a professional, and they will champion you for your diligence. You must not procrastinate, and you must be able to deliver fast. The sooner you can deliver, the sooner they can sell, and the sooner you can make another film with your profits!

CHAPTER 17
HORROR FILM FESTIVALS

> **❝ Cinema should make you forget you are sitting in a theater. ❞**
> —ROMAN POLANSKI

Now that your film is completed, it's time to hit the horror genre festival circuit. After all, this is why we make films to begin with, so people can see our work. These fiendish fests are the most popular in October. The audiences and filmmakers who attend these events usually know their genre well and are voracious for a great horror flick. You need to get exposure and create a buzz around your film to ignite the interest of a distributor or sales agent. It is also a great way to get genre press coverage, both online and print.

FESTIVAL CREDIBILITY: CHECK BEFORE YOU SUBMIT!

From my personal experience and having spent thousands of dollars on submission fees, postage, and raw materials, there seems to be a lot of film festivals that are scams or unprofessional backyard operations. I have written checks to festivals that didn't have the professional courtesy to provide me with a rejection letter or email but were quick to cash my check. Others turned out to be held in VFW halls or backyard barbeques. Don't make the mistake of sending your film to as many festivals as possible and then waiting in front of your email box to see who accepts it. You must do your homework and target the best ones, especially the genre-specific ones. These are the questions I always ask before I submit:

1. How many years has the festival been in operation?

2. What companies are sponsoring the festival?

3. Who are the celebrity guests?

4. What is the venue and what projection systems are they using?

5. How many days is the festival?

6. What is the festival's programming history, and have they played independent films that are similar in content and budget level as my film?

7. Does the festival have any censorship rules?

If all those questions cannot be answered to your satisfaction, save your money for your next movie! Always choose the festival you want your film to play at, don't let them choose you. You're the filmmaker, and without you and your film, there is no festival.

SUBMIT EARLY & SAVE

In our busy lives it's easy to procrastinate, but in the world of film festivals early submissions save money. However, don't submit too early, especially if your film is still in postproduction. You should never submit a work-in-progress film for consideration, even if the festival rules say it is okay.

Actor Andre "Chyna" McCoy, actor Rick Irvin, actress Shirley To, and producer/composer Jojo Draven at a film festival in Los Angeles supporting GHOST MONTH.

I have done this several times and wasted hundreds of dollars in submission fees, and I regret it. I once submitted the trailer and the first 20 minutes of my feature film in progress to meet an entry deadline. I assumed they could see from the trailer and the first few scenes how cool it was for the festival—dumb idea. It's really ridiculous to send an unfinished work of any kind to a panel of judges and assume they will understand that the music is only temporary, the bad audio will be fixed in the mix, the sound FX are missing but coming soon, and the CGI killer dolls will be in place before the festival opens.

PRESS KITS TO DIE FOR

Press kits are promotional booklets for a film that are submitted to the festival with your entry form or upon their request. It's like a sales brochure promoting and informing people about your project. This can be done as a traditional hard copy press kit or an electronic press kit (EPK), or both. EPKs are a popular and preferred method when submitting online—using a popular service like Withoutabox.com—but I always do both. My hard copy and EPK versions for my films always contain the following:

1. **Cover sheet:** This should contain the title logo, production company, director, writer, star actors (if any), and contact information for you or the person representing your film.

2. **One-sheet artwork:** You need to have artwork for your film, even if it's only temporary. This is crucial, especially in the horror genre.

3. **Synopsis:** This should be one concise description of the plot of your film and should be no longer than one page.

4. **Cast and crew information:** You should list your lead actors and include their minibiography and a brief filmography. For the crew you should include the producer, director, writer, cinematographer, makeup FX artist, composer, and any other notable person with credits worth mentioning. This should only be one page, and don't be modest!

5. **Statement of the director:** The director's statement is a short statement that explains why you made the film and your vision, but this is usually optional.

6. **News and media coverage:** You should include any news, press, or reviews for your film and always highlight the best first.

7. **Technical information:** This is a technical description of your film and should include things such as shooting format (35mm, 16mm, digital), aspect ratio (16×9, 4×3), sound format (5.1, stereo), running time, language, and MPAA rating, if applicable.

8. **Production still photos:** These can be color or black and white images and should be professionally shot.

9. **Production notes:** You should mention anything you think is noteworthy about the production in this section. If you are telling a story about how you shot the ending of your film on your uncle's farm during a tornado, that is not worth mentioning!

10. **Trailer DVD and online version:** You must have a trailer ready for your film before you submit. I always have a separate DVD and an online version.

The items you should include may be different from film to film, so you should always check with the festival and review their guidelines before submitting. It's important to present this kit in the most professional way possible and always check for grammatical errors and spelling.

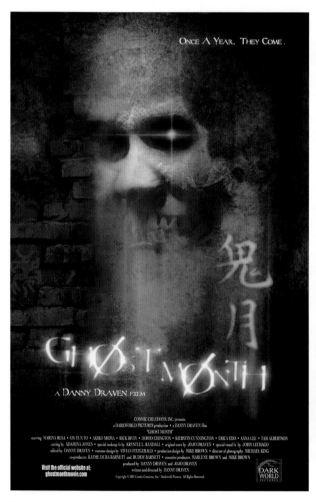

Festival flyer for GHOST MONTH (front).

Festival flyer for GHOST MONTH (back).

You only get one chance to impress, so don't be modest, but don't be pretentious either and claim your film is "the most disturbing film ever made," or "the next chapter in horror," or other hackneyed phrases. Leave that to your distributor.

SUBMITTING ONLINE

Withoutabox.com is an online service that saves you time and money by organizing all your festival submissions in one place. It is the preferred way to submit to festivals online. You can create your electronic press kit, include a trailer and video clips, and track your submission status from your own account. There are tens of thousands of people in 80 countries that use the system, and Withoutabox.com also sends you regular email updates on new festivals. It's also *free*! I use this service for all my online submissions and it really is fantastic—I don't get paid to say that.

Withoutabox.com

PROMOTE YOUR FILM

Film festivals do their own promotion to get as many people to attend as possible, but you also need to help them fill the seats. You need to tell *everyone* you know and enlist the cast, crew, and all your friends to promote! It's also smart to create your own full-color flyers promoting your film at the festival; the flyers should be complete with date, screening time, address, and directions. Keep in mind that most strangers you invite will probably not show up, especially in Los Angeles where a yes is usually a no, so you must campaign for your film even harder to pack the house. If you don't want to promote, imagine yourself sitting in a theater with 10 people, a few cast members, and your mom. Embarrassing, isn't it?

The premiere of DEATHBED and DAHMER at the Palace theater in downtown Los Angeles.

THE ACCOLADES OF HORROR

Don't Be a Sore Loser or Arrogant Winner! – Not everyone will win an award at a festival, and if that person is you, don't get angry or feel like you deserved it more than the others. I've overheard conversations at festivals of jealous competitors trashing the movies that won while they are still in the lobby. I've seen movies sweep up all the awards but never get distribution or go with a bum company. I've seen people who win and ignore everyone else the rest of the night as they all congratulate one another profusely. I like to think all the movies are judged fairly and unbiased—and I think most are—but nepotism and favoritism in this business is real, so prepare yourself.

It is a very rewarding experience when you win an award of any kind, especially without bribing or sleeping with anyone. Winning an award certainly adds marketing value and credibility to your film. It lets a potential buyer know that it was good enough to be selected and recognized by your peers as exceptional. When a distributor puts a campaign together, they will advertise your film as award-winning, and you'll see the festival wreaths on your box cover. Even if you don't win, just getting accepted as an official selection is a bonus and should be exploited. However, keep your ego in check and don't believe your own hype.

Best director award for GHOST MONTH.   Best cinematography award for GHOST MONTH.   Official selection for GHOST MONTH.

NETWORKING & SCHMOOZING

Film festivals are just that—festivals. They're an organized series of movies to celebrate the art of filmmaking. It's not a festival that is only about *your* movie. It's not a wrap party, either. I have seen a lot of filmmakers only attend the festival 10 minutes before their film screens, leave without staying for tea, then return during the award ceremony to claim their certain victory. Those filmmakers have no tact. You should have respect for your colleagues and take an interest in other people's work and stories and hopefully make lasting connections for future endeavors.

A horror film festival is a lot of fun because the participants are usually fans of the genre, so immediately you have something in common. I have met future investors, producers, reviewers, actors, people who owe me money, and fans asking me to sign movies from years ago at these festivals. Never underestimate any person you meet. Bring a stack of business cards, and make sure you don't leave until you've handed them all out. You should attend the parties and participate in the Q&A panels. Be personable, polite, and respectful to other people's projects and you'll be just fine. Have fun. Don't be a self-absorbed chucklehead.

FILM FESTIVAL NIGHTMARES

Quality Control & Protecting Your Presentation – One of the most embarrassing moments of my life was at a film festival. I was screening my new movie for the first time at a supposedly prestigious theater, and the cast, crew, and my friends and family were in attendance. As the theater filled and the lights dimmed, I was horrified when the projectionist rewound the first 10 minutes of my film in front of the audience. After that insult, the film began and I wanted to scream when I saw the image was no longer pristine because it was being projected by archaic, uncalibrated equipment. The result was a very ugly, muddy, and washed out image on-screen. I spent the entire time seeing 2 years of work being presented to my peers in a disastrous manner. During the film, I tracked down the projectionist and complained. He then proceeded to adjust the brightness, contrast, and volume during a dramatic sequence! This cost me my pride and probably an immediate distribution deal.

For the audience's sake and your own, you *must* be selective about how your movie is exhibited, both visually and aurally. Unless you are screening a film print, festivals will most likely project your film from a VHS (don't do this!), DVD-R, miniDV, DVCAM, or Digi Beta tape in standard stereo. That is fine if their equipment is top notch, but keep in mind that any time you take a standard definition source and project it onto a 10- to 20-foot screen, you will notice a considerable quality drop. It will no longer be as beautiful and pristine as it was on your home TV, especially when the projection equipment is something out of antiquity. For maximum quality, always screen from a film print or an HD source with 5.1 surround sound. The projection system must be capable of HD input/output. I recommend showing your film off a Blu-ray disc (BD-R), HDCAM, or HDCAM SR master, or even an HD QuickTime movie output directly from a hard drive to an HD projector. This works fabulously.

AUDIENCE REACTIONS – A film festival is the perfect place to watch your film for the first time with a live audience of strangers to observe their reactions. When I screen my movies at festivals, I don't watch the film; I know it better than anyone. I watch the people. I look around and notice everything and everyone. Do people laugh where they are supposed to laugh? Do they jump at the right moments? Is anyone texting or checking email on their cell phone? Using the film festival as a test screening is also a great opportunity to decide on final editorial changes based on observations and constructive feedback from your colleagues.

LIST OF HORROR FILM FESTIVALS (DOWNLOAD)

Visit the companion web site at http://booksite.focalpress.com/companion/Draven.

INTERVIEW BOX

ANDREA BEESLEY-BROWN FESTIVAL DIRECTOR,
International Horror & Sci-Fi Film Festival

Actress Adrienne King (FRIDAY THE 13TH) and festival director Andrea Beesley-Brown. Photo Credit: Bradley Thornber (2008)

www.horrorscifi.com

Founded in 2004 by Brian Pulido and the Phoenix Film Foundation, the International Horror & Sci-Fi Film Festival is Arizona's premier genre film festival highlighting new and classic horror and sci-fi films from around the globe. Produced mostly by volunteer staff, it runs in October annually and awards filmmakers who excel in the genres of horror and sci-fi as well as celebrating cult classics and new releases.

DRAVEN: *What are the common mistakes you see filmmakers make when submitting to a film festival?*

BEESLEY-BROWN: Presentation. It's not necessarily the thing that we take into

continued on the next page

continued from the previous page

consideration the most, but we do like to look at the whole package of the film, the press kit, how thorough the submission is and its overall presentation.

DRAVEN: *Once accepted to the festival, what should all filmmakers have ready and why?*

BEESLEY-BROWN: Filmmakers should have their media materials ready. For our festival we are able to promote the films heavily in advance through print media (posters, postcards) on display at the venue and also should have a trailer available to upload online to our web site and begin the online promotion engine.

DRAVEN: *What does the festival look for in a horror film in order to be accepted to the festival?*

BEESLEY-BROWN: Originality and ingenuity in the script. We look for innovative storytelling and a strong horror narrative. Films that will thrill, scare, and haunt the viewer in a way that they haven't seen before.

Film critic Craig Outhier and actor Jeffrey Combs (RE-ANIMATOR) doing a Q&A.
Photo Credit: Bradley Thornber (2008).

DRAVEN: *Can you give us a glimpse of how the judging process works, and what criteria may be used to determine the winners?*

BEESLEY-BROWN: Each film is reviewed in full twice by members of our viewing committee. After that, the top films are forwarded to the program directors of each genre to consider and make the final choices. Every film submitted is watched at least twice, and many others are viewed three or four times.

DRAVEN: *Do film acquisitions executives lurk in the audiences at your festival, or is it mainly horror and sci-fi fans?*

BEESLEY-BROWN: With our festival, I would say a strong majority of the audience are horror and sci-fi fans; however, on occasions we will have acquisition executives from various distribution companies, not lurk but openly network with filmmakers.

DRAVEN: *Do the winners of awards from festivals like yours, who then display "Best Picture" or "Best Actor" on the box art usually help the film in terms of sales or finding distribution?*

BEESLEY-BROWN: We hope so! As our festival grows and gains notoriety each year, our hope is that award winners can use their accolades to further their film's sales and distribution chances.

DRAVEN: *There seems to be a never-ending list of genre film festivals emerging every year. A low-budget filmmaker can spend thousands in expensive submission fess and press kits just trying to get accepted. What criteria can filmmakers use to judge the quality of a film festival and make sure it's not a backyard operation?*

BEESLEY-BROWN: I would suggest filmmakers do their research on the founders and organizers of the event. Do they have legitimate and ample experience? What guests have they worked with (as far as talent)? Communicate with previous filmmakers who have attended and get their feedback. What studio films are they showing, and how long have they been in operation?

DRAVEN: *What is a press kit, and why is it important for a film festival?*

BEESLEY-BROWN: A press kit is a visual and tangible advertisement of the film, and it is very important. Since the filmmaker isn't able to submit their film in person, they need to make an impact on the judge immediately. With snappy graphics, a solid letter, trailer DVD and professional photos, a press kit can instantly grasp the attention of a judge who has hundreds of submissions to review.

DRAVEN: *What is your advice for a filmmaker who wants to network at the festival?*

BEESLEY-BROWN: Bring business cards and a smile! Take all the opportunities that you can to mix and mingle at parties, Q&A sessions, with fans and festival organizers. What better way to promote your product than to be an active part of the festival?

DRAVEN: *Does a film with a star or a higher production budget get priority over microbudget productions?*

BEESLEY-BROWN: We program the best films, period. We want to provide our audiences with the best quality out there disregarding the filmmaker's budget. Many times, the big-budget movies will get blown away by a small film with a great story. Therefore, lower budget films with more powerful acting and narrative will often prevail.

CHAPTER 18

SELF-PROMOTION & MARKETING

> **❝ Searchers after horror haunt strange, far places. ❞**
>
> **—H. P. LOVECRAFT**

There is an old philosophical riddle: if a tree falls in a forest with no one to hear it, then does it make a sound? It's a perplexing question. It seems obvious that of course it makes a sound, but what is sound other than energy stimulating your eardrums and your brain interpreting it as sound? Sound is only sound if there is someone there to hear it, and if no one is there to see, hear, touch, or smell the tree, then how could its existence occur?

I have always thought of self-promotion and marketing this way. It has forced me to roll up my sleeves and make a sound that someone will hear. You must make a sound in the forest of the film world, which is already overcrowded, otherwise there will be no one there to hear you, or in this case see your film! After all, this is why we make films, for them to be seen (and heard!) by as many people as possible.

I know this may seem obvious, but make sure your film is ready to be promoted first. You don't want to promote a product you haven't shot yet or that is still in postproduction. It's best to wait until you are completely done and ready to deliver before you unveil your project to the world. In the horror business you must strike while the iron is hot.

INTERNET MARKETING

The key to successful Internet marketing is to get your film in front of the right group of people, and in this case it's horror fans. If you Google any horror-themed subject, you immediately get thousands of web sites, message boards, chat rooms, blogs, and so on. It seems endless. So where do you start? I always start at the top sites and work my way down from there. In general, you need to congregate where they do, advertise where they lurk, and entice them to see your film any way you can. The Internet has opened a worldwide portal for independents to be seen, and your computer is your access to the world stage. So, let's get started.

IMDb.com

The IMDb (Internet Movie Database) is the premiere place to find out about any person or movie in the business and beyond. It's both a blessing and a curse for filmmakers.

First and foremost, make sure you enter your movie data and photos into the IMDb yourself. It's vital to make sure the information is accurate and doesn't give away too much private information about your film. I have had nightmares with information being posted by crew members, cast, and even fans who leak confidential information. It's crucial not to post any information that you may later want to change. The IMDb, and the information that is posted, can ruin you and your film. The IMDb has never retracted information I've requested. You should control your flow of information as much as possible.

SOCIAL NETWORKING SITES

Social networking web sites are where you can interact with people who have similar interests as you. You should create a dedicated page just for your film. Usually, you set up an account or profile, upload videos, audio, and pictures, and start networking and marketing. It's as simple as that.

MySpace.com

By now everyone has heard of MySpace, and for good reasons. MySpace has a special free account especially for filmmakers, which allows you to upload videos, photos, have a blog, and add friends to your profile, who can post comments.

Facebook.com

This is a free social networking web site. You can upload pictures and video. It's a fact that studios, such as Miramax and Warner Bros., even use it to promote films.

FearNet.com

FearNet.com is a multiplatform horror network on the Internet. They have over 125,000 registered users who participate in horror-themed chats, blogs, and community services online. You can create your own account and upload videos (trailers!), photos (artwork!), and much more. This is a fantastic way to get direct exposure to horror fans!

FearNet.com

Other Social Networking Resources

- Friendster.com
- Bebo.com
- Flickr.com

Blogs & Social Bookmarking Resources

- WordPress.org
- CreateBlog.com

- Blogger.com

- LiveJournal.com

- MovableType.net

- Digg.com

- reddit.com

- StumbleUpon.com

VIDEO SHARING SITES

To promote your film, you need to get your trailer on every video web site you can muster. Before you do so, it's important to tag the end of your trailer with a web site plug; otherwise, your trailer may filter through the Internet but leave people without a place to get more information on your film.

YouTube.com

YouTube is a leader in online video sharing. YouTube allows users to share videos across the Internet through web sites, mobile devices (e.g., iPhone), blogs, and email. You can create your own channel and upload your trailer and clips to promote your film and link the video in a variety of mediums.

Metacafe.com

This is a community-based video sharing web site that specializes in short-form, original entertainment. It's a great place to upload your trailer and get it seen and rated. They have a program called Producer Rewards where content creators get paid for original content based on views and ratings.

Revver.com

This is an online media network that supports free and unlimited sharing of media. They pair videos with targeted ads and track them as they spread across the Internet. They serve millions of videos a month to a wide audience, and they also share the advertising revenue with you.

HULU.com

Hulu is an online video service that allows users to enjoy great videos on Hulu.com and on 35 other popular Web sites across the Web. Hulu videos are available on AOL, IMDb, MSN, MySpace, and Yahoo! in the U.S. as well as a growing network of personal blogs, fan sites, and other Web sites where users choose to embed the Hulu video player.

Other Video Sharing Resources

- GUBA.com

- SPIKE.com

- Vimeo.com

- Veoh.com

- blip.tv

- iklipz.com

- Video.Google.com

- Video.Yahoo.com

- Video.AOL.com

- FearNet.com

- Openfilm.com

MAILING LISTS

When you are self-distributing, email mailing lists are gold. This keeps you in personal communication with your own fan base, which you'll need to build over time. Sometimes you can partner with web sites, companies, or individuals who have large email lists or web traffic to help promote your film. If you can gain access to large email lists targeted at horror fans, this is ideal.

ONLINE PRESS RELEASES

When you are ready to tell the world about your film, it's a good idea to send out a highly visible press release that will get placed in all the important news sources on the Internet. A fantastic way to do this is to use a news and press release distribution service like PRWeb.com. They do charge a fee, but it's worth it.

HORROR MOVIE WEB SITE

An independent film, no matter what the budget, needs a web site. The web site can be as simple or as elaborate as you wish, and these days it is inexpensive to create one. This site acts as a representative of your film to the entire world, and that's exactly how you should think of it.

It's important to feature all the important elements of your film and keep the site up to date at all times. I have been randomly contacted by distributors, producers, reviewers, and foreign buyers through my movie web site more than any other method.

HORROR MOVIE WEB SITE CHECKLIST

1. THE DOMAIN NAME – You need an easy-to-remember domain name dedicated to your film. You can register your domain name at places such as Register.com or GoDaddy.com

The official GHOST MONTH movie web site main menu (www.ghostmonthmovie.com)

2. THE HOSTING SERVICE – You must choose a hosting service that can handle high traffic and video content with no problems.

3. TRAILER – I like to make available small, medium, large, HD, and iPhone/iPod versions of all trailers.

4. ARTWORK AND STILLS GALLERY – It's always great to have plenty of artwork and stills from the film available for press reasons.

5. MOVIE CLIPS – Chose some clips from your film, but don't give away too much of the story.

6. PRESS KIT – You should have an easy to download press kit available at all times.

7. MOVIE STATUS – It's good to mention what rights are sold and what territories are still available. Any DVD release dates or purchasing information should be posted.

8. CONTACT INFORMATION – You must have this in a visible spot. Be professional, and make sure all your business correspondence is with your email address for your movie (e.g., lastname@ yourmoviename.com).

9. SEARCH ENGINE/LINK PAGE SUBMISSIONS – You must submit your new domain name to all the major search engines. There are specialty horror search engines such as HorrorFind.com, Cryptcrawl.com, Horror.net, and EverythingScary. com. There are thousands of horror-themed web sites on the Internet; you should get posted on as many link pages as you can. Roll up your sleeves!

SCARY MERCHANDISE

I always create as much merchandise as possible, usually just to give away. The more people you can give pens, hats, shirts, stickers, and other creative things to, the better. People are walking billboards, and everyone loves to get something free! You never know where merchandise may end up. For example, for my ultralow-budget film DARKWALKER (2003), producer Chuck Williams licensed the rights to Bump In The Night Productions to create the DARKWALKER Halloween mask. The mask has since been featured in the Universal Studios hit film KNOCKED UP (2007) and then again on *The Girls Next Door* (2008) in the episode "Scream Test" on E! Channel. See what I mean?

The official DARKWALKER mask.
Sculpted by Chuck Jarman
(www.bumpinthenightproductions.com)

The official DARKWALKER soundtrack CD.
Music by Jojo Draven (www.jojodraven.com)

The DARKWALKER trading card.
Terror Cards by Previn Wong (www.TerrorCards.com)

PROMOTIONAL SCREENINGS

It's a great idea to have your own special screening of the film. You should invite as many industry people (especially distributors, producer reps, and sales agents) to the event as possible. They may or may not show up because most like to screen on a DVD at their office, but it doesn't hurt to ask. It's always professional to screen it at the best place you can afford, with drinks and finger foods for guests, as well as plenty of hand-outs with your movie's information on it.

I have also taken the opportunity at film festivals/screenings to shoot audience reactions after the film is over. It's a man-on-the-street style interview. I then use the footage to help create a buzz or use in a promo video for sales. Leave your parents at home for this one, and ask permission before you stick a camera in someone's face.

HORROR CONVENTIONS & SPECIAL EVENTS

Horror movies have a loyal audience; they always have. It amazes me the amount of horror conventions that pop up every year and the established ones that keep chugging along. This is a great way to promote your film directly to the fans. You can get your own table or booth and hand out flyers, pens, T-shirts, and have the cast in attendance. You can also screen your film at some of these events. I have also met several distributors this way who seem to comb these events looking for product to release.

HORROR CONVENTIONS LIST (DOWNLOAD)

web file: Horror_Conventions_Listing.pdf

HORROR FILM REVIEWS

Everyone's a critic, so it's not hard to get your indie horror film reviewed these days. There are countless online reviewers and some fantastic horror magazines on the market, although the latter usually prefer movies that have studio distribution.

The point of getting a review is to hopefully get one that is good enough to use quotes for marketing and promoting your film. It is very popular to place quotes on the final box art, especially if the person, magazine, or reviewer is well-known. For example, on the cover of my film GHOST MONTH, they used the quote: "The GRUDGE meets THE HAUNTING IN CONNECTICUT in this terrifying supernatural shocker!" —Stuart Alson, Independent Film Quarterly.

There are good reviews and bad ones for all films, no matter how well done the film is, but you can't please everyone. It's true that because you are making a low-budget film, you're more of a target for critical reviews, whether it's technical or performance related, or they just don't like you personally. I'm no stranger to personal attacks, but sometimes a reviewer's invective overshadows their journalism, or lack of it. For example, one chucklehead said of one of my really early films: "I'd love to see Danny Draven suplexed into a swimming pool full of Vietnamise [yes, he spelled it wrong] Bird Eating Tarantulas…" My point is not to take anything personally, especially from people who can't write or spell check, like this guy. We live in a world where everyone has a voice and opinion through the Internet, and when you put your movie out into the world, you're game. At the end of the day you must choose the people you want to review your film; don't send it to just anyone. You can judge your success by the quality of the people who review your film.

Like the riddle of the tree, it's up to you to make sure people are in the proverbial forest as the tree falls and that they experience the event with all their senses. I spend a lot of time promoting my films, and I usually have studio distribution, but they seem to always do the bare minimum. It's a lot of hard work and time consuming, but if you can dedicate a certain amount of time to your film each week promoting and marketing it, you'll see it pay off in the long run. In independent filmmaking, I have always had the philosophy that the best help is always self-help.

Horror producer/director Charles Band takes promoting his products to the road with his Full Moon Horror Road Show, which he does yearly. For more info go to: www.fullmoonroadshow.com

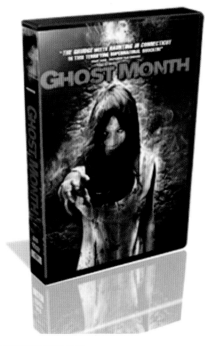

GHOST MONTH DVD.
Image courtesy of North American Motion Pictures

THE TOP HORROR MAGAZINES TO REVIEW YOUR FILM

Fangoria magazine
fangoriaonline.com

Rue Morgue magazine
rue-morgue.com

GoreZone magazine
gorezone.co.uk

VideoScope magazine
videoscopemag.com

HorrorHound magazine
horrorhound.com

HORROR MAGAZINE & WEB SITE LIST (DOWNLOAD)

web file: Horror_Magazine_Listing.pdf

INTERVIEW BOX

HERSCHELL GORDON LEWIS DIRECTOR
"The Godfather of Gore"

Herschell Gordon Lewis

www.herschellgordonlewis.com

HERSCHELL GORDON LEWIS—The incredibly popular, violent horror films of recent decades, such as TEXAS CHAINSAW MASSACRE, FRIDAY THE 13TH, and A NIGHTMARE ON ELM STREET, owe much of their existence to the undisputed Godfather of Gore, Herschell Gordon Lewis. In 1963, Lewis, with his monumental splatter movie BLOOD FEAST, single-handedly changed the face of horror cinema forever. As well as virtually inventing the gore generation, Lewis also produced a number of exploitation movies, as well as sampling the full gamut of exploitation subjects ranging from wife swapping and ESP to rock 'n' roll and LSD. A TASTE OF BLOOD (1967) details all these, plus gore classics such as TWO THOUSAND MANIACS (1964), THE GORE GORE GIRLS (1972), COLOR ME BLOOD RED (1965), and THE WIZARD OF GORE (1970), placing them in context amid the roots and development of the exploitation film.

DRAVEN: *Your film BLOOD FEAST (1963) is generally recognized as the first splatter film. In modern times, we have computers to help us do digital gore FX and make deaths even more realistic to the eye. In the gross-out wars of Hollywood, have you ever felt that filmmakers go too far?*

LEWIS: On the contrary, I feel they don't go far enough. Too many splatter films are derivative. We get the feeling we're watching the same tired effects over and over again. More to a negative point, these offerings are humorless. Ugh.

continued on the next page

continued from the previous page

DRAVEN: *There are a lot of movies being made for little money but generating high returns because of great titles, trailers, art campaigns, and concepts. What are the three most important elements in a horror movie marketing campaign, and why?*

LEWIS: The three most important elements: (1) showmanship on the level of P. T. Barnum, (2) promise of an experience the moviegoer hasn't ever enjoyed before, (3) wording that maximizes the relationship between producer and viewer.

DRAVEN: *What is it in the human psyche that attracts people to violent films, and is this a good or a bad thing?*

Herschell Gordon Lewis directing on set.

LEWIS: Bloodlust is implicit in the human psyche. Psychologists have proved over and over again that being able to satisfy that bloodlust as a spectator is a powerful preventive against the need to satisfy bloodlust by aggressive action.

DRAVEN: *What are your thoughts on the state of the horror genre today? Is it better or worse than when you were making films?*

LEWIS: Since I intend to make another movie, I'd say, competitively, it's worse. Imagination seems to have gone the way of all flesh.

DRAVEN: *What is your advice for independent filmmakers trying to self-distribute and market their movies online?*

LEWIS: Before you make that first phone call or send that first email, be positive you have an adequate answer to the self-question: Do I have a salable product, and if not, what can I do to make it salable?

DRAVEN: *What advice can you give new filmmakers who want to start their career in low-budget horror films?*

LEWIS: Don't let your ego drive the product. What *you* think is entertaining may be light-years removed from what an outsider regards as entertaining.

CHAPTER 19

THE FUTURE OF HORROR

Talent is cheaper than table salt. What separates the talented individual from the successful one is a lot of hard work.

—STEPHEN KING

So what is the future of horror movies?

We've had the Asian-horror craze, the torture porn, and countless remakes of 1970s and 1980s horror classics. At some point, sequels and the horror franchises will run dry. Studios are big business, and they're in it to make money. This is why we see them regurgitate the same formulaic films over and over again. When horror movies become more mainstream and less independent, we may be in trouble.

SUBJECT MATTER

I will say one thing I know is true. The horror film has always been an ideal artistic outlet for exploring the nature of violence and the current events of our world. This paves the way for a whole new breed of upcoming horror filmmakers to tell original stories. Whatever society is struggling through during any given era is a good place to start with a horror film. For example, consider our post-9/11 world, our fears of terrorism, germ warfare, cloning, or just the guy next door who commits a murder. I can think of plenty of horror movies already. There is also a plethora of unproduced novels, short stories, and classical literature waiting for someone to bring them to life or reinvent them for a new generation of horror fans.

BEWARE OF TRENDS

Horror trends come and go like fall and spring fashions. If you are thinking of making a horror film, whatever you do *don't follow trends*. By the time you write, shoot, deliver, and sell your film, that trend will either be waning or already gone. You will always be left behind with a movie everyone has already seen or is tired of. It has been said that Hollywood churns out sequels and remakes because they have run out of fresh ideas.

When I made CRYPTZ (2002) for Full Moon Pictures, it was a time in the straight-to-video business when urban horror films were very a popular trend. In those days the video stores practically preordered the films from indie distributors with which they had selling/buying relationships. We started the project in December 2001, and it was written, shot, posted, and at Blockbuster by April 2002 on DVD. We followed trends, and in this case it was successful but only because the film already had a home for distribution. During the shooting of CRYPTZ, I was also prepping to shoot another urban horror film called THE GRIM RAPPER, a film once again to fill a trend, which I eventually turned down. The world was spared from a killer rapper using evil music from his boom-box to explode the heads of his victims.

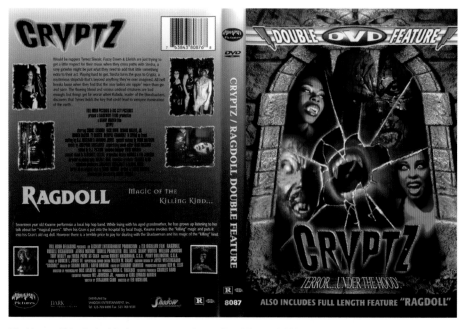

Blockbuster Video's double feature artwork for my film CRYPTZ (2002). The movie was made to fill a trend in the urban horror market.

FUTURE

From a technological standpoint, I think we are going to see many more 3-D horror films in the coming decades. James Cameron has pioneered the way, and the indie filmmaker will follow behind. We have surround sound, so it seems fitting that the next step in film's evolution is a visual surround, or 3-D films. Examples of 3-D horror films that have been made recently are SCAR 3-D (2009), MY BLOODY VALENTINE 3-D (2009), or PIRANNA 3-D (2010). In the music world, the rock band U2 is doing this more and more with their live stage shows.

So, you read this book and hopefully learned a few things, but now what? Where do you go from here? Well, all I can say is it's up to you. You must make your own path. Take what knowledge you can from this book and others and get your butt on the set. It's our imagination, originality, and sheer unbreakable determination and drive that makes a great indie film. The horror film isn't going anywhere. Horror is not dead.

THE FUTURE OF HORROR IS YOU!

Tony Timpone
Photo Credit: Jonathan McPhail

TONY TIMPONE *FANGORIA* MAGAZINE EDITOR & CHIEF, AUTHOR, PRODUCER

www.fangoria.com

Since 1979, *Fangoria* magazine has been the leading publication devoted to horror entertainment. The magazines are carried on newsstands and bookstores all over the world and have inspired generations of genre filmmakers and authors. *Fangoria* has been featured in scores of TV shows (*Amazing Stories*, *Late Night with Jimmy Fallon*), movies (GREMLINS, FRIDAY THE 13TH: PART III, MY NAME IS BRUCE) and documentaries (GOING TO PIECES, HIS NAME WAS JASON, HORROR BUSINESS). The magazine is currently under the umbrella of Fangoria Entertainment, which has spawned and/or coproduced horror

continued on the next page

continued from the previous page

conventions (www.fangocon.com), a popular web site (www.fangoria.com), several DVD labels, TV specials (*Fuse Fangoria Chainsaw Awards*), movies (CHILDREN OF THE NIGHT, SEVERED TIES, MINDWARP), books (*Fangoria's Best Horror Films, 100 Best Horror Films You've Never Seen*), comics (*Bump, Beyond the Valley of the Rage*), trading cards, T-shirts, and much more.

DRAVEN: *What is the current state of the horror genre? Is horror dead or in a revival phase, and why?*

TIMPONE: Horror is in better shape than ever. For example, looking at the industry trade bible *Variety* as a guide, 7 out of the top 50 movies playing the weekend of February 13–16, 2009, were horror or dark genre films: FRIDAY THE 13TH, CORALINE, MY BLOODY VALENTINE 3-D, TWILIGHT, THE UNBORN, UNDERWORLD: RISE OF THE LYCANS, and THE UNINVITED. More people are seeing new horror films than ever before, fueled by the marketplace expansion by women turning out to see these movies in record numbers. For example, on opening weekend, 57 percent of the audience for the brutal THE LAST HOUSE ON THE LEFT remake was female. That's extraordinary when you consider the film's extreme subject matter and the fact that just 15 years ago, horror was a male-dominated genre.

DRAVEN: *No one on earth sees more independent horror films than staff at* Fangoria. *In your experience at the magazine, what are the biggest pitfalls you see when reviewing horror films, both ultralow-budget and studio films? Is it production quality, script, character, gore, or something else, and why?*

Fangoria magazine issue 276

TIMPONE: The big problem is usually story/screenplay and the inclusion of characters we care about. I want to be moved both emotionally and viscerally when I see a horror film, and not enough effort is put into those areas by filmmakers big and small. We have to identify with the characters. For me, everything else is secondary. Next, it's crucial, especially for low-budget films, that convincing/talented actors be hired to carry the film. Nothing pulls me out of a movie faster than amateur acting.

DRAVEN: *With the advent of new 3-D horror films, such as the remake of MY BLOODY VALENTINE 3-D (2009), do you think this is* the new frontier for the horror film experience, and why?

TIMPONE: Theater owners and studios have to compete with home entertainment systems that are almost as good as your average multiplex these days, so it is important for them to expand upon the moviegoing experience and give the audience more bang for their buck. The 3-D systems today are much more sophisticated and immersive than the ones from the old days and the films less gimmicky, like the wonderful CORALINE. We will see more 3-D and IMAX market penetration in the years ahead.

DRAVEN: *It seems to me that a lot of independent horror films and distributors are using B to Z level actors with a name value, even if that person is only in the film for a few minutes. Do you think this recycling of actors approach helps a movie in terms of fan response and sales, or is it hurting the genre, and why?*

TIMPONE: For a fan, seeing a familiar genre face can make the difference in picking up a film for rental or purchase. But sometimes, hiring low-rent actors will actually hurt the film from getting a distributor or finding their way into Blockbuster. I've heard stories from buyers who refuse to acquire C. Thomas Howell movies, for example, because he has been appearing in so many terrible Z-grade films in recent years.

DRAVEN: *As the longtime editor and chief of* Fangoria *magazine and an author, producer, and horror scholar, what is it about the genre you love so much, and where do you think the future of horror will take us?*

TIMPONE: I always loved horror films because they are an escape from the mundane. I also seek an emotional engagement when I see a film, and horror movies, when done right, deliver that in spades, having viewers laughing and screaming and gasping for air.

Horror films are more popular than ever, and across many categories: from hard R slashers like FRIDAY THE 13TH to PG-13 supernatural romances like TWILIGHT. Sure, we will see a lot more remakes and TWILIGHT wannabes over the next few years, but as long as there is the occasional surprise like MARTYRS, INSIDE, CLOVERFIELD, LET THE RIGHT ONE IN, THE HOST, 28 DAYS LATER, THE ORPHANGE, SPLINTER, and PAN'S LABYRINTH, the genre will continue to grow and challenge us.

Fangoria magazine issue 282

INDEX